Gender, Poverty and Livelihood in the Eastern Himalayas

T0347739

The Eastern Himalaya region covers a geographical area that spans five nations and has diverse landscapes, a multitude of ethnic groups and a rich variety of flora and fauna. The region is relatively poor in terms of GDP and per capita income; industrialisation and infrastructure is under-developed; climate-induced disasters are frequent; and maternal and infant mortality rates are high. Economic constraints combined with restrictive cultural norms create barriers for women in education, employment and decision-making, thus further entrenching unequal gender relations.

This book explores the ways in which gender-sensitive and inclusive policies can be developed to address the basic issues of marginalisation, livelihood, poverty and vulnerability in the Eastern Himalayas. The chapters in the volume touch upon current concerns, such as the economic and social challenges faced by women, their control over resources, questions of patriarchy, discrimination, gender rights and equity, information, empowerment and participation, and women as agents of change.

This volume will be useful to researchers and scholars in gender studies, sociology and social anthropology, development studies, economic and human geography, politics, northeast and Himalayan studies, South Asian studies, as well as policymakers and those in the development sector and non-governmental organisations.

Sanjoy Hazarika is the Director of the Commonwealth Human Rights Initiative (CHRI) and was the founder of the Centre for North East Studies and Policy Research, Jamia Millia Islamia, New Delhi, India.

Reshmi Banerjee is Academic Visitor at the Asian Studies Centre (Programme on Modern Burmese Studies), St Antony's College, University of Oxford, UK.

Gender, Poverty and Livelihood in the Eastern Himalayas

Edited by Sanjoy Hazarika
and Reshmi Banerjee

Routledge
Taylor & Francis Group

LONDON AND NEW YORK

First published 2018
by Routledge

2 Park Square, Milton Park, Abingdon, Oxfordshire OX14 4RN
52 Vanderbilt Avenue, New York, NY 10017

*Routledge is an imprint of the Taylor & Francis Group,
an informa business*

First issued in paperback 2019

British Library Cataloguing-in-Publication Data
A catalogue record for this book is available from the British Library

Library of Congress Cataloging-in-Publication Data
A catalog record has been requested for this book

ISBN: 978-1-138-69642-6 (hbk)
ISBN: 978-0-367-89018-6 (pbk)

Typeset in Sabon
by Apex CoVantage, LLC

Contents

List of figures		vii
List of tables		viii
List of contributors		ix
Acknowledgements		xii

Introduction 1
SANJOY HAZARIKA AND RESHMI BANERJEE

1 The Eastern Himalaya and the Mongoloid myth 12
GEORGE VAN DRIEM

2 Access to water and gender rights in India: contextualising the various debates through the study of a mountain village in Sikkim 42
JWALA D. THAPA

3 Challenges to women as food and risk managers in the context of floods: a case study from Tinsukia 67
SARAH MARIE NISCHALKE AND SUMAN BISHT

4 'Constructed' images of gender and gender roles in the Northeastern Himalayas: virtual and actual 85
SUBHADRA MITRA CHANNA

5 Towards a research collaboration with indigenous communities in India 102
TARA DOUGLAS

6 Female MGNREGA workers and poverty reduction
in Sikkim   121
MARCHANG REIMEINGAM

7 Women in the land of Jade: issues and interventions   147
RESHMI BANERJEE

Index   169

Figures

1.1 Geographical distribution of Trans-Himalayan languages   19

1.2 Geographical distribution of the major Trans-Himalayan subgroups   20

1.3 Thirty out of forty-two Trans-Himalayan subgroups lie south of the Himalayan divide, seven to the north and east, and five (Tshangla, Bodish, Nungish, Lolo-Burmese and Kachinic) straddle both flanks of the Himalayas   22

1.4 Geographical distribution of Hmong-Mien   23

1.5 Geographical distribution of Kradai   24

1.6 Geographical distribution of Austronesian   25

1.7 Geographical distribution of Austroasiatic   26

1.8 The 2012 Benares Recension: a revised East Asian phylogeny   27

1.9 After the Last Glacial Maximum, the Y chromosomal haplogroup O (M175) split into the subclades O1 (MSY2.2), O2 (M268) and O3 (M122)   29

1.10 Paternal lineages branching into new subclades   30

5.1 The two young Thangka artists, Palzor Sherpa and Tashi Lepcha, from Sikkim creating the artwork for the folktale from Sikkim in the *Tales of the Tribes* animation series   115

5.2 Manipur workshop team   115

5.3 Young animation students of the National Institute of Design experiment with Gond artwork for the animated Gond folktale 'Manjoor Jhali' in the *Tales of the Tribes* collection during a workshop in 2012   116

Tables

6.1 Share of completed work under MGNREGA
    in Sikkim, India   125

6.2 Usually employed as a casual labour in the total
    employment and casual labour households in
    Sikkim and in India   127

6.3 Employment generated under MGNREGA in Sikkim   129

6.4 Share of MGNREG work classified by social groups in
    Sikkim and in India, 2009/10   131

6.5 Minimum wage rate for MGNREGA workers and
    index number of wage, Northeast India   135

6.6 Average wage/salary earnings per day received by different
    employees of 15–59 years in Sikkim and in India   137

6.7 Number and share of population below poverty line in
    Sikkim and in India   139

6.8 Worker population ratio of Sikkim and India   141

Contributors

Reshmi Banerjee is an Academic Visitor at the Asian Studies Centre (Programme on Modern Burmese Studies), St Antony's College, University of Oxford, UK. She was previously a research associate at the Centre of Southeast Asian Studies (CSEAS), School of Oriental and African Studies (SOAS), University of London, UK and Visiting Professor at the Centre for North East Studies and Policy Research, Jamia Millia Islamia, New Delhi, India. She is co-editor of the book *Climate Change in the Eastern Himalaya: Impact on Livelihoods, Growth and Poverty* (2015). She has been a post-doctoral fellow at the University of Indonesia (UI) in Jakarta, a researcher in the Indonesian Institute of Sciences (LIPI), and Fellow at the Rajiv Gandhi Institute for Contemporary Studies (RGICS). She has also taught at University of Delhi and the University of Indonesia.

Suman Bisht completed her doctorate from the Department of Sociology, Delhi School of Economics, University of Delhi, India. She has expertise in health, livelihood and climate change with a strong background in gender and more than sixteen years of experience working across different sectors such as health, gender-based violence, natural resource management, migration and others. She has worked with university, research organisations, national and international NGOs, grass-roots organisations and women's groups in India and outside, including Rwanda, Sri Lanka, China, Nepal and Vietnam. She has worked in senior program management positions in international organizations, developing, managing, and implementing development programmes with a clear gender focus. She joined ICIMOD (International Centre for Integrated Mountain Development) as a senior gender specialist in January 2012 and is currently working as Program Coordinator for AdaptHimal, Nepal.

Subhadra Mitra Channa taught Anthropology at the University of Delhi, India. Her areas of interest include marginalisation and identity, gender, religion and cosmology, ecology and landscapes. She has received several prestigious international awards and fellowships. She was Charles Wallace Fellow to UK (Queen's University, Belfast 2000), Visiting Professor to MSH, Paris (2002), Fulbright visiting lecturer to Auburn University, Alabama, USA (2003) and Fulbright Scholar-in-Residence to University of Southern California, USA (2008/9). She is the author/editor of nine books and has more than fifty scholarly published papers. She was President of the Indian Anthropological Association, editor of the journal 'Indian Anthropologist'; Chair of the Commission on the Anthropology of Women (IUAES) and is presently Vice President of IUAES. Her important publications include *Gender in South Asia* (2013) and *The Inner and Outer Selves* (2013), *Life as a Dalit* (2013), *Gender Livelihood and Environment* (2015).

Tara Douglas is co-founder and Secretary of the Adivasi Arts Trust (www.adivasiartstrust.org). She has conducted several screening programmes and creative workshops with school children in UK. She has also conducted animation workshops in Nagaland, Sikkim, Manipur, Arunachal Pradesh, Madhya Pradesh and Gujarat for indigenous participants, artists and storytellers. She completed a Doctorate of Professional Practice on 'Tales of the tribes: animation as a tool for indigenous representation' at Bournemouth University, UK. This practice-led research produced in a new collection of short animation films made in collaboration with indigenous communities in India called the *Tales of the Tribes*.

George van Driem has written several grammars of languages of the Himalayas (Limbu, Dumi, Dzongkha and Bumthang) and authored a two-volume ethnolinguistic handbook entitled *Languages of the Himalayas* (2001). In Bhutan, he discovered two languages previously unknown to science (Black Mountain Mönpa and Gongduk). He also collaborates with linguists and population geneticists to reconstruct human population prehistory. His doctorate students and postdoctoral scholars conduct pioneering work in the Asian heartland. He directs the Linguistics Institute at the University of Bern, Switzerland, where he is also the Chair of Historical Linguistics.

Sanjoy Hazarika is Director at Commonwealth Human Rights Initiative (CHRI) and was founder of the Centre for North East Studies and Policy Research, Jamia Millia Islamia, New Delhi, India. He is Chairman of the Task Force that promotes educational opportunities and welfare of students from the northeast region belonging to SCs, STs and PwDs, Ministry of Human Resource Development, Government of India, and member of the Executive Council of Nagaland University and the Society of Indian Institute of Advanced Study, Shimla. He has authored several books and contributed articles and papers to newspapers and journals. Some of his books include *The State Strikes Back: India and the Naga Insurgency* (2009), *Writing on the Wall: Reflections on the North-East* (2008), *Rites of Passage* (2000), *The Regeneration of India* (1995) and *Strangers of the Mist* (1994).

Sarah Marie Nischalke is a food security expert with a focus on mountain food and nutrition security, farming systems, gender and climate change adaptation. From 2012 to 2014, she worked as a food security analyst in the Himalayas at the International Centre for Integrated Mountain Development, Nepal. She has a doctorate in Human Geography and is currently working at the Center for Development Research in Bonn, Germany as Senior Researcher with a gender focus in agriculture in Eastern Africa (Ethiopia and Madagascar).

Marchang Reimeingam completed her doctorate in Economics from Jawaharlal Nehru University, New Delhi, India. He is Assistant Professor in the Centre for Study of Social Change and Development (CSSCD) in the Institute for Social and Economic Change (ISEC), Bengaluru, India. Before joining the ISEC, he was Assistant Professor of Economics in the Central University of Sikkim, Gangtok and Research Associate in the Institute for Human Development, New Delhi. His broad areas of interest in research include labour issues, migration studies, human resource development, regional economy and regional development.

Jwala D. Thapa is a research scholar in the West Bengal National University of Juridical Sciences (WB NUJS), Kolkata, India. Her doctoral research is based on the issue of mountain environment and the approach of the Indian environmental legal system to mountain areas of India, specifically focusing on Sikkim. She has also authored papers in several journals as well as presented papers in national and international conferences. She was formerly a Law Clerk and Research Assistant in the office of the Hon'ble Justice Asok Kumar Ganguly, Supreme Court of India, New Delhi, India.

Acknowledgements

This edited volume, *Gender, Poverty and Livelihood in the Eastern Himalayas*, is a collection of academic papers which were presented at the international conference entitled 'The Eastern Himalaya: gender, poverty and livelihoods' held in the Centre for North East Studies and Policy Research, Jamia Millia Islamia, New Delhi in February 2014. We are deeply grateful to the administration of Jamia Millia Islamia, especially Prof. S. M. Sajid (the then officiating Vice Chancellor), Prof. Shahid Ashraf (the Registrar) and Dr Abdul Malik (the Joint Registrar) for their support. We are also deeply grateful to the Government of Sikkim whose funding through the Sikkim Studies Programme was crucial for the successful organisation of this conference. We would also like to thank the performers of the fourth North East Annual Day, namely The Homecoming (rock band from Jamia), Minute of Decay (the all-girls band from Manipur), Toshan Nongbet and the Band, Brahmaputra Bihu Group and finally Girish and the Chronicles. We also extend our deep appreciation for the support provided by the faculty and staff from the Centre for North East Studies and Policy Research as well as the volunteers who helped conduct the programme. We thank our esteemed participants who presented their papers, chaired sessions and finally contributed their chapters to this edited volume.

Introduction

Sanjoy Hazarika and Reshmi Banerjee

The Eastern Himalayan region is a unique area with diversified land-scapes, a multitude of ethnic groups and a rich variety of flora and fauna. It spans not only parts of India's East and Northeast but also parts of Nepal, all of Bhutan, the Chin and Rakhine states in Myanmar, parts of Yunnan Province in China as well as the Sagaing Region. It is poor in terms of GDP and per capita income with underdeveloped industrialisation and poor infrastructural linkages. It has also witnessed high maternal and infant mortality rates, climate change, natural disasters, political turmoil, armed conflicts which in turn has impacted the livelihoods and well-beings of the population. Women in all poor regions are the worst affected as they face a double vulnerability: first of being women and second of being poor. Limited accessibility to economic resources (do not own land, have no access to credit and are often not gainfully employed) and lack of social opportunities (discriminated in education, health, knowledge and information networks, skill development and social support networks) and political and legal rights (non-participation and exclusion in decision-making processes) expose women to greater risks and vulnerabilities. Cultural constraints, issues of caste, class and ethnicity further combine to create a situation where women face a complex range of challenges which require serious thought and some meaningful but immediate action. Gita Sen comments that 'gender systems, structures and biases, and forms of oppression and subordination work at multiple levels and are both powerful and resistant to change' (Sen 2000: 272). Gendered inequality continues to be high and the empowerment of women remains an aspiration.

In many parts of Asia and Africa, women are involved in subsistence agriculture where finding food and water for the entire family is one of their primary tasks. They are also burdened with the responsibility of looking after the children and the elderly. These become their daily chores, which results in little or no leisure time. Women face food and nutrition insecurity along with shortages of water. They often have to travel long distances (away from their comfort zones), especially in areas of conflict, making them extremely vulnerable to sexual attacks, markedly when they access open spaces to 'answer nature's call'. Women are the main users of water but they are scarcely consulted in the design and management of water programmes. They also tend to spend a lot of time in collecting fuel for cooking with an Indian woman spending 2–7 hours in a day, whereas in Sub-Saharan Africa, 20 kg of fuel wood is carried on an average of 5 km per day by many (Skinner 2011). The World Health Organization has observed that 30 per cent or more of women's daily energy intake is spent in fetching water in India and Africa. Moreover, long hours of walking not only leaves them exhausted but also results in injury of various types to the vertebral column (World Health Organization 2012). With desertification in many areas predicted to happen, women could face increasing hardships in the coming years to their lives and dignity.

A study of five villages in Assam's Karbi Anglong and Meghalaya's East Garo Hills revealed that women had to go far to fetch water as springs close to the villages were drying up. Moreover, women were facing more pressure as men were going out in search of wage labour opportunities with the decline in agriculture (Macchi *et al.* 2011). They tend to dominate the informal sector with their lower educational levels and lesser mobility, thus restricting their entry in the non-agricultural and nonfarm sectors. Bina Agarwal thus observes that women tend to get lower wage rates and lower average real wage earnings in both agriculture and non-agriculture. Moreover, there was a distinction between legal and social recognition, with the former not necessarily translating into practice, thus the difference between recognition and enforcement (Agarwal 2002). There is an urgent need for legal awareness and legal aid for women which will enable them to get accessibility to their rights and benefits.

Bharati Borah (a social scientist based in the Majuli Island on the Brahmaputra River in Assam) observed that limited opportunities for women are available as wage labourers because of which it was forcing women to go to the nearby towns which in turn was rendering them vulnerable to pressure (Borah *et al.* 2012). Land rights can be a very important factor in women's empowerment in India. Kartik C. Roy observed that both legal and customary land rights can be an important instrument for tribal women to enjoy substantive freedom, but sadly the rural women in India who are largely illiterate have no knowledge or awareness of their inheritance rights (Roy 2008: 70–73).

Moreover, in the agrarian countryside, moneylenders are not ready to give loans to women as they cannot provide or offer any collateral. Livelihood diversification, anyway, is a gendered process as women's greater burden of domestic work along with limited time and mobility creates restrictions for them. Further Deepak K. Mishra observes that the 'gendered nuances of livelihood diversification are intensified in mountain ecology' (Mishra 2012: 137). This, according to him, is due to various factors like resource specificity and multiple overlapping hierarchies, i.e. between men and women, plains and hills as well as within communities and finally between the state and the communities (ibid.).

Various studies reveal not only the challenges faced by women but also the initiatives taken by them. A study in West Bengal (after Storm AILA) revealed that women were forced to go deeper into the jungles to collect honey, shrimps and other non-timber forest products as the men had migrated. Thus, the women were not only prone to tiger and crocodile attacks but also were left with no time to look after their vegetable gardens which was crucial for food security (Kapoor 2011). Meanwhile in Bastar, Chhattisgarh, Gond and other areas, Adivasi women are entering into new occupations as they require it to increase their economic resilience. Thus, they are venturing beyond agriculture into making terracotta, metal and wood sculpture (Kelkar 2009). Yet, one finds that women are given the charge of 'home gardens' among the Lepchas and the Nagas (called *leeden sing* by the Lepchas) and not the 'wet terrace fields', as the former is usually small in size and produces minor crops (like vegetables, herbs and traditional crops) whereas the latter produces the major crop (wet rice) and consists of a larger area. Thus, male and female domains are clearly marked out in spite of the fact that women play a major role in sowing, transplanting, weeding, harvesting, seed selection in the wet terraced fields. (Goodrich 2012: 171).

There is not only a need to include and expand the gender and asset question by including land, jewellery, house/homestead, livestock, savings, energy infrastructure but also women need to have rights to new technology like planters, rainwater harvesting, grinding mills which can go a long way in increasing their productivity (Kelkar 2013: 63). Groups of women have been in a position to take land on lease through the initiatives of the Deccan Development Society which has made them stronger. In Andhra Pradesh, Integrated Tribal Development Authority and Scheduled Caste Development Corporation have successfully transferred land to the landless (by purchasing land from the willing owners who wanted to lease it) and all such transfers were made in the names of women and free of charge. In Bangladesh too, women have fought for their user rights over fish ponds, have improved their livelihoods and well-beings of their households through their income from fish culture and built assets like cattle, shops and taken land on lease (ibid.: 73–76).

Women also tend to suffer more during natural disasters. Climate change is not gender neutral. Women are often not warned, cannot swim nor can they leave their homes. Women made up 55–70 per cent of the tsunami victims in Indonesia's Banda Aceh in 2004. Many female headed poor households (35% in rural India, 15% in Bangladesh and 10% in Nepal), living in lowlands or along river banks or on steep slopes are subject to recurring floods. Their roles as caregivers and food providers are not only affected but also the resultant migration and displacement leads to loss of livelihoods and economic assets/opportunities. Additional problems are posed when there is degradation of natural resources and decline in agrarian productivity (WEDO 1997: 317, 318). The World Disasters Report recognises that women and girls are at a higher risk of sexual violence, exploitation and abuse, trafficking and domestic violence in disasters. Women's insecurity not only can increase when there is biodiversity loss but also when contamination of drinking water in the coastal areas leads to pregnant women getting affected with pre-eclampsia, eclampsia and hypertension as has occurred in Bangladesh (World Health Organization 2010). Even in emergency responses, the privacy and sanitary needs of women are neglected as was evident in the camps of displaced people in post-tsunami Aceh, Indonesia, where lack of closed bathrooms prevented women from cleaning themselves which in turn impacted their reproductive health. Also since the management committees consist of men, the issues of women are often ignored (Ariyabandu 2009: 10). They were not consulted nor were they involved in the decisions being taken.

Women often do not have the opportunities for negotiation and thus receive inadequate compensation and relief after a major disaster. They spend months in relief camps, waiting for proper rehabilitation. The breakdown of the local security systems and the normal social protection systems during disasters are used by the organised traffickers to trap vulnerable women. Women in the mountains are particularly vulnerable as they are first more prone to climate and nature induced disasters and second lack transport and communication facilities along with readily available health and education (Nellemann *et al.* 2011). Mountains are by definition fragile and this landscape has been made more fragile by deforestation, dam and road construction, tourism industry. The communities in general, living in these areas, suffer from 'inequalities of opportunities' as compared to their lowland neighbours. The women of this region – in particular, widows, orphans, female heads of households, disabled and ailing – face extreme difficulties during periods of crisis. Women along with men are 'key social actors/players' in laying down the foundation of hazard resilient communities. This is also recognized by strategies which strengthen women's capacity in disaster response and hazard reduction (Mehta 2009: 61–65).

The absence of peace in parts of the region has further affected the socio-economic and psychological conditions. Women have faced the brunt of violence and yet their voices remain unheard. Despite protests, their issues and concerns remain unaddressed as they lack inadequate representation in the governing institutions, whether it is the national parliament, state legislatures and local councils or Panchayat Raj Institutions. Even customary and traditional institutions exclude women and are largely not gender neutral. Yet, women in this Himalayan belt have an innate knowledge of the local terrain, local crops and wild edible varieties, seed selection, manure application, pest management, postharvest processing and value addition. This wisdom is all part of the oral traditions which need to be highlighted in the future (Kapoor 2011).

Women have a crucial role to play not only as conservers of biodiversity but also as peacemakers. Paula Banerjee rightly points out that peacemaking has actually helped in the creation of spaces for women in the public sphere, but the 'political nature' of the work of peacemaking is not recognised by the majoritarian leadership; thus women are not only redefining peace but are also defined by the politics of peace (Banerjee 2010: 156). Women continue to however remain more visible in the arena of social reform: fighting against drug addiction, alcoholism, HIV infection and men are less involved in these endeavours. Women, thus, continue to function within a delineated space without sometimes realising that political empowerment is required to bring policy changes/designs which are necessary for removing these social evils (Nag 2006: 225, 226).

Gender-sensitive and -inclusive policies are needed for this region to tackle marginalisation, poverty and vulnerability. However, gender-disaggregated data is extremely scarce. Also, there is absence of involvement and participation of men in the entire debate. Sylvia Chant thus mentions the 'missing men' to highlight this issue by stating that 'men and gender relations remain largely absent from policy responses to women's poverty' (Chant 1997: 185). A strong foundation of gender justice is needed. Specific policies and projects especially targeting rural women should be designed and implemented.

Saraswati Raju observes that it is not women's participation in economically productive activities but the recognition that society places on women that gives her and increases their 'worth'. For Raju, workforce participation, sex ratios, marriage, health indicators, mortality differentials etc. are essentially the 'outcomes' of 'worth' which is spatially produced (Raju 2011: 39). The state of Kerala is characterised by a 'gender paradox' where women as collectives and as individuals have not exercised much influence although the state is a highly politicised space. Women of the state not only have little influence in the development processes which can impact them but they also have low levels of participation in the political and public sphere. This is in spite of the fact that the state is much better off than other states of India in terms of social development index but the element of powerlessness still persists. There has been limited empowerment of women in terms of autonomy, agency, mobility and self-confidence (Erwer 2011: 137, 138).

In Northeast India, even now, there is limited participation of women in state assemblies, autonomous district councils, urban durbars and village councils. Rosemary Dzuvichu observes that in spite of the contribution of Naga women in the economy, they do not find their space and voice in institutions like the traditional village councils, village judiciary or the apex Tribal Hohos. Women have not only 'no rights' to land, ancestral property or inheritance but also they have no control over the sale of large animals, animal products or fresh stock. This is in contrast to the women in the Andes of Latin America who are not only the owners but also the major livestock managers (Dzuvichu 2013: 175–177).

Education needs to facilitate the process of awareness amongst women regarding their capabilities and possibilities of inclusion. The school system is often kept outside the arena of gender reform with stress being laid on working with local women and women's organisations in local communities. Thus, gender education reforms do not function uniformly both within a country and across countries (Arnot and Fennell 2008: 4). Women often internalise the view that they do not deserve education and the social context/environment further prevents the aspects of learning, participation and achievement. Elaine Unterhalter states that 'equality is thus an aspect of equal regard as much as equal resources to address need' (Unterhalter 2008: 25). According to Amartya Sen, political freedoms, economic facilities, social opportunities, transparency guarantees and protective security – all these rights and opportunities not only help in improving the capability of a person but also are complementary to each other (Sen 2006: 507, 508). Women's development in the future is also thus connected with providing them with such varied and distinct types of freedom.

This edited volume, *Gender, Poverty and Livelihood in the Eastern Himalayas,* is a collection of academic papers which were presented in the international conference titled 'The Eastern Himalaya: gender, poverty and livelihoods' held in the Centre for North East Studies and Policy Research, Jamia Millia Islamia, New Delhi in February 2014. The book is an attempt to capture the issues and challenges affecting women of this region; it tries to delve into not only their political, economic and environmental vulnerability but also explores their role as active agents of change. One needs to address the basic problem of marginalisation and exclusion of women by making them equal partners in the political processes and developmental initiatives. The publication brings together a group of esteemed scholars who have tried to give voice to some of these critical concerns.

Themes of the book

The opening chapter is a monograph by George van Driem titled 'The Eastern Himalaya and the Mongoloid myth' which sets the tone for the book. The historical linguist and population geneticist provides a detailed view of the region, both in its spatial and temporal dimensions. The tale of ethnogenesis in the Eastern Himalaya and Asian ethnolinguistic prehistory is presented on the basis of the 2012 Benares Recension of the East Asian linguistic theory along with findings of population genetics. The chapter highlights the distinct nature of our maternal and paternal lineages and sheds light on the peopling of eastern Eurasia, Australasia, the Indian Ocean and the Pacific. It interestingly shows that the Eastern Himalaya holds the key to an understanding of the ethnolinguistic prehistory of well over half of the planet's surface and captures the importance of this region.

Chapter 2 studies the aspect of access to water and gender rights in India. Titled 'Access to water and gender rights in India: contextualising the various debates through the study of a mountain village in Sikkim' by Jwala D. Thapa, it looks at the various debates that exist currently in the case of the rights of women and their access to water for domestic use. It tries to further analyse whether any differences exist in the debates based on topography. It asks the question as to whether policies with respect to rights to water need to be made not only gender sensitive but also topography sensitive. It delves into the issues of traditional space, introduction of modern technology and the role of women as equal partners to accessibility and management of water.

Sarah Marie Nischalke and Suman Bisht in Chapter 3 bring out the challenges faced by women during floods as food and risk managers by taking the case study of Tinsukia in Assam. The chapter titled 'Challenges to women as food and risk managers in the context of floods: a case study from Tinsukia' is based both on quantitative and qualitative data collected in different localities in the district. Women are highly disadvantaged in their rights, knowledge, time and resources. They are extremely vulnerable and are at a higher risk to suffer from disasters than men. The chapter highlights not only the vulnerability of women but also the need to set up gender- and climate-sensitive agricultural systems.

Gender roles and construction all across the world are deeply embedded and informed by the political/historical context of any society. Chapter 4 of the book titled ' "Constructed" images of gender and gender roles in the Northeastern Himalayas: virtual and actual' by Subhadra Mitra Channa observes that the relative isolation of the Northeast from the caste-based patriarchal norms of mainland India, its historical association with East Asia and the major modes of subsistence- all have had a cumulative impact on gender roles and associated expectations. Although these roles are not static, yet even in their dynamism, they respond in a manner which seems to be informed by the cultural experiences in which they are embedded. Northeast India is at the receiving end of stigmatised gender constructs and negative images. Images are virtual, but the social impact is real. The chapter studies the context of such constructs that are both stereotypical and hierarchical.

Chapter 5 presents a discussion on appropriate research methodologies within the context of research on indigenous representation carried out by a person located outside the indigenous community to foster self-reflexivity and sensitive interaction with indigenous communities for collaborative projects. Tara Douglas in her chapter 'Towards a research collaboration with indigenous communities in India' explores the *Tales of the Tribes*, which is a research project that investigates historical and contemporary indigenous representation and proposes the appropriation of animation as a tool to re-engage with their own heritage and reinvigorate it for future generations.

Chapter 6 of the book titled 'Female MGNREGA workers and poverty reduction in Sikkim' by Marchang Reimeingam looks at the extent of female participation in rural work through the MGNREGA (Mahatma Gandhi National Rural Employment Guarantee Scheme) scheme and its link with poverty reduction in the state. It is based on secondary data from the Ministry of Rural Development, National Sample Survey and Planning Commission, Government of India. Rates of employment, participation, income status and overall well-being are studied in poverty reduction and rural development. The last chapter of the book takes us across the border to Myanmar. In this chapter, titled 'Women in the land of Jade: issues and interventions', Reshmi Banerjee chronologically traces the role and relevance of women in the country. She examines not only the socio-economic and political challenges faced by women both before and after independence but also the inherent paradoxes and ambivalence in society towards them. The chapter also delves into the repression, fear and control faced during the military regime along with the issues of violence against women, trafficking, migration, livelihoods of rural women, displacement. Various positive interventions for improving the condition of women have been attempted and the chapter hopes to initiate awareness and concern as they are the first step towards creating a more empowering environment for women in the future.

References

Agarwal, B. 2002. *Are We Not Peasants Too? Land Rights and Women's Claims in India*, Retrieved from: http://ccc.uchicago.edu/docs/AreWeNotPeasantsToo.pdf

Ariyabandu, M. M. 2009. 'Sex, gender and gender relations in disasters', in E. Enarson and P. G. Dhar Chakrabarti (eds.), *Women, Gender and Disaster: Global Issues and Initiatives*. New Delhi: Sage, p. 10.

Arnot, M. and S. Fennell. 2008. '(Re)visiting education and development agendas-contemporary gender research', in S. Fennell and M. Arnot (eds.), *Gender Education and Equality in a Global Context-Conceptual Frameworks and Policy Perspectives*. London: Routledge, p. 4.

Banerjee, P. 2010. *Borders, Histories, Existences: Gender and Beyond*. New Delhi: Sage, p. 156.

Borah, A., S. Devi and M. Medhi. 2012. *Impact of Climate Change on Marginalized Women: An Exploratory Study Across 6 Districts in Assam*. Guwahati: CESPR, RGVN and INECC, Retrieved from: ASSAM Study Impact%20of%20Climate%20Change%20on%20Marginalized%20Women.pdf

Chant, S. 1997. 'The "feminization of poverty" and the "feminization" of anti-poverty programmes: room for revision?', in N. Visvanathan, L. Duggan, N. Wiegersma and L. Nisonoff (eds.), *The Women, Gender and Development Reader*. Nova Scotia: Fernwood Publishing Ltd, p. 185.

Dzuvichu, R. 2013. 'Gender and livestock in Nagaland', in G. Kelkar and M. Krishnaraj (eds.), *Women, Land and Power in Asia*. New Delhi: Routledge, pp. 175–177.

Erwer, M. 2011. 'Emerging feminist space politicizes violence against women', in S. Raju (ed.), *Gendered Geographies: Space and Place in South Asia*. New Delhi: Oxford, pp. 137, 138.

Goodrich, C.G. 2012. 'Gender dynamics in agro-biodiversity conservation in Sikkim and Nagaland', in S. Krishna (ed.), *Agriculture and a Changing Environment in Northeastern India*. New Delhi: Routledge, p. 171.

Kapoor, A. 2011. *Engendering the Climate for Change – Policies and Practices for Gender – Just Adaptation.* New Delhi: Supported by Alternative Futures, Heinrich Boll Foundation and Christian Aid, Retrieved from: Engendering_the_Climate_for_Change(1)-HeinrichBollFoundation.pdf

Kelkar, G. 2009. *Adivasi Women – Engaging with Climate Change.* New Delhi: UNIFEM, IFAD and the Christensen Fund, Retrieved from: adivasi_women_engaging_with_climate_change_1-UNIFEM-GovindKelkar.pdf

Kelkar, G. 2013. 'Gender and productive assets: Implications for women's economic security and productivity', in G. Kelkar and M. Krishnaraj (eds.), *Women, Land and Power in Asia*. New Delhi: Routledge, pp. 63–76.

Macchi, M., A. M. Gurung, B. Hoermann and D. Choudhury. 2011. *Climate Variability and Change in the Himalayas: Community Perceptions and Responses.* Kathmandu: ICIMOD, Retrieved from: http://gender-climate.org/wp-content/uploads/docs/publications/icimod-climate_variability_and_change_in_the_himalayas.pdf

Mehta, M. 2009. 'Reducing disaster risk through community resilience in the Himalayas', in E. Enarson and P. G. Dhar Chakrabarti (eds.), *Women, Gender and Disaster: Global Issues and Initiatives*. New Delhi: Sage, pp. 61–65.

Mishra, D. K. 2012. 'Livelihood diversification: Farming, forest-use and gender in Northeastern India', in S. Krishna (ed.), *Agriculture and a Changing Environment in Northeastern India*. New Delhi: Routledge, p. 137.

Nag, S. 2006. 'Her masters' voice – women, peacemaking and the genderisation of politics', in P. Biswas and C. J. Thomas (eds.), *Peace in India's North-East – Meaning, Metaphor and Method*. New Delhi: Regency, pp. 225, 226.

Nellemann, C., R. Verma and L. Hislop. 2011. *Women at the Frontline of Climate Change – Gender Risks and Hopes – A Rapid Response Assessment.* UNEP, GRID Arendal, ICIMOD and CICERO, Retrieved from: rra_gender_screen.pdf

Raju, S. 2011. 'Reclaiming spaces and places: The making of gendered geography of India', in S. Raju (ed.), *Gendered Geographies: Space and Place in South Asia*. New Delhi: Oxford, p. 39.

Roy, K. C. 2008. 'Institutions and gender empowerment in India', in K. Roy, H. Blomqvist and C. Clark (eds.), *Institutions and Gender Empowerment in the Global Economy*. Singapore: World Scientific Publishing Co Pte Ltd, pp. 70–73.

Sen, A. 2006. 'Development as freedom', in B. Agarwal, J. Humphries and I. Robeyns (eds.), *Capabilities, Freedom, and Equality – Amartya Sen's Work from a Gender Perspective*. New Delhi: Oxford, pp. 507, 508.

Sen, G. 2000. 'Engendering poverty alleviation: Challenges and opportunities', in S. Razavi (ed.), *Gendered Poverty and Well Being*. Oxford: Blackwell, p. 272.

Skinner, E. 2011. *Gender and Climate Change – Overview Report*. Institute of Development Studies, Retrieved from: 2011_10_BRIDGE_Gender_and_climate_change.pdf

Unterhalter, E. 2008. 'Global values and gender equality in education: Needs, rights and capabilities', in S. Fennell and M. Arnot (eds.), *Gender Education and Equality in a Global Context: Conceptual Frameworks and Policy Perspectives*. London: Routledge, p. 25.

WEDO (The Women's Environment and Development Organization). 1997. 'Gender, climate change and human security: Lessons from Senegal', in N. Visvanathan, L. Duggan, N. Wiegersma and L. Nisonoff (eds.), *The Women, Gender and Development Reader*. Nova Scotia: Fernwood Publishing Ltd, pp. 317, 318.

World Health Organization. 2010. *Gender, Climate Change and Health*. World Health Organization, Retrieved from: GenderClimateChangeHealthfinal-WHO.pdf

World Health Organization. 2012. *Mainstreaming Gender in Health Adaptation to Climate Change Programmes (User's Guide)*. Geneva: World Health Organization, Retrieved from: Mainstreaming_Gender_Climate.pdf

1 The Eastern Himalaya and the Mongoloid myth

George van Driem

1. Defining the Eastern Himalaya

In the west, the Himalayas are punctuated by the Tirič Mīr in the Hindu Kush at 7,708 m and by the K2 in the Qarāqoram at 8,661 m. In the east, the Himalayas are punctuated by the Ganŝ dKar-po [kʰɑ̃ kɑːpɔ̄] in eastern Tibet at 6,740 m and the Hkakabo Razi in northern Burma at 5,881 m. The Himalayan massif runs a vast length of over 3,600 km from the Hazārahjāt highlands in the west to the Liángshān in the east. The Eastern Himalaya can be said to encompass the eastern half of the Himalayas, beginning from the Dhaulāgiri 8,167 m in central Nepal on eastward. The Kālī Gaṇḍakī River, which flows just at the foot of the Dhaulāgiri, bisects the great Himalayan range into two halves of roughly equal length.

Although the Himalayas are the highest mountain range on our planet, they form no watershed, since many of the rivers are of greater antiquity than the mountains themselves. The Himalayas only began to rise long after the Tethys Sea shrivelled up some 35 million years ago and the once insular habitat of the Indian subcontinent had fused with the Eurasian mainland. Like a number of other prominent Himalayan rivers, the Kālī Gaṇḍakī runs right through the Himalayas, originating on the Tibetan plateau and coursing down through the mountains onto the Gangetic plain. This dramatic invagination at the very centre of the Himalayan range is prominently visible to any airplane passenger flying across the Gangetic plain. For ethnolinguistic phylogeography, the Kālī Gaṇḍakī demarcates a vast region known as the Eastern Himalaya, which extends eastward all the way into the Indo-Burmese borderlands and the Chinese provinces of Yúnnán and Sìchuān and constitutes an area of pivotal importance to population prehistory.

2. The Mongoloid myth

As a species, we have always been obsessed with how we look and in which ways we appear to be similar or different from one another. The ancient Hindu caste system and the apartheid system of South Africa were just two of many systems based on our perceptions of caste, tribe and race. Even before the Portuguese first set foot in Japan in 1542, Europeans were trying to come to grips with the human phenotypical diversity which they observed in the peoples whom they met on their voyages across the seas. Today we understand that in scientific terms, there is actually no such thing as race (Cavalli-Sforza *et al.* 1994). We are all members of one large human family. The relationship between genes, their phenotypical expression and their pleiotropic interplay is inordinately complex, and our individual differences often tend to be larger than the differences between groups.

Historically, long before the discovery of the molecular mechanisms underlying genetics, scholars resorted to superficial classifications in their attempts to understand human diversity. Classification was conducted on the basis of somatology, which involved crude observations about external appearance. In 1758, in the famous tenth edition of his *Systema Naturæ*, Carl Linnæus distinguished between four geographical subspecies of *Homo sapiens*, i.e. *europaeus, afer, asiaticus* and *americanus*. Later, Johann Friedrich Blumenbach, in a dissertation which he defended at Göttingen in 1775, distinguished between what he imagined were five human races, namely the 'white' *Caucasiae,* the 'yellow' *Mongolicae,* the 'black' *Aethiopicae,* the 'red' *Americanae* and the 'brown' *Malaicae* (1776 [1795]: xxiii, xxiv). With his coinages, Blumenbach single-handedly invented the 'Mongoloid' and 'Caucasoid' races. With regard to his *Varietas Caucasia,* Blumenbach opined:

> The name of this variety is taken from the Caucasus mountains, as well as, indeed, most of the southern flank thereof, in the Georgian area, where the most beautiful race of men is to be found and in whom all the physiological reasons converge so that it may be presumed that the first human beings are likely to have been native to this region.
>
> (1795/1776: 303)[1]

Later, Johann Christian Erxleben recognised four of the same races as Blumenbach but under different names, with his *Homo sapiens europaeus, asiaticus, afer* and *americanus* (1777: 1, 2) corresponding to Blumenbach's *Varietas Caucasia, Mongolica, Aethiopica* and *Americana* (1795 [1776]: 304, 307, 310, 319) respectively. As opposed to Blumenbach's *Varietas Malaica,* Erxleben distinguished no separate Malay race, but he made finer distinctions in northern Asia, distinguishing a more northerly *Homo sapiens tatarus* from the Chinese phenotype, which he termed *Homo sapiens asiaticus,* and he grouped Lapps, Samoyeds and other Uralic peoples under a distinct heading named *Homo sapiens lappo.* In France in 1801, Julien-Joseph Virey basically followed Blumenbach in recognising five races, but he outdid Erxleben in his attempts further to subclassify within these races.[2]

Taking his inspiration from Blumenbach, the German scholar Christoph Meiners (1747–1810), on the basis of the descriptions in Dutch and Russian accounts of the peoples encountered in other parts of the world, set up a classification of races based on what he imagined where the *uralte Stammvölker* or racial prototypes of mankind. His cogitations were published posthumously in three volumes. In the second volume, *der alte Mongolische Stamm* or 'the Mongoloid race' was designated by Meiners as one of the main races of mankind. He wrote:

> In physiognomy and physique, the Mongol diverges as much from the usual form as does the Negro. If any nation merits being recognised as a racial prototype, then it should rightfully be the Mongol, who differs so markedly from all other Asian peoples in his physical and moral nature.
>
> (1813, 2: 61)[3]

Meiners described the cruelty of the invading hordes led by Genghis Khan as being inherent to the 'moral nature' of the Mongoloid race, conveniently overlooking the historically well-documented cruelties of Western and other peoples. The serendipity of the nomenclatural choices made by Blumenbach (1795 [1776]) and Meiners (1813) gave rise to the Mongoloid myth. If the Mongols were the primordial tribe from which all peoples of the Mongoloid race descended, then it was logical to think that the homeland of all Mongoloids lay in Mongolia.

Jean Baptiste Bory de Saint-Vincent (1825: 323–325) subsequently introduced the term *Homo sapiens sinicus* for the Chinese, who he thought distinct from proper Mongoloids, but the 'Chinese race' would later vanish from subsequent classificatory schemes because the Chinese came to be seen by such early physical anthropologists as a mixture of the Northeast Asian 'Tungids' and the 'Palaeomongoloids' of the Himalayas and Southeast Asia.[4]

I have often been told by people in Nepal and northeastern India that their ancestors came from Mongolia. Some even adorn their lorries, cars and motorcycles with captions like 'Mongol' or 'Mongolian'. When I ask them why they think so, they tell me that they are members of the Mongoloid race or मंगोल जाति *Mangol jāti*, which, as the name tells us, must have originated in Mongolia. I do not have the heart to tell them that the very idea was dreamt up by a German scholar in Göttingen in the early 1770s, who was just imaginatively trying to make sense of human diversity, though he had no expertise or specialist knowledge to do so.

People in the West suffer from the same obsolete ideas. A friend of mine from Abkhazia, who happens to be a renowned linguist, was travelling in the United States of America with a colleague of his from the Republic of Georgia. Whilst driving a rented car, they were pulled over by a police officer. The obese and heavily armed man in uniform demanded to see my friend's driving licence and then asked them, 'Are you folks Arabs?' The policeman spoke with a heavy American accent and pronounced the word Arabs as ['eɪræːbz]. Since Abkhazia and Georgia both lie in the Caucasus, my friend responded, 'No, Sir, we are both Caucasians'. This response somehow displeased the police officer, who asserted, '*I* am a Caucasian!'. My friend coolly responded, 'No, Sir, you are not a Caucasian, and you do not look particularly like a Caucasian. *We* are Caucasians.' The exasperated policeman spluttered, '. . . but . . . but I am white!'

In the aftermath, my friend had to explain to the American policeman where the Caucasus Mountains lay and who the Caucasians were. However, he did not go as far as to explain that the idea that Europeans were purportedly Caucasian originated with Blumenbach in the early 1770s. Like the Mongoloid, the Caucasoid was another one of his racial prototypes. Americans who apply for a driving licence, take a Scholastic Aptitude Test or fill in any number of other official forms are often asked to specify their race. A person of European ancestry often checks a box saying that he or she is a 'Caucasian'. Some people from Asia and Africa are baffled by these racial questions and by the choices of race on offer, which differ from one form to another, and then end up having to decide whether they are 'coloured' or belong to some other 'race'. Although the topic of race is taboo in America, American society is both riddled with antique modes of thinking about race and very much in denial about widely held racist assumptions.

By contrast, indigenous peoples of Nepal, Sikkim, Bhutan and north-eastern India have a legitimate interest in their ancestry. Native people of the Eastern Himalaya share a natural and logical curiosity about why they appear to be different from the Brahmins and Chetris of Nepal and from the majority of Indians in India. We are all interested in where we came from, and both historical linguistics and population genetics can shed some light on this question. Before we examine some of the new insights from the field of ethnolinguistic phylogeography, a number of caveats should be noted.

3.   Language and genes

There is a long lineage of scholars from Julius von Klaproth and Friedrich Max Müller (1872) who, since the early nineteenth century, have stressed that language and biological ancestry are two different things. There have been others too, like Sir William Jones, who from time immemorial have confounded language and race. Generally, people throughout history have been inclined to speak the language spoken by their parents, but the language which we happen to speak today may very well not be the language of our parents. Since genes are invariably inherited by offspring from their biological parents, a probabilistic correlation may therefore exist between language and genes in human populations, though this need not necessarily be so.

Historical linguistics and human population genetics present two distinct windows on the past. At the same time, the time depth accessible to historical linguistics is an order of magnitude shallower than the time depth accessible to genetics. Language families represent the maximal time depth accessible to historical linguists because the relatedness of languages belonging to a recognised linguistic phylum represents the limit of what can be demonstrated by the comparative method. This epistemological barrier represents the linguistic event horizon. Languages and genes are independent, but correlations may exist between chromosomal markers and language. Yet, these relationships should not be confused with identity. The correlation of a particular genetic marker with the distribution of a certain language family must not be simplistically equated with populations speaking languages of a particular linguistic phylum.

Moreover, we must also take into account the potential skewing effects of natural selection, gene surfing, recurrent bottlenecks during range expansion and the sexually asymmetrical introgression of resident genes into incursive populations. Factors such as ancient population structure and possible ancient Y chromosomal introgression could also affect inferences and interpretations based on any single Y chromosomal locus when attempting to reconstruct migrations and elucidate the geographical origins of populations (Mendez *et al.* 2013; van Driem 2012b). Even with all these caveats in place, we must be especially aware of all provisos and qualifications included in our inferences and working hypotheses when attempting to understand East Asian ethnolinguistic phylogeography.

4. Father tongues

When studying the distribution of maternally inherited markers in the mitochondrial DNA and paternally inherited markers on the Y chromosome, population geneticists soon found that it was easier to find statistically relevant correlations between the language of a particular community and the paternally inherited markers prevalent in that community than between the language and the most salient maternally inherited markers found in that speech community. This Father Tongue correlation had already been described by Poloni *et al.* (1997, 2000) before the appearance of the seminal articles on Y chromosomal phylogeography by Underhill *et al.* (2000, 2001). Subsequent work, e.g. Karafet *et al.* (2008), further refined the resolution of the Y chromosomal haplogroup tree.

The inference was made that paternally inherited polymorphisms may serve as markers for linguistic dispersals in the past and that a correlation of Y chromosomal markers with language may point towards male-biased linguistic intrusions. The Father Tongue correlation is ubiquitous but not universal. Its preponderance allows us to deduce that a mother teaching her children their father's tongue must have been a prevalent and recurrent pattern in linguistic prehistory. It is reasonable to infer that some mechanisms of language change may be inherent to this pathway of transmission. Phylogenies of autosomal single nucleotide polymorphisms in whole genome studies are making headway (Li *et al.* 2008), but it is still too early to tell to what extent correlations of autosomal markers with language phyla will be identified that are as salient as the currently observed Father Tongue correlations.

There are a number of reasons why we might expect this outcome. Initial human colonisation of any part of the planet must have involved both sexes in order for a population of progeny to establish itself. Once a population is in place, however, subsequent migrations could have been heavily gender-biased. Subsequently, male intruders could impose their language whilst availing themselves of the womenfolk already in place. By contrast, correlations between maternal lineages and linguistic phylogeography discerned to date have been underwhelming. The Father Tongue hypothesis suggests that linguistic dispersals were, at least in most parts of the world, posterior to initial human colonisation and that many linguistic dispersals were predominantly later male-biased intrusions. Such patterns are observed worldwide.

The correlation of Niger–Congo languages with Y chromosomal haplogroups is a striking example (Wood *et al.* 2005). Likewise, the martial and male-biased historical spread of Hàn Chinese during the sinification of southern China, recounted in detail in the Chinese chronicles, is just as faithfully reflected in the genetic evidence (Wen *et al.* 2004). A recent common ancestry between native Americans and indigenous Altaians is also based preponderantly on the shared Y chromosomal heritage and is not quite as well reflected in the mitochondrial lineages (Dulik *et al.* 2012). The saliency of Y chromosomal haplogroups in tribal and caste populations in India contrasts with the comparatively featureless nature and antiquity of the mitochondrial landscape (Thanseem *et al.* 2006; Thangaraj *et al.* 2006a).

Previously, it has been proposed that the spread of Y chromosomal R subclades is likely to be linked to the dispersal of Indo-European from an original homeland in the Pontic–Caspian steppe (van Driem 2007, 2012b), but the unfolding story of Y chromosomal R lineages will no doubt turn out to be complex (Underhill *et al.* 2010). In order to be conclusive, a fine-mesh study of populations inhabiting the Western Himalayan region should be undertaken. Similarly, it has been proposed that the Y chromosomal lineage L, which shows a great diversity of subclades on the Iranian highland, can be identified as the possible marker of a patrilingual dispersal of Elamo-Dravidian emanating from a region which included the Bactria and Margiana of later prehistory (van Driem 2012b), and that one of these Y chromosomal L subclades will appear to be correlated with the patrilingual spread of Dravidian languages from the Indus Valley into southern India (van Driem 2014b). I have also proposed that haplogroup Q, an offspring clade of Y chromosomal haplogroup P, could be a marker for the Greater Yenisseian linguistic phylum (van Driem 2008, 2014b).

Populations forming local exceptions to the Father Tongue correlation, such as the Hungarians and the Balti, have been discussed elsewhere (van Driem 2012b, 2014b). Even in areas of the globe where the Father Tongue correlation does not hold, such as Tibetan-speaking Baltistan, we can observe that the main Y chromosomal haplogroups are more recent arrivals than the main maternal lineages. In the following sections, the ancestry of the native peoples of the Eastern Himalaya is explained. In so doing, we focus on the identification of the paternal haplogroup O2a (M95) with the spread of Austroasiatic, haplogroup O3a3c (M134) with Trans-Himalayan, haplogroup O3a3b (M7) lineage with Hmong-Mien and O1 (MSY2.2) with Austro-Tai (van Driem 2007, 2012b, 2014b). Against the background of the East Asian linguistic theory, linguistic ancestry will be seen to correlate well with paternal ancestry.

5. The Trans-Himalayan family and the Sino-Tibetan myth

The second most populous linguistic phylum on the planet is Trans-Himalayan or Tibeto-Burman. Most speakers of Trans-Himalayan languages today live to the north and east of the Himalayas (Figure 1.1), but

Figure 1.1 Geographical distribution of Trans-Himalayan languages.

Note: Maps in this chapter are not to scale.

Source: Dr. Chr. Enderle[5]

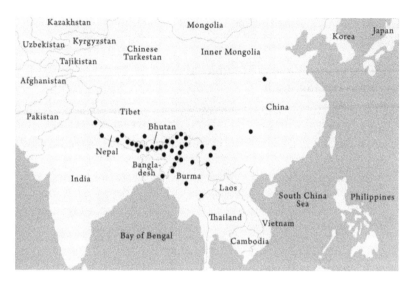

Figure 1.2 Geographical distribution of the major Trans-Himalayan subgroups. Each dot represents not just one language, but the putative
historical geographical centre of each of forty-two major linguistic
subgroups.

Source: Author

most of the over 300 different languages and three-fourths of the major
Trans-Himalayan subgroups are located to the south of the Himalayan
divide (Figure 1.2). The Trans-Himalayan linguistic phylum was first recognised by Klaproth in 1823, who identified the family as consisting of
Tibetan, Chinese, Burmese and related languages. This linguistic phylum
was called Tibeto-Burman by scholars in the British Isles, e.g. Hodgson
(1857), Cust (1878), Forbes (1878), Houghton (1896).

   In addition to the Mongoloid myth, another widespread myth which
has only recently come to be dispelled is the Sino-Tibetan myth. Until
1924, Sino-Tibetan was called Indo-Chinese, a hypothetical language
family containing all the languages of Asia and Oceania, including Japanese, the Polynesian languages and even all the languages of Papua
New Guinea. The theory was dreamt up by a Scotsman called John
Caspar Leyden, who made a meteoric career as a British civil servant
in Asia during the Napoleonic wars but then died at the age of 35 in
Indonesia. The idea that all Asian and Oceanic languages shared some
'common mixed origin' appealed to British colonial authorities.

The Indo-Chinese tree came to be whittled down in size over time but also became tinged with racist ideologies. The rebranding of the theory in 1924 as Sino-Tibetan helped to disguise the racist underpinnings of the model. Aside from its tainted history, the Sino-Tibetan family tree itself was false and consisted of two branches, one of which was Sino-Daic. When the Kradai or Daic languages were finally removed from Sino-Tibetan, the reduced Sino-Tibetan tree still represented a false phylogeny, uniting all non-Sinitic languages into a single subgroup which Sino-Tibetanists misleadingly labelled 'Tibeto-Burman'. No Sino-Tibetanist has ever been able to adduce any historical linguistic evidence for this taxon and therefore for the family tree.[6]

Sino-Tibetan was assailed by scholars who proposed other models, e.g. Sino-Burman (Ramstedt 1957), Sino-Himalayan (Bodman 1973, 1980) and Sino-Kiranti (Starostin 1994). Finally, even Jim Matisoff, the retired Berkeley professor who once championed the model, has now publicly recanted the Sino-Tibetan phylogenetic model on three occasions.[7] This step ought to be lauded as a noble act on his part because he had previously defended the Indo-Chinese family tree ever since, as a student at Columbia University in the 1960s, he inherited the antiquated model from his mentor Paul Benedict. The ability to change one's mind in the face of evidence, or the lack thereof, is a defining trait of a scientist.

The Sino-Tibetan myth must be ousted as a false theory because this model has continued to mislead a number of scholars even in recent years. Yet, dispelling myths can be an arduous task because of the tenacity with which such narratives can take hold of the human mind. Today the default model remains Klaproth's original Tibeto-Burman linguistic family, augmented by all the linguistic subgroups which have come to be recognised by linguists since 1823 to the present day (Figure 1.3). Since 2004, the newer name Trans-Himalayan has been gaining currency for Tibeto-Burman because this neutral geographical name accurately reflects the pivotal concentration and distribution of main subgroups of the linguistic phylum.

6. The East Asian linguistic theory

Following in the footsteps of scholars such as Witsen (1692) and Hadrianus Relandus (1706, 1707, 1708), Klaproth challenged conventional wisdom in 1823 by proposing a polyphyletic view of Asian language families. In assailing the dominant biblically inspired paradigm of a single gargantuan language family encompassing all Asian languages, Klaproth was able to distinguish the contours of many of the known

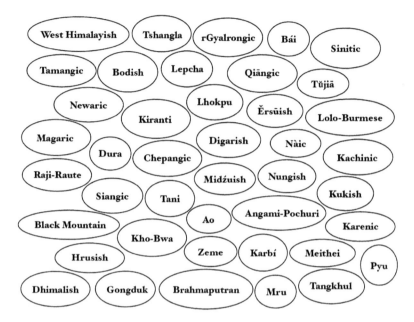

Figure 1.3 Thirty out of forty-two Trans-Himalayan subgroups lie south of the Himalayan divide, seven to the north and east, and five (Tshangla, Bodish, Nungish, Lolo-Burmese and Kachinic) straddle both flanks of the Himalayas.

Source: Author

Asian linguistic phyla. The five major linguistic phyla recognised today which form part of the East Asian story are Trans-Himalayan, Hmong-Mien, Kradai, Austronesian and Austroasiatic (Figures 1.1, 1.4–1.7).

Once Klaproth's polyphyletic view had been in place for nearly a century, scholars began to discern possible long-distance relationships between the recognised language families. We might say that for linguistic taxonomy, Klaproth's centrifugal step was gradually followed by a series of centripetal steps. Gustave Schlegel (1901, 1902) agreed with Klaproth in assessing Kradai to be unrelated to Sinitic, merely replete with Sinitic loans, and argued instead that Kradai was related to Austronesian. Schlegel's old theory was taken up by Benedict (1942, 1975, 1976, 1990) under the guise of 'Austro-Thai', though this putative genetic link constituted just an ingredient in Benedict's grand and poorly supported 'Japanese/Austro-Tai'.

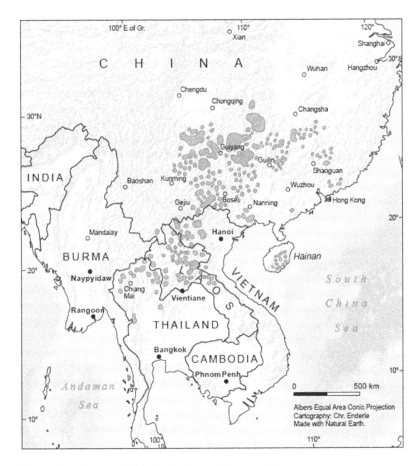

Figure 1.4 Geographical distribution of Hmong-Mien.

Source: Dr. Chr. Enderle

Weera Ostapirat (2005, 2013) was the first to present methodologically sound and cogent historical comparative evidence that Kradai and Austronesian represent coordinate branches of an Austro-Tai family. The coordinate branches of Ostapirat's Austro-Tai represent an ancient migration from what today is southern China across the Taiwan Strait to Formosa, where the Austronesian linguistic phylum established itself, whilst the proto-language ancestral to today's Kradai language communities remained behind on the mainland. Much later, the Formosan exodus led to the spread of the Malayo-Polynesian

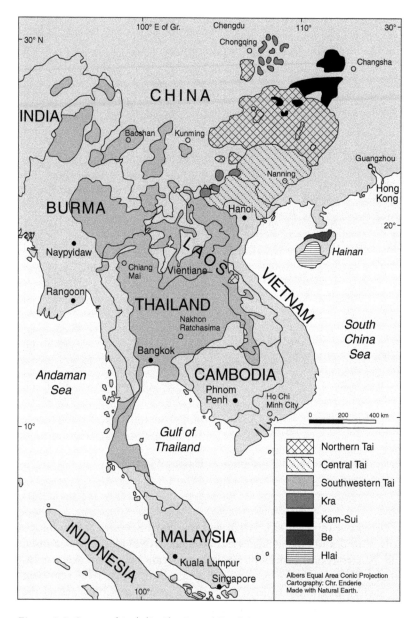

Figure 1.5 Geographical distribution of Kradai.

Source: Dr. Chr. Enderle

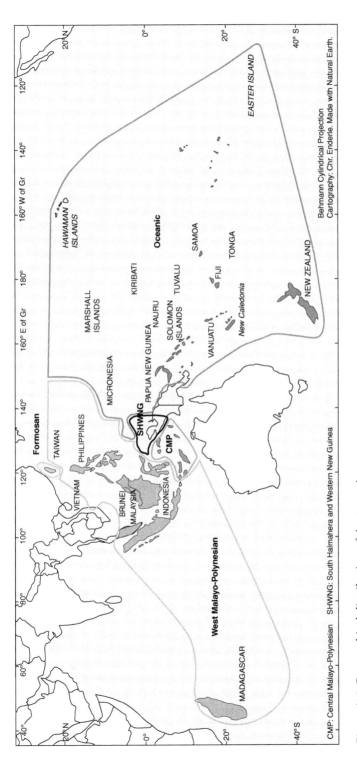

Figure 1.6 Geographical distribution of Austronesian.

CMP: Central Malayo-Polynesian   SHWNG: South Halmahera and Western New Guinea

Source: Dr. Chr. Enderle

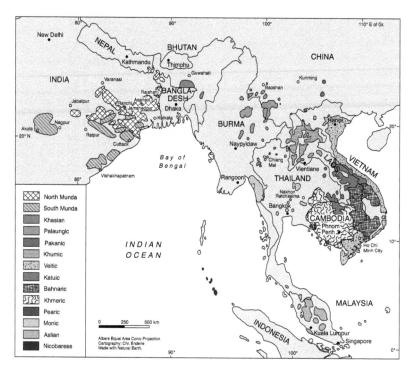

Figure 1.7 Geographical distribution of Austroasiatic.
Source: Dr. Chr. Enderle

branch throughout the Philippines, the Malay Peninsula, the Indonesian Archipelago, Madagascar and Oceania.

By uniting Kradai and Austronesian into Austro-Tai, Ostapirat reduced the five major linguistic phyla to just four: Austro-Tai, Trans-Himalayan, Hmong-Mien and Austroasiatic. Decades ago, transgressing the linguistic event horizon, Wilhelm Schmidt (1906) proposed an Austric macrofamily, uniting Austroasiatic and Austronesian, based on morphological evidence drawn especially from Nicobarese. Lawrence Reid became a proponent of Schmidt's theory but also envisaged an even larger macrofamily, proposing that Austric 'as a language family may eventually need to be abandoned in favour of a wider language family which can be shown to include both Austronesian and Austroasiatic languages but not necessarily as sisters of a common ancestor' (Reid 2005: 150).

Conrady (1916, 1922) and Wulff (1934, 1942) each proposed a superfamily consisting of Austroasiatic, Austronesian, Kradai and Tibeto-Burman. Benedict (1942), Blust (1996) and Peiros (1998) proposed an

Austric superfamily comprising Austroasiatic, Austronesian, Kradai and possibly Hmong-Mien. Then in 2001 at Périgueux, a year before he died of congestive heart failure in Hawai'i, Stanley Starosta proposed the East Asian linguistic phylum encompassing Kradai, Austronesian, Tibeto-Burman, Hmong-Mien and Austroasiatic. Starosta's evidence was meagre, yet primarily morphological in nature. The ancient morphological processes shared by the families of this phylum, according to Starosta, were an agentive prefix *<m->, a patient suffix *<-n>, an instrumental prefix <s-> and a perfective prefix *<n->. The East Asian word was ostensibly disyllablic and exhibited the canonical structure cvcvc.

Starosta's posthumously published East Asian phylogeny was marred by editorial errors (Starosta 2005: 183), which were later corrected (van Driem 2005: 322). A theory of linguistic relationship at this time depth lies at the frontier of what can be empirically demonstrated to the satisfaction of a methodologically rigorous historical linguist. This hypothesis will therefore remain an informed conjecture until solid historical linguistic evidence either further supports or overturns the model. At Benares in 2012, I presented the tweaked East Asian family tree depicted in Figure 1.8. The revised phylogeny is based on historical linguistic intuitions and other types of information about population prehistory (van Driem 2014b).

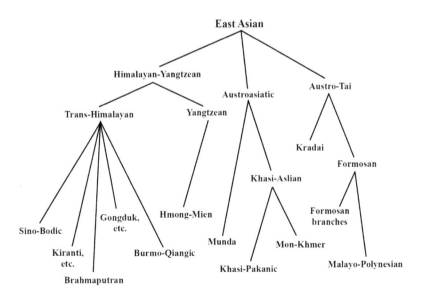

Figure 1.8 The 2012 Benares Recension: a revised East Asian phylogeny.
Source: Author

7.   East Asian and the Eastern Himalayan homeland

The populations today speaking languages of the Trans-Himalayan, Hmong-Mien, Austroasiatic and Austro-Tai linguistic phyla are characterised by a preponderance of the Y-chromosomal haplogroup O. In fact, the four linguistic phyla are each characterised by a particular subclade of O, suggesting both a paternal spread of these language families as well as a time depth for the putative East Asian language family coeval with the antiquity of the paternal haplogroup O itself.

There is good reason to believe that the geographical locus of the ancestral haplogroup NO (M214) lay in the Eastern Himalaya. When the two paternal lineages N and O split up, the bearers of haplogroup N set out for East Asia just after the Last Glacial Maximum, braving ice and tundra, and, in a grand counterclockwise sweep, gradually migrated across northern Eurasia as far west as Lappland (Rootsi *et al.* 2007; Derenko *et al.* 2007; Mirabal *et al.* 2009). I have identified this clade with the paternal spread of Michael Fortescue's Uralo-Siberian linguistic phylum (van Driem 2014b). The ancestral clade N* (M231) is still found in the highest frequency in northern Burma, Yúnnán and Sìchuān.

The fraternal clade O, which appears to be a marker for the linguistic ancestors of the hypothetical East Asian linguistic phylum, remained behind in the Eastern Himalaya. As temperature and humidity increased after the Last Glacial Maximum, the Y chromosomal haplogroup O (M175) split up into the subclades O1 (MSY2.2), O2 (M268) and O3 (M122). The three subclades can be putatively assigned to three geographical loci along an east–west axis for the sake of argument and without any claim to geographical precision. Whereas the haplogroup O1 (MSY2.2) moved to the drainage of the Pearl River and its tributaries in what today is Guǎngdōng, the bearers of haplogroup O2 (M268) moved to southern Yúnnán, whilst bearers of the O3 (M122) haplogroup remained in the southeastern Himalayas, expanding their range initially only into adjacent parts of northeastern India and northern Burma (Figure 1.9). The O2 (M268) clade split into O2a (M95) and O2b (M176), an event which took place just before the linguistic event horizon.

Asian rice, perhaps both *japonica* and *indica* rice, may have first been domesticated roughly in the area hypothetically imputed to O2 (M268), which would have included southern Yúnnán (van Driem 2011a, 2012a; Figure 1.9). The bearers of the subclade O2a (M95) became the *Stammväter* of the Austroasiatics (van Driem 2007; Chaubey *et al.* 2010). The Austroasiatics spread from this locus initially

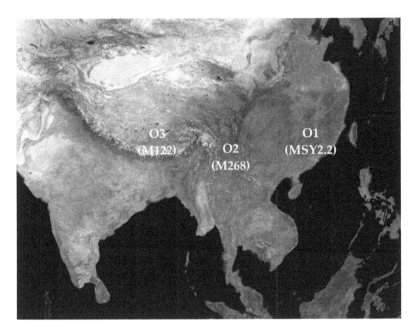

Figure 1.9 After the Last Glacial Maximum, the Y chromosomal haplogroup O (M175) split into the subclades O1 (MSY2.2), O2 (M268) and O3 (M122). Bearers of the O2 (M268) paternal lineage domesticated Asian rice.

Source: Author

to the Salween drainage in northeastern Burma and to the area that today is northern Thailand and western Laos. In time, the Austroasiatics would spread as far as the Mekong delta, the Malay Peninsula, the Nicobars and later even into eastern India, where they would introduce both their language and their paternal lineage to indigenous peoples of the subcontinent (Figure 1.10). Despite its prevalence in Munda populations, the topology of haplogroup O2a does not support a South Asian origin for this paternal lineage (Kumar *et al.* 2007; Chaubey *et al.* 2010). Once again the mitochondrial background is of greater antiquity, and the paternal lineage appears to be the signature for the spread of the language phylum and its adoption by resident populations (Thangaraj *et al.* 2006a; Kumar *et al.* 2006).

Since we have associated the paternal lineage O2a (M95), which is a derivative clade of haplogroup O2 (M268), with the Austroasiatic

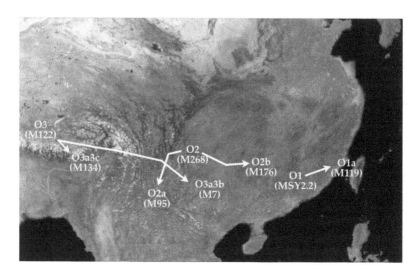

Figure 1.10 Paternal lineages branching into new subclades. Each event involved a linguistic bottleneck leading to language families that today are reconstructible as distinct linguistic phyla. The O1 (MSY2.2) lineage gave rise to the O1a (M119) subclade, which moved eastward to the Fújiàn hill tracts and across the strait to Formosa, which so became the *Urheimat* of the Austronesians. Bearers of O3a3b (M7) became the Proto-Hmong-Mien. In the Eastern Himalaya, the bearers of haplogroup O3a3c (M134) expanded and became the Trans-Himalayans. Haplogroup O2a (M95) is the Proto-Austroasiatic paternal lineage. The para-Austroasiatic fraternal clade O2b (M176) spread eastward, sowing seed along the way.

Source: Author

language phylum, we might conjecture that Asian rice, perhaps both *japonica* and *indica* rice, was first domesticated roughly in the general area hypothetically imputed to O2 (M268). Whilst the bearers of the O2a (M95) haplogroup became the *Stammväter* of the Austroasiatics, the other derivative paternal subclade O2b (M176) spread eastward, where they introduced rice agriculture to the areas south of the Yangtze. Though the bearers of the O2b (M176) haplogroup continued to sow seed as they continued to move ever further eastward, they left little or no linguistic traces, except perhaps an Austroasiatic name for the Yangtze River in Chinese (Pulleyblank 1983). This para-Austroasiatic paternal lineage moved as far as the Korean Peninsula and represents the second major wave of peopling attested in the Japanese genome (Jin *et al.* 2009; Karafet *et al.* 2009).

We can identify the O2b (M176) lineage with the Yayoi people, who introduced rice agriculture to Japan, perhaps as early as the second millennium BC, during the final phase of the Jōmon period (Tanaka *et al.* 2004; Hammer *et al.* 2006). The Yayoi appear also to have introduced other crops of continental inspiration to the Japanese archipelago such as millet, wheat and melons. The gracile Yayoi immigrants soon outnumbered the more robust and less populous Jōmon, who had been the first anatomically modern humans to populate Japan. The Y chromosomal haplogroup O2b and other O haplogroups in Japan are later arrivals but account for more than half of all Japanese paternal lineages, with their highest frequencies in Kyūshū. A Father Tongue theory for Altaic which assumes no close affinity between Altaic and Uralo-Siberian entails that an antique C haplogroup, perhaps C3, represents an early trace of a paternally disseminated linguistic phylum at a great time depth. Much of this old linguistic stratum was lost long ago. The remnants of this Father Tongue survive in Japan as Japanese and elsewhere in Asia as the other languages of the Altaic language family, i.e. Korean, Tungusic, Mongolic and Turkic.[8] Another Father Tongue, anciently introduced to Japan by the bearers of the Y chromosomal haplogroup D2 (M55), survives today as Ainu.

At the dawn of the Holocene in the Eastern Himalaya, haplogroup O3 (M122) gave rise to the ancestral Trans-Himalayan paternal lineage O3a3c (M134) and the original Hmong-Mien paternal lineage O3a3b (M7). The bearers of the polymorphism O3a3c (M134) stayed behind in the area comprising Nepal, Sikkim, Bhutan, northeastern India, southeastern Tibet and northern Burma, whilst the bearers of the O3a3b (M7) lineage migrated eastward to settle in the areas south of the Yangtze. On their way, the early Hmong-Mien encountered the ancient Austroasiatics, from whom they adopted rice agriculture. The intimate interaction between ancient Austroasiatics and the early Hmong-Mien not only involved the sharing of knowledge about rice agriculture technology, but also left a genetic trace in the high frequencies of haplogroup O2a (M95) in today's Hmong-Mien and of haplogroup O3a3b (M7) in today's Austroasiatic populations.

On the basis of these Y chromosomal haplogroup frequencies, Cai *et al.* (2011: 8) observed that Austroasiatics and Hmong-Mien 'are closely related genetically' and ventured to speculate about 'a Mon-Khmer origin of Hmong-Mien populations'. It would be more precise to infer that the incidence of haplogroup O3a3b (M7) in Austroasiatic language communities of Southeast Asia indicates a significant

Hmong-Mien paternal contribution to the early Austroasiatic populations whose descendants settled in Southeast Asia, whereas the incidence of haplogroup O3a3b (M7) in Austroasiatic communities of
the Indian subcontinent is undetectably low. On the other hand, the
incidence of Y chromosomal haplogroup O2a amongst the Hmong-
Mien appears to indicate a slightly more modest Austroasiatic paternal
contribution to Hmong-Mien populations than vice versa.

As the Hmong-Mien moved eastward, the bearers of haplogroup
O2b (M176) likewise continued to move east. Even further east, the
O1 (MYS2.2) paternal lineage gave rise to the O1a (M119) subclade,
which moved from the Pearl River drainage eastward to the Mǐn River
drainage in the hill tracts of Fújiàn and across the strait to Formosa,
which consequently became the *Urheimat* of the Austronesians (cf.
Abdulla *et al.* 2009). Back west in the Eastern Himalaya, the bearers of Y chromosomal haplogroup O3a3c (M134) expanded further
throughout Sìchuān and Yúnnán, north and northwest across the
Tibetan plateau as well as further westward across the Himalayas and
southward into the Indo-Burmese borderlands. In the southwest on the
Brahmaputra Plain, the early Tibeto-Burmans encountered Austroasiatics, who had preceded them.

If we assume a linguistic dispersal in which languages were spread
by populations in which a particular paternal lineage was dominant,
then the Malayo-Polynesian expansion via the Philippines into insular
Southeast Asia must have entailed the introduction of Austronesian
by bearers of the Y chromosomal haplogroup O1a (M119) to resident communities, in which an originally Austroasiatic paternal lineage O2a (M95) was and would remain dominant even after linguistic
assimilation, and other older paternal lineages also persisted (Karafet
et al. 2005; Li *et al.* 2008). Similarly, Malagasy is linguistically clearly
Austronesian, but genetically the Malagasy trace both their maternal
and paternal ancestries equally to Borneo and to the African mainland
(Hurles *et al.* 2005).

The ancestral Trans-Himalayan paternal lineage O3a3c (M134)
spread from the Eastern Himalaya in a northeasterly direction across
East Asia to the North China Plain. Subsequently, at a far shallower
time depth, the Tibeto-Burman paternal lineage O3a3c (M134) spread
from the Yellow River basin into what today is southern China, beginning with the Hàn expansion southward during the Qín dynasty in the
third century BC. The ancestral Tibeto-Burman paternal lineage O3a3c
(M134) is intrusively present in the Korean Peninsula and beyond,
although Uralo-Siberian populations such as the Evenki predominantly retain the paternal lineage N. The distribution map of major

Trans-Himalayan linguistic subgroups shows the centre of linguistic phylogenetic diversity to be rooted squarely in the Eastern Himalaya, with outliers trailing off towards the Loess plains of the Yellow River basin in the northeast. This geographical projection of Trans-Himalayan linguistic diversity appears to reflect the spread of the paternal O3a3c (M134) lineage putatively associated with this linguistic dispersal.

Molecular genetic findings shed light both on ethnolinguistic prehistory and its unrecorded sociolinguistic dimensions, and often population geneticists find molecular corroboration of what some linguists and ethnographers have been claiming for centuries. Although paternal ancestry only represents a very small segment of our ancestry, emerging autosomal findings appear, at least in part, to corroborate the reconstruction presented here for meridional East Asia (Chaubey *et al.* 2010; Jinam *et al.* 2013). Correlations between linguistic, archaeology and genetics must inform a chronologically layered view of ethnolinguistic prehistory (Bellwood *et al.* 2011; van Driem 2011b).

The Eastern Himalaya from the Dhaulāgiri to the Liángshān and more particularly the region comprising Nepal, Sikkim, Bhutan, southeastern Tibet and northeastern India furnished the cradle for the ethnogenesis of all East Asian language families: Trans-Himalayan, Hmong-Mien, Austroasiatic and Austro-Tai. At even greater time depths, the Uralo-Siberian and Altaic linguistic phyla too may have ultimately originated in the Eastern Himalaya. In the hoary past, when our anatomically modern ancestors emerged from Africa on their way to East Asia, Southeast Asia, Oceania, Siberia, the Americas and even Lappland, many of these ancestors must at one point have passed through the Eastern Himalayan region and crossed the mighty Brahmaputra.

Notes

1 Nomen huic varietati a Caucaso monte, tum quos vicinia eius et maxime quidem australis plaga pulcherrimam hominum stirpem, Georgianam foveat; tum quod et omnes physiologicae rationes in eo conspirent, in eandem regionem, si uspiam, primos humani generis avtochthones verisimillime ponendes esse.

2 Julien-Joseph Virey distinguished 'cinq races principales' (all in Tome I: 124). The first race is 'la celtique', which has various types ranging from 'les scandinaves' in the northwest to the 'scythes, persans, arabes, maures . . . et même les indous cisgangetiques' in the southeast (pp. 129–131), whereas 'la racine originelle des mongols se partagent en trois branches' (pp. 131, 132), i.e. those 'qui embrasse presque toute la circonférence du pole arctique . . . esquimaux. tschutchis, kamtschadales . . . koriaques, ostiaques, gakates, jukagres, samoïedes . . . lapons'. 'La seconde division' comprised 'les éleuths et calmouks . . . les tunguses, baskirks, kosaques vrais . . . kirguis, tschouvaches,

burattes, soongarés . . . tous les peuples mantcheoux du nord de la Chine, et les tribus tangutiques du Thibet' (pp. 133, 134). 'Les mogols méridionaux' comprised 'les chinois, les japonais, les corésiens, tonquinois, cochinchinois, les habitans d'Iesso, plusieurs thibetains, siamois, etc.' (p. 135). The third race comprised 'les tribus malaies' throughout insular Southeast Asia and Madagascar (pp. 136, 137). The fourth race was 'l'espèce nègre', which comprised sub-Saharan Africa as well as the people 'de la nouvelle Hollande [i.e. Australia] . . . et la nouvelle Calédonie'. Virey named the fifth race 'caraïbe', which was disseminated throughout the Americas.

3 Die Gesichts – und Körperbildung der Mongolen steht von der gewöhnlichen Form eben so sehr ab, als die der Neger. Und wenn irgend eine Nation verdient, als uraltes Stammvolk betrachtet zu werden; so kommt dieser Nahme mit recht den von allen anderen Asiatischen Völkern, der körperlichen und moralischen Beschaffenheit nach so sehr verschiedenen Mongolen zu.

4 Jean Baptiste Bory de Saint-Vincent (1825: 297) distinguished the 'Espèce Sinique, *Homo sinicus*. Presque toujours, mais improprement confondue avec la précédente sous le nom Mongole' (comprising 'Coréens, Japonais, Chinois, Tonkinois, Cochinchinois, Siamois, et des Hommes qui peuplent l'empire du Birman') as distinct from the Tungid type, which he inappropriately labelled 'Espèce Scythique, *Homo scythicus*' (p. 296), comprising 'Turcomans, Kirguises, Cosaques, Tartares, Kalmouks, Mongols et Mantchoux' (p. 294). Bory de Saint-Vincent also distinguished 'Espèce Hïndoue, *Homo indicus*' (p. 300) and 'Espèce Hyperboréenne, *Homo hyperboreus*', comprising '. . . les Ostiaks, les Tonguses et les Jakoutes . . . les Jukaghires, les Tchoutchis, les Kouriaques, et quelques hordes de Kamtschadales . . .'.

5 The figures drawn by Dr. Chr. Enderle are reproduced from George van Driem's contribution to *Nepal: An Introduction to the Natural History, Ecology and Human Environment in the Himalayas* (2015) with the gracious permission of the editors Colin Pendry and Georg Miehe.

6 This long episode in linguistic history has been recounted elsewhere (van Driem 2014a).

7 The first such pronouncement took place on 29 October 2009 at the 4th International Conference on Austroasiatic Linguistics at Mahidol University, the second on 24 February 2012 in a talk entitled 'The present state of Sino-Tibetan studies: Progress and outstanding issues' at a special seminar for the Hakubi Project and Centre for Southeast Asian Studies at Kyōto University and the third on 26 October 2012 at the 45th International Conference for Sino-Tibetan Languages and Linguistics at Nanyang Technological University in Singapore.

8 Martine Robbeets (2014) applies 'Altaic', the traditional name of this linguistic phylum, just to the language family comprising only Tungusic, Mongolic and Turkic, and she has introduced the new label 'Trans-Eurasian' for the linguistic phylum encompassing Japonic, Koreanic and 'Altaic' *sensu* Robbeets.

References

Abdulla, M. A., I. Ahmed, A. Assawamakin, J. Bhak, S. K. Brahmachari, G. C. Calacal, A. Chaurasia, C.-H. Chen, J. Chen, Y.-T. Chen, J. Chu, E. M. C. Cutiongco-de la Paz, M. C. A. de Ungria, F. C. Delfin, J. Edo, S. Fuchareon, H.

Ghang, T. Gojobori, J. Han, S.-F. Ho, B. P. Hoh, W. Huang, H. Inoko, P. Jha, T. A. Jinam, J. Lì, J. Jung, D. Kangwanpong, J. Kampuansai, G. C. Kennedy, P. Khurana, H.-L. Kim, K. Kim, S. Kim, W.-Y. Kim, K. Kimm, R. Kimura, T. Koike, S. Kulawonganunchai, V. Kumar, P. S. Lai, J.-Y. Lee, S. Lee, E. T. Liu, P. P. Majumder, K. K. Mandapati, S. Marzuki, W. Mitchell, M. Mukerji, K. Naritomi, C. Ngamphiw, N. Niikawa, N. Nishida, B. Oh, S. Oh, J. Ohashi, A. Oka, R. Ong, C. D. Padilla, P. Palittapongarnpim, H. B. Perdigon, M. E. Phipps, E. Png, Y. Sakaki, J. M. Salvador, Y. Sandraling, V. Scaria, M. Seielstad, M. R. Sidek, A. Sinha, M. Srikummool, H. Sudoyo, S. Sugano, H. Suryadi, Y. Suzuki, K. A. Tabbada, A. Tan, K. Tokunaga, S. Tongsima, L. P. Villamor, E. Wang, Y. Wang, H. Wang, J.-Y. Wu, H. Xiao, S. Xu, J. O. Yang, Y. Y. Shugart, H.-S. Yoo, W. Yuan, G. Zhao, B. A. Zilfalil and The Indian Genome Variation Consortium. 2009. 'Mapping human genetic diversity in Asia', *Science*, 326: 1541–1545.

Bellwood, P., G. Chambers, M. Ross and H.-C. Hung. 2011. 'Are "cultures" inherited: Multidisciplinary perspectives on the origins and migrations of Austronesian-speaking peoples prior to 1000 BC', in B. W. Roberts and M. van der Linden (eds.), *Investigating Archaeological Cultures: Material Culture, Variability and Transmission*. Dordrecht: Springer, pp. 321–354.

Benedict, P. K. 1942. 'Thai, Kadai, and Indonesia: A new alignment in southeastern Asia', *American Anthropologist*, 44: 576–601.

Benedict, P. K. 1975. *Austro-Thai: Language and Culture, with a Glossary of Roots*. New Haven: Human Relations Area Files.

Benedict, P. K. 1976. 'Sino-Tibetan: Another look', *Journal of the American Oriental Society*, 96 (2): 167–197.

Benedict, P. K. 1990. *Japanese/Austro-Tai*. Ann Arbor: Karoma Publishers.

Blumenbach, J. F. 1795 [originally 1776]. *De generis hvmani varietate nativa. Editio tertia*. Göttingen: Vandenhoek & Ruprecht.

Blust, R. 1996. 'Beyond the Austronesian homeland: The Austric hypothesis and its implications for archaeology', in W. H. Goodenough (ed.), *Prehistoric Settlement of the Pacific*. Philadelphia: American Philosophical Society, pp. 117–160.

Bodman, N. C. 1973. 'Some Chinese reflexes of Sino-Tibetan s-clusters', *Journal of Chinese Linguistics*, 1 (3): 383–396.

Bodman, N. C. 1980. 'Proto-Chinese and Sino-Tibetan: Data towards establishing the nature of the relationship', in F. van Coetsem and L. R. Waugh (eds.), *Contributions to Historical Linguistics: Issues and Materials*. Leiden: E.J. Brill, pp. 34–199.

Bory de Saint-Vincent, Jean Baptiste. 1825. *Dictionnaire classique d'histoire naturelle. Tome Huitieme*. Paris: Rey et Gravier.

Cai, X., Z. Qin, B. Wen, S. Xu, Y. Wang, Y. Lu, L. Wei, C. Wang, S. Li, X. Huang, H. Li? and the Genographic Consortium. 2011. 'Human migration through bottlenecks from Southeast Asia into East Asia during Last Glacial Maximum revealed by Y chromosomes', *Public Library of Science*, 6 (8): e24282.

Cavalli-Sforza, L. L., P. Menozzi and A. Piazza. 1994. *The History and Geography of Human Genes*. Princeton, NJ: Princeton University Press.

Chaubey, G., M. Metspalu, Y. Choi, R. Mägi, I. G. Romero, S. Rootsi, P. Soares, M. van Oven, D. M. Behar, S. Rootsi, G. Hudjashov, C. B. Mallick, M. Karmin, M. Nelis, J. Parik, A. G. Reddy, E. Metspalu, G. van Driem, Y. Xue, C. Tyler-Smith, K. Thangaraj, L. Singh, M. Remm, M. B. Richards, M. M. Lahr, M. Kayser, R. Villems and T. Kivisild. 2010. 'Population genetic structure in Indian Austroasiatic speakers: The role of landscape barriers and sex-specific admixture', *Molecular Biology and Evolution*, 28 (2): 1013–1024.

Conrady, A. 1916. 'Eine merkwürdige Beziehung zwischen den austrischen und den indochinesischen Sprachen', in *Aufsätze zur Kultur – und Sprachgeschichte vornehmlich des Orients: Ernst Kuhn zum 70. Geburtstage am 7. Februar 1916 gewidmet von Freunden und Schülern*. München: Verlag von M. & H. Marcus, pp. 475–504.

Conrady, A. 1922. 'Neue austrisch-indochinesische Parallelen', in *Asia Major: Hirth Anniversary Volume*. London: Robsthan and Company, pp. 23–66.

Cust, R. N. 1878. *A Sketch of the Modern Languages of East India*. London: Trübner and Company.

Derenko, M., B. Malyarchuk, G. Denisova, M. Wozniak, T. Grzybowski, I. Dambueva and I. Zakharov. 2007. 'Y-chromosome haplogroup N dispersal from south Siberia to Europe', *Journal of Human Genetics*, 52: 763–770.

Dulik, M. C., S. I. Zhadanov, L. P. Osipova, A. Askapuli, L. Gau, O. Gokcumen, S. Rubinstein and T. G. Schurr. 2012. 'Mitochondrial DNA and Y chromosome variation provides evidence for a recent common ancestry between native Americans and indigenous Altaians', *American Journal of Human Genetics*, 90 (2): 229–246.

Erxleben, J. C. P. 1777. *Systema regni animalis per Classes, ordines, Genera, Species, Varietates cvm Synonymia et Historia Animalivm*. Leipzig: Weygand.

Forbes, C. J. F. S. 1878. 'On Tibeto-Burman languages', *Journal of the Royal Asiatic Society of Great Britain and Ireland*, 10: 210–227.

Hammer, M. F., T. M. Karafet, H. Park, K. Omoto, S. Harihara, M. Stoneking and S. Horai. 2006. 'Dual origins of the Japanese: Common ground for hunter-gather and farmer Y chromosomes', *Journal of Human Genetics*, 51: 47–58.

Hodgson, B. H. 1857. 'Comparative vocabulary of the languages of the broken tribes of Népál', *Journal of the Asiatic Society of Bengal*, 26: 317–371.

Houghton, B. 1896. 'Outlines of Tibeto-Burman linguistic palæontology', *Journal of the Royal Asiatic Society*, January: 23–55.

Hurles, M. E., B. C. Sykes, M. A. Jobling and P. Forster. 2005. 'The dual origin of the Malagasy in Island Southeast Asia and East Africa: Evidence from maternal and paternal lineages', *American Journal of Human Genetics*, 76: 894–901.

Jin, H.-J., C. Tyler-Smith and W. Kim. 2009. 'The peopling of Korea revealed by analyses of mitochondrial DNA and Y-chromosomal markers', *Public Library of Science PLoS One*, 4 (1): e4210.

Jinam, T. A., L.-C. Hong, M. E. Phipps, M. Stoneking, M. Ameen, J. Edo and HUGO Pan-Asian SNP Consortium and Naruya Satou. 2013. 'Evolutionary history of continental Southeast Asian: "Early train" hypothesis based on genetic analysis of mitochondrial and autosomal DNA data', *Molecular Biology and Evolution*, 29 (11): 3513–3527.

Karafet, T. M., J. S. Lansing, A. J. Redd and J. C. Watkins. 2005. 'Balinese Y-chromosome perspective on the peopling of Indonesia: Genetic contributions from pre-Neolithic hunter-gatherers, Austronesian farmers and Indian traders', *Human Biology*, 77 (1): 93–114.

Karafet, T. M., F. L. Mendez, M. B. Meilerman, P. A. Underhill, S. L. Zegura and M. F. Hammer. 2008. 'New binary polymorphisms reshape and increase resolution of the human Y-chromosomal haplogroup tree', *Genome Research*, 18: 830–838.

Karafet, T. M., S. L. Zegura and M. F. Hammer. 2009. 'Y-chromosome Japanese roots', in P. N. Peregrine, I. Peiros and M. Feldman (eds.), *Ancient Human Migrations: A Multidisciplinary Approach*. Salt Lake City: University of Utah Press, pp. 137–148.

Kumar, V., B. T. Langstieh, S. Biswas, J. P. Babu, T. N. Rao, K. Thangaraj, A. G. Reddy, L. Singh and B. M. Reddy. 2006. 'Asian and non-Asian origins of Mon-Khmer and Mundari speaking Austroasiatic populations of India', *American Journal of Human Biology*, 18: 461–469.

Kumar, V., A. N. S. Reddy, J. P. Babu, T. N. Rao, B. T. Langstieh, K. Thangaraj, A. G. Reddy, L. Singh and B. M. Reddy. 2007. 'Y-chromosome evidence suggests a common paternal heritage of Austro-Asiatic populations', *BioMed Central Evolutionary Biology*, 7: 47, doi:10.1186/1471-2148-7-47.

Li, J. Z., D. M. Absher, H. Tang, A. M. Southwick, A. M. Casto, S. Ramachandran, H. M. Cann, G. S. Barsh, M. Feldman, L. L. Cavalli-Sforza and R. M. Myers. 2008. 'Worldwide human relationships inferred from genome-wide patterns of variation', *Science*, 319: 1100–1104.

Lǐ Huī, B. W., S.-J. Chen, B. Su, P. Pramoonjago, Y. Liu, S. Pan, Z. Qin, W. Liu, X. Cheng, N. Yang, X. Li, D. Tran, D. Lu, M.-T. Hsu, R. Deka, S. Marzuki, C.-C. Tan and J. Lì. 2008. 'Paternal genetic affinity between western Austronesians and Daic populations', *BMC Evolutionary Biology*, 8: 146, doi:10.1186/1471-2148-8-146.

Linnæus, C. 1758. *Systema Naturæ per Regna tria Naturæ, secundum Classes, Ordines, Genera, Species, cum characteristibus, differentiis synonymis, locis*. (Editio Decima). Holmiæ: Laurentius Salvius.

Meiners, C. 1813 [posthumous]. *Untersuchungen über die Verschiedenheiten der Menschennaturen (die verschiedenen Menschenarten) in Asien und in den Südländern, in den Ostindischen und Südseeinseln, nebst einer historischen Vergleichung der vormahligen und gegenwärtigen Bewohner dieser Continente und Eylande*. Tübingen: in der J.G. Cotta'schen Buchhandlung.

Mendez, F. L., T. Krahn, B. Schrack, A.-M. Krahn, K. R. Veeramah, A. E. Woerner, F. L. M. Fomine, N. Bradman, M. G. Thomas, T. M. Karafet and M. F. Hammer. 2013. 'An African American paternal lineage adds an extremely ancient root to the human Y chromosome phylogenetic tree', *American Journal of Human Genetics*, 92: 454–459.

Mirabal, S., M. Reguiero, A. M. Cadenas, L. L. Cavalli-Sforza, P. A. Underhill, D. A. Verbenko, S. A. Limborska and R. J. Herrera. 2009. 'Y chromosome distribution within the geo-linguistic landscape of northwestern Russia', *European Journal of Human Genetics*, 17: 1260–1273.

Müller, F. M. 1872. *Über die Resultate der Sprachwissenschaft: Vorlesung gehalten in der kaiserlichen Universitæt zu Strassburg am* XXIII. *Mai* MDCCCLXXII. Strassburg: Karl J. Trübner, und London: Trübner & Co.

Ostapirat, W. 2005. 'Kra-Dai and Austronesian: Notes on phonological correspondences and vocabulary distribution', in L. Sagart, R. Blench and A. Sanchez-Mazas (eds.), *The Peopling of East Asia: Putting Together Archaeology, Linguistics and Genetics*. London: Routledge Curzon, pp. 107–131.

Ostapirat, W. 2013. 'Austro-Tai revisited', *23rd Annual Meeting of the Southeast Asian Linguistic Society*, 29 May 2013, Chulalongkorn University, Bangkok, Thailand.

Peiros, I. 1998. *Comparative Linguistics in Southeast Asia*. Canberra: Pacific Linguistics.

Poloni, E. S., N. Ray, S. Schneider and A. Langaney. 2000. 'Languages and genes: Modes of transmission observed through the analysis of male-specific and female-specific genes', in J.-L. Dessalles and L. Ghadakpour (eds.), *Proceedings: Evolution of Language, 3rd International Conference 3–6 April 2000*. Paris: École Nationale Supérieure des Télécommunications, pp. 185–186.

Poloni, E. S., O. Semino, G. Passarino, A. S. Santachiara-Benerecetti, I. Dupanloup, A. Langaney and L. Excoffier. 1997. 'Human genetic affinities for Y chromosome P49a,f/*Taq*I haplotypes show strong correspondence with linguistics', *American Journal of Human Genetics*, 61: 1015–1035 (cf. the erratum published in 1998 in the *American Journal of Human Genetics*, 62: 1267).

Pulleyblank, E. G. 1983. 'The Chinese and their neighbours in prehistoric and early historic times', in D. N. Keightley (ed.), *The Origins of Chinese Civilization*. Berkeley: University of California Press, pp. 411–466.

Ramstedt, G. J. 1957 [posthumous]. *Einführung in die altaische Sprachwissenschaft: Lautlehre* (Suomalais-Ugrilaisen Seuran Toimituksia, Mémoires de la Société Finno-Ougrienne, 104, 1). Helsinki: Suomalais-Ugrilaisen Seura.

Reid, L. A. 2005. 'The current status of Austric: A review and evaluation of the lexical and morphosyntactic evidence', in L. Sagart, R. Blench and A. Sanchez-Mazas (eds.), *The Peopling of East Asia: Putting Together Archaeology, Linguistics and Genetics*. London: Routledge Curzon, pp. 132–160.

Relandus, H. [Adriaan van Reeland]. 1706, 1707, 1708. *Dissertationum Miscellanearum, Pars Prima, Pars Altera, Pars Tertia et Ultima*. Trajecti ad Rhenum: Gulielmus Broedelet.

Robbeets, M. 2014. 'The Japanese inflectional paradigm in a Trans-Eurasian perspective', in M. Robbeets and W. Bisang (eds.), *Paradigm Change in the Trans-Eurasian Languages and Beyond*. Amsterdam: John Benjamins, pp. 197–232.

Rootsi, S., L. A. Zhivotovsky, M. Baldovič, M. Kayser, I. A. Kutuev, R. Khusainova, M. A. Bermisheva, M. Gubina, S. A. Federova, A.-M. Ilumäe, E. K. Khusnutdinova, M. I. Voevoda, L. P. Osipova, M. Stoneking, A. A. Lin, V. Ferak, J. Parik, T. Kivisild, P. A. Underhill and R. Villems. 2007. 'A counterclockwise northern route of the Y-chromosome haplogroup N from Southeast Asia towards Europe', *European Journal of Human Genetics*, 15: 204–211.

Schlegel, G. 1901. Review: '*Elements of Siamese Grammar* by O. Frankfurter, Ph.D., Bangkok: Printed at the American Presbyterian Mission Press, Leipzig, Karl W. Hiersemann, 1900', *T'oung Pao* (Série II), 2: 76–87.

Schlegel, G. 1902. *Siamese Studies* (T'oung Pao, New Series II, Volume II, Supplement). Leiden: Henri Cordier and Gustave Schlegel.

Schmidt, W. 1906. 'Die Mon-Khmer Völker, ein Bindeglied zwischen Völkern Zentral-Asiens und Austronesiens', *Archiv für Anthropologie, Neue Folge*, 5: 59–109.

Starosta, S. 2005 [posthumous]. 'Proto-East-Asian and the origin and dispersal of languages of East and Southeast Asia and the Pacific', in L. Sagart, R. Blench and A. Sanchez-Mazas (eds.), *The Peopling of East Asia: Putting Together Archaeology, Lingtuistics and Genetics*. London: Routledge Curzon, pp. 182–197.

Starostin, S. A. 1994. 'The reconstruction of Proto-Kiranti', *Paper Presented at the 27ème Congrès International sur les Langues et la Linguistique Sino-Tibétaines*, 14 octobre 1994, Centre International d'Études Pédagogiques à Sèvres, Sèvres, France.

Tanaka, M., V. M. Cabrera, A. M. González, J. M. Larruga, T. Takeyasu, N. Fuku, L.-J. Guo, R. Hirose, Y. Fujita, M. Kurata, K.-I. Shinoda, K. Umetso, Y. Yamada, Y. Oshida, Y. Sato, N. Hattori, Y. Mizuno, Y. Arai, N. Hirose, S. Ohta, O. Ogawa, Y. Tanaka, R. Kawamori, M. Shamoto-Nagai, W. Maruyama, H. Shimokata, R. Suzuki and H. Shimodaira. 2004. 'Mitochondrial genome variation in eastern Asia and the peopling of Japan', *Genome Research*, 10A: 1832–1850.

Thangaraj, K., G. Chaubey, V. Kumar Singh, A. Vanniarajan, I. Thanseem, A. G. Reddy and L. Singh. 2006a. '*In situ* origin of deep rooting lineages of mitochondrial macrohaplogroup M in India', *BMC Genomics*, 7: 151, doi:10.1186/1471-2164-7-151.

Thangaraj, K., V. Sridhar, T. Kivisild, A. G. Reddy, G. Chaubey, V. Kumar Singh, S. Kaur, P. Agrawal, A. Rai, J. Gupta, C. B. Mallick, N. Kumar, T. P. Velavan, R. Suganthan, D. Udaykumar, R. Kumar, R. Mishra, A. Khan, C. Annapurna and L. Singh. 2006b. 'Different population histories of the Mundari- and Mon-Khmer-speaking Austro-Asiatic tribes inferred from the mtDNA 9-bp deletion/insertion polymorphism in Indian populations', *Human Genetics*, 119 (1–2): 223, 224.

Thanseem, I., K. Thangaraj, G. Chaubey, V. Kumar Singh, L. V. K. S. Bhaskar, B. M. Reddy, A. G. Reddy and L. Singh. 2006. 'Genetic affinities among the lower castes and tribal groups of India: Inference from Y chromsome and mitochondrial DNA', *BMC Genetiocs*, 7: 42, doi:10.1186/1471-2156-7-42.

Underhill, P. A., N. M. Myres, S. Rootsi, M. Metspalu, L. A. Zhivotovsky, R. J. King, A. A. Lin, C.-E. T. Chow, O. Semino, V. Battaglia, I. Kutuev, M. Järve, G. Chaubey, Q. Ayub, A. Mohyuddin, S. Q. Mehdi, S. Sengupta, E. I. Rogaev, E. K. Khusnutdinova, A. Pshenichnov, O. Balanovsky, E. Balanovska, N. Jeran, D. H. Augustin, M. Baldovič, R. J. Herrera, K. Thangaraj, V. Singh, L. Singh, P. Majumder, P. Rudan, D. Primorac, R. Villems and T. Kivisild. 2010. 'Separating the post-glacial coancestry of European and Asian Y chromosomes within haplogroup R1a', *European Journal of Human Genetics*, 18: 479–484.

Underhill, P. A., G. Passarino, A. A. Lin, P. Shen, M. Mirazón-Lahr, R. A. Foley, P. J. Oefner and L. L. Cavalli-Sforza. 2001. 'The phylogeography of Y chromosome binary haplotypes and the origins of modern human populations', *Annals of Human Genetics*, 65: 4–62.

Underhill, P. A., P. Shen, A. A. Lin, J. Lì, G. Passarino, W. H. Yang, E. Kauffman, B. Bonné-Tamir, J. Bertranpetit, P. Francalacci, M. Ibrahim, T. Jenkins, J. R. Kidd, S. Q. Mehdi, M. T. Seielstad, R. S. Wells, A. Piazza, R. W. Davis, M. W. Feldman, L. L. Cavalli-Sforza and P. J. Oefner. 2000. 'Y chromosome sequence variation and the history of human populations', *Nature Genetics*, 26: 358–361.

van Driem, G. 2005. 'Sino-Austronesian vs. Sino-Caucasian, Sino-Bodic vs. Sino-Tibetan, and Tibeto-Burman as default theory', in Y. P. Yadava, G. Bhattarai, R. R. Lohani, B. Prasain and K. Parajuli (eds.), *Contemporary Issues in Nepalese Linguistics*. Kathmandu: Linguistic Society of Nepal, pp. 285–338.

van Driem, G. 2007. 'Austroasiatic phylogeny and the Austroasiatic homeland in light of recent population genetic studies', *Mon-Khmer Studies*, 37: 1–14.

van Driem, G. 2008. 'Reflections on the ethnolinguistic prehistory of the greater Himalayan region', in B. Huber, M. Volkart and P. Widmer (eds.), *Chomolangma, Demawend und Kasbek: Festschrift für Roland Bielmeier zu seinem 65. Geburtstag* (2 vols., Vol. 1). Halle: International Institute for Tibetan and Buddhist Studies, pp. 39–59.

van Driem, G. 2011a. 'Rice and the Austroasiatic and Hmong-Mien homelands', in N. J. Enfield (ed.), *Dynamics of Human Diversity: The Case of Mainland Southeast Asia*. Canberra: Pacific Linguistics, pp. 361–389.

van Driem, G. 2011b. 'The Trans-Himalayan phylum and its implications for population prehistory', *Communication on Contemporary Anthropology*, 5: 135–142.

van Driem, G. 2012a. 'The ethnolinguistic identity of the domesticators of Asian rice', *Comptes Rendus Palevol*, 11 (2): 117–132.

van Driem, G. 2012b. 'Etyma, shouldered adzes and molecular variants', in A. Ender, A. Leemann and B. Wälchli (eds.), *Methods in Contemporary Linguistics*. Berlin: Mouton de Gruyter, pp. 335–361.

van Driem, G. 2014a. 'Trans-Himalayan', in N. Hill and T. Owen-Smith (eds.), *Trans-Himalayan Linguistics*. Berlin: Mouton de Gruyter, pp. 11–40.

van Driem, G. 2014b. 'A prehistoric thoroughfare between the Ganges and the Himalayas', in T. Jamir and M. Hazarika (eds.), *50 Years after Daojali-Hading: Emerging Perspectives in the Archaeology of Northeast India*. New Delhi: Research India Press, pp. 60–98.

Virey, J.-J. 1801 [An IX]. *Histoire naturelle du genre humain, ou Recherches sur ses principaux Fondemens physiques et moraux; précédées d'un Discours sur la nature des êtres organiques, et sur l'ensemble de leur physiologie. On y a joint une dissertation sur le sauvage de l'Aveyron* (deux tomes). Paris: F. Dufart.

von Klaproth, J. H. 1823. *Asia Polyglotta*. Paris: A. Schubart.

Wen, B., L. Hui, L. Daru, S. Xiufeng, Z. Feng, H. Yungang, L. Feng, G. Yang, M. Xianyun, Z. Liang, Q. Ji, T. Jingze, J. Jianzhong, H. Wei, R. Deka, S. Bīng, R. Chakroborty and J. Lì. 2004. 'Genetic evidence supports demic diffusion of Han culture', *Nature*, 431 (7006): 302–305.

Witsen, N. 1692. *Noord en Oost Tartarye, ofte Bondig Ontwerp van eenige dier Landen en Volken, welke voormaels bekent zijn geweest, beneffens verscheide tot noch toe onbekende, en meest nooit voorheen beschreven Tartersche en Nabuurige Gewesten, Landstreeken, Steden, Rivieren, en Plaetzen, in de Noorder en Oostelykste Gedeelten van Asia en Europa* (2 vol.). Amsterdam: François Halma.

Wood, E. T., D. A. Stover, C. Ehret, G. Destro-Bisol, G. Spedini, H. McLeiod, L. Louie, M. Bamshad, B. I. Strassmann, H. Soodyall and M. F. Hammer. 2005. 'Contrasting patterns of Y chromosome and mtDNA variation in Africa: Evidence for sex-biased demographic processes', *European Journal of Human Genetics*, 13: 867–876.

Wulff, K. 1934. *Chinesisch und Tai: Sprachvergleichende Untersuchungen*. Copenhagen: Levin & Munksgaard.

Wulff, K. 1942 [posthumous]. *Über das Verhältnis des Malay-Polynesischen zum Indochinesischen*. Copenhagen: Munksgaard.

2 Access to water and gender rights in India

Contextualising the various debates through the study of a mountain village in Sikkim

Jwala D. Thapa

1. Introduction

Principle 3 of the Dublin Principles 1992[1] recognises the important role women play in the provision, management and safeguarding of water all over the world. The crucial role of women in making provisions for drinking, sanitation and other domestic purposes in households in rural India is also a very well-known fact. Due to the lack of proper access, it is also well known that women travel many kilometres and for the greater part of a day to ensure the fulfilment of the daily domestic requirement of water (Lahiri-Dutt 2009: 275). Understandably, while it is the prerogative of the government to ensure that the population in general do not suffer from water scarcity problems, it is also expected that such initiatives be taken keeping in mind the difficulties faced by women due to lack of proper access to water. In spite of this, the Draft National Water Policy 2012 of India does not separately recognise the need to identify and solve the difficulties of women with respect to access to water.

Women all over India face different kinds of problems in carrying out their role as the managers and providers of water. Also, India being a vast country with different topographical variations, problems of accessibility to water also changes with changes in geographical variations. Additionally throwing in social and cultural considerations, a blanket approach to understanding, analysing and resolving water issues vis-à-vis women only create more problems.

In this chapter, the author has looked into various debates that exist in India with respect to the right to water of women in India and tried to analyse these debates through a field study in a mountain village of Sikkim. The principal aim was to contextualise these debates in order to identify any differences that may occur in the difficulties faced by women with a change in topography and with some alterations in cultural underpinnings. The study also aimed at understanding whether a separate approach needs to be adopted when it comes to mountain women.

Although the study is not representative of all mountain women, as it was conducted in only two sample villages in the Namchi-Assangthang area, it has yielded interesting insights into some common problems that are faced by women of the mountains and how a different approach might be needed in national policymaking and the legislative frameworks that might transpire with respect to water accessibility. In her fieldwork related to water quality and quantity analysis in the East and South Districts of Sikkim, Archana Tiwari identifies that Namchi-Assangthang area, the focus areas of this chapter, are one of the most drought prone areas (Tiwari 2012: 41).[2]

2.   Methodology

The author has used the doctrinal method of research for conducting a literature review of the major existing narratives to form a background for the fieldwork. Subsequently, the unstructured interview technique was used to collect data and conduct a qualitative study through a comparison with the narratives culled out through the doctrinal study. It is also important to mention here that literature on gender studies of Sikkimese women are rare and also most feminist narratives on mountain women have been focused on women of Nepal and Western Indian Himalayas. Since these have been used extensively in this chapter, this liberty is justified on two common but broad grounds: that these narratives are about women of the mountains and that these women profess Hinduism, which as a religion inculcate similar attitudes towards water as an element of nature.

The focus of this study has been the two villages of Ahley Ward (No. 4) and Dumigaon Ward (No. 5) which fall under the administrative block of Assangthang-Sambung (GPO) in Namchi, South District, Sikkim.[3] These villages were selected due to their proximity to the town of Namchi, which is the administrative headquarters of the South District of Sikkim, a district which has historically had water access and availability issues, especially significant during the winter season.[4] These villages were also selected because of their lack of proper modern state-sponsored water supply systems as opposed to the adjoining villages in the Assangthang-Sambung (GPO) area.

A preliminary field visit was made to understand the nature of the field, the population and to meet the contact persons. Soon after, a week-long visit was made to observe the behaviour of women and other members of the family in water collection. Interviews were also conducted at the same time with all sections of the population but focusing primarily on the women. The main water sources of the two villages became the nerve centre of the research to understand the frequency of water collection and the main actors involved in the same. The whole process occurred in the month of July–August which coincides with the monsoon rains in the Sikkim Himalayas and leads to abundance in water flows in streams, rivers, brooks, ponds and a result of a high rise in the water table.

3. Preliminary framework adapted after the first field visit

The villagers of Ahley Gaon and Dumi Gaon primarily belong to the Tibeto-Burmese groups of Rai, Magar, Lepcha and Bhutia and the Indo-Aryan groups of Bahun, Chettri, Kami and Damai. While the Bahuns and Chettris are Hindus belonging to the upper caste Brahmins and Kshatriyas respectively, the latter two are scheduled castes as per the Hindu varna system. A majority of the population follow the Hindu religion, while a small number of the populace are Buddhists and Christians. The Rais and Magars, who are in the majority in the two villages, are followers of Vaishnavism[5] and observe the strict tenets of the Hindu religion like the caste system, vegetarianism etc., even though they are not recognised as belonging within the folds of the Hindu varna system.[6]

The families of the two villages comprise about a hundred households in total with an average of five members per family and a couple of female-headed households. Most of the population, including both men and women equally, are involved in regular agricultural work and other seasonal employment like those under the Mahatma Gandhi National Rural Employment Guarantee Scheme (MGN-REGA), while some of them are employed with the government in small jobs.[7]

The social set up in the villages is such – like in any other mountain villages in Sikkim, especially amongst the Tibeto-Burmese populace – that for women working outside the domestic sphere, there is no social sanction or it is not frowned upon. Hence, employment opportunities for women, especially under gender-sensitive projects like those under the MGNREGA, are welcomed without any social restraints and resistance. Since women have been more visible in the community sphere as compared to their counterparts in the plains as well as those amongst the Indo-Aryan communities in the mountains itself, absorption of changes in the employment trends are also not questioned by the male members. Hence, men do not perceive this as a threat to their role as providers. Apart from their employment outside the domestic sphere, these women still perform gendered activities like cooking, cleaning in addition to their reproductive functions.

The farming activities are based on the *khetala*[8] system whereby farm labour is used on a rotational system involving all the village members. Hence, in-migratory farm labour is absent and so is outmigration. The relative nature of the availability of male–female employment opportunities in the villages is such that most of the households subsist comfortably on the annual crops and income from other job opportunities.[9] The agricultural production is focused on maize, millet, soya bean, ginger, cherry chillies (*dalley*) and seasonal vegetables.[10] These seasonal crops coincide with the weather and generally crops like maize, pulses, soya bean and vegetables are grown during the wet seasons, while the winter seasons are for crops like ginger, tubers and millet. However, the global change in weather patterns has made it difficult for the otherwise hardworking farmers of these two villages to sustain on agriculture and farming alone.

Water access and water management system in the two villages

The agricultural activity is mostly rain fed and the two villages suffer from a generally dry and windy weather with acute water shortage during the winter seasons.[11] Monsoons bring abundant water in the two villages and this leads to the sprouting of water from the ground aquifers in all places, a phenomenon known as *mulphutnu* (Khawas 2004: 9). Although rice is not grown, terraced farming which is more associated with rice cultivation is also practised in these two villages in accordance with the mountainous topography although most of them are dry fields which are all rain fed.

A village woman of Dumi Gaon narrated a local legend whereby there is a belief that all those places through which the river Rangeet (the second biggest river of Sikkim) flows has been cursed to be dry. One cannot but see some semblance of truth in the legend as those parts of the South and West Districts of Sikkim through which the river flows face acute dryness and water shortages.[12] Ahley Gaon and Dumi Gaon are no exceptions to this legend and the flowing river can in fact be 'heard' from both these places and also seen from many points of these villages.

Bio-folklores such as these are common in Sikkim, as in other parts of India, especially amongst the Hindu and Buddhist populace. For the

Hindus, water sources like rivers, springs, ponds and brooks are sacred spaces where a high degree of purity is attached to the maintenance of these community places. In those places from which springs erupt, *bar* and *peepal* trees are planted, representing the Hindu deities Vishnu and Laxmi respectively, and pujas are performed regularly to appease the gods and goddesses turning these places into sacred groves. Sometimes such sacred groves themselves have water sources relegating them to the status of highly sacred water sources.[13] The sacredness associated with water sources is such that meat, clothes with menstrual blood and other kinds of human waste are not washed in the streams and ponds as it is believed that these activities will anger the deities and might lead to the drying up of the water or 'shifting' of the water source to another place. Most of the times, people do not walk or trample on the *mohaan*,[14] *mul* or the sources from which the water flows or erupts as this part of the water source is considered the place in which the deities, who bless the place with water, reside. In case of still-water ponds, people never put their body parts inside or wash anything in it, in the same belief of its sacredness and hence, water is always scooped out with clean *gagris* or metal tumblers.

The village of Ahley Gaon was named after an *ahal*, a pond that rests on the top of the village, ensconced between hillocks on a low water table area. The *ahal* is an aquatic sacred grove for the villagers, a *devithan*, literally translated as a 'goddess place' or a place where the 'female' deity of the forest dwell.[15] The oral storytelling tradition of this village has preserved stories like that of the sightings of a *devi* in the night atop a tiger. One can never whistle, talk or speak loudly in the vicinity as it could disturb the goddess and make her angry. A story also goes that a middle-aged woman was washing millet to make *chang*[16] when she was sucked into the watery vortex of the pond and her body was never found. The village, being historically steeped in the Vaishnavite Hindu tradition, considered it a punishment for the woman for trying to make an alcoholic drink.

These beliefs and practices are positive community habits as they in fact ensure that such community water sources remain uncontaminated. However, sometimes these beliefs verge on the extreme where discriminatory practices prevail with respect to villagers belonging to the scheduled castes who are considered untouchables.[17] They are not allowed to collect water from these sources or at many a times, when the upper caste members are in the vicinity, they have to stand aside and wait for their turn or collect water when no one is around. Changes in social milieu and awareness brought about by the legal regulation of such practices have however been able to dilute such discrimination although not in attitudes.[18]

The villagers, for the purpose of this study, were interviewed specifically with respect to access to water for drinking and other domestic purposes. In much of the households, there were state-provided facilities of water harvesting tanks. This water was considered unsafe and impure for drinking because it was rainwater that fell stagnant for a long period of time during storage.[19] They were also not aware of any other methods of water purification, except boiling, although they spoke of some villages nearby using alum and lime to clarify the harvested rainwater before being boiled for drinking. Hence, the harvested water was mainly used for washing, irrigation of kitchen and corner gardens, feeding cattle, sanitation and for all other purposes except drinking.

The villages had also been provided with tanks, newly set up by the Agriculture and Horticulture Department, to harvest rainwater for irrigating vegetable and fruit gardens/orchards.

Hence, the provision with respect to drinking water was the most neglected. The villagers informed that with respect to drinking water, the state leaves it upon the villagers to find a 'source' of drinking water and then puts the onus on the villagers to apply to the concerned department for a water supply network. The state then provides pipes, cement and other construction materials as well as labour for the construction of the supply. Most of the times, the state provides them with a cemented water dispensing system with a metal tap outside the homes on a fixed budget and a plan calculated per household. Those with money use the same water supply system to build extra tanks for water storage and divert the pipes inside the kitchens, bathrooms etc., replicating the urbanised water dispensing system of the towns of Sikkim which is an added luxury in the other villages and something unimaginable in the two villages of this study.

Water sources in Ahley Gaon Ward

Till date, in the village of Ahley Gaon, there have been two instances of state-provided water supply system but they remain useless as the villagers are unable to find a water source. The main source of water for the village is a *dhara*[20] or a mountain stream which feeds the water needs of all the families in the entire mountain slope.

Ahley Gaon had not been able to create/find any other source of water to feed the state-provided water supply system, creating acute difficulties for at least twenty-six families living above the level of the *dhara* stream. Most of the time, water for drinking and household use is fetched in *gagris* and jerrycans and stored on a daily basis. However, the families below the *dhara* source do not face much difficulty as they used personal plastic CVC pipes to channelise water to their individual homes. Hence, the focus of the interview became of the difficulties of women above the *dhara* source since they are not able to channelise the water upstream to their homes.

Water sources in Dumi Gaon Ward

With respect to the other village, which has about seventy-six families throughout the mountain slope and of which about ten were interviewed, the village did have the same nature of state-provided provisions with respect to rainwater harvesting. However, the village had water sources at frequent intervals towards a downward slope of the mountain, starting at the higher parts above the densely populated parts of the village. Hence, the whole village was somehow able to manage having drinking water right at their houses by channelising them through the use of personal CVC pipes. Also, the village had a perennial source of water at the top part of the mountain slope in the form of two *kuas* (ponds), namely *Dumi Kua* and *Bar Kua* of which the latter supplied the major quantity of drinking water through the personalised CVC pipe system.

In fact, the state-built water supply system did try to use the *Bar Kua* at one point of time but failed as the pond was a sufficient source only during the monsoons. Here, the state-supplied water system that sourced water through the Namchi town from Ravangla also did not work as the water supply depleted and became insignificant by the time it reached the village. This was also the case in Ahley Gaon where the water supplied from Namchi did go to a nearby village, from a system that ran through but above the village, but village politics and power struggle ensured that they did not get even a drop from the supply system. Villagers from Ahley Gaon admitted to 'stealing' water during the night, many a times by diverting the water flow through CVC pipes which sustained until the theft was discovered.[21] The villages being close-knit and having a strong sense of community, such instances become full-blown issues where the perpetrators are harshly dealt with, sometimes with social ostracisation which is a very serious punishment in the rural context. These matters are seriously dealt with because the water is not just for the purpose of drinking but also for agrarian purposes and hence, it amounts to economic losses.

Both the villages however faced similar patterns with respect to availability of water on a seasonal basis with the months of January till about May being the harshest period when natural water sources in the mountains dry up due to depletion of the water table. It is in these periods that the debates of water access and management and role of women could have been studied best.[22] However, the interview in the village of Ahley Ward revealed substantial findings which the author felt did not vary much with those in the harsh periods of water scarcity because the villagers have to depend on the *dhara* all year round for drinking water as well as the use of collected water for sanitation and other domestic purposes. Much of the findings were similar to the findings relating to water availability and access of people of Dumi Gaon Ward during the periods of water scarcity from natural sources.

Hence, the comparison of the existing debates with respect to role of women and water access was made by highlighting some major issues with respect to drinking water in the following areas:

1   Collection of water
2   Use and management
3   Role in policy decisions relating to state-made provisions for water both through traditional and formal methods

Collection of water

Studies of role of women in collection of water done in the plain areas of India project a traditional picture of a long line of women in colourful clothes, walking miles in search of portable water. Men are not depicted as involved in the collection of water. The interview as well as observation of these two villages revealed that in these mountain villages, collection of water is almost an equally divided task with no gender differentiation. The most important reason for this being that the mountain topography meant that men, being stronger, were able to cover the distance faster and with a bigger load. Thus, if a woman made a trip to the *dhara* to and fro carrying a 10-L *gagri*, a man was more efficient because he could carry two at a time.

Hence, the responsibility with respect to collection was about the availability of free time taken off from the daily subsistence work, farm work and other commitments, regardless of gender. However, keeping in mind the physiological differences between men and women and the still persisting traditional domestic roles of these women, their workload did not seem less in totality. Hence, their relief from the role of water collectors depended on the good nature and benevolence of the male adult members of the household.

However, the interviews did reveal a section which was a casualty to the difficult access to and availability of water – children. Most households had school-going children and because some were too young to help in farming or in the kitchen, the responsibility of water collection fell on their young shoulders. Regardless of gender, children in these villages were responsible for collection of water before leaving for school and after coming back from school. Regardless of the economic status of their parents within the village community, children are expected to stock up water to be used by the parents for domestic use. They found recycled, 5-L plastic jerrycans as the most convenient modes of carrying water. The holidays, which left them with ample time at their disposal, was spent fetching water during periods of the day which could have been spent on study, preparation for school curriculum or play. On an average, children of both villages travel about 6 km up and down the mountain to collect water.

Use and management

Women in India have been delegated the traditional role of not just collection of drinking water but also its use and management. This is because women do most of the domestic work and hence, ensuring economical use of water falls within their domain. This also includes educating children about water use as a part of their upbringing and hence, children seemed to have a very high regard for the value of water as an important natural resource.

In this study, the findings were mixed in this aspect rather than being entirely projected towards women. Due to the active involvement of women, men and children in water collection, the knowledge about its efficient use and management in daily use is prevalent because collection of water in a mountainous topography is affected by the decisions of all members of the household. However, in comparisons between men and women, it is the women who still ensure that the daily water supply in the household subsists and this is done by frequent trips to the *dhara*, almost on an hourly basis. This is continued through the use of the labour of children at the first instance and then the women as their work hours are more flexible as compared to the men who are still considered primary breadwinners. Also, because women are involved in the cooking of meals for the whole family, sometimes with the help of young daughters, the females of the households keep an eye on the availability of water in the house. Hence, it is mostly the prerogative of the women to manage and educate about the use of water at the level of a household.

The women also spoke of the general belief in the connection between womanly behaviour and water use. They said that the way in which a woman manages the water in the house is the signs of her being a *lacchini* (one who brings good luck) or an *alachinni* (one who brings bad luck). Indiscriminate use of water is considered the signs of a bad homemaker and a luckless woman. Thus, if a woman used water sparingly and with much economy, it was considered a sign of her being endowed with good virtues that bring good luck to the household. In a traditional social set-up, such beliefs are crucial in determining and maintaining their respectable position in the household. Hence, a house in which the *gagri*s are full of water all the time was considered a house which was blessed with luck and prosperity.

Thus, women are the first in the line of efficient water management and ensuring a steady supply of water in the house was a reflection of their being properly domesticated women, an important component of a mountain woman's secure place in a household. It also meant that the women made frequent trips to the *dhara* daily since males go out into the fields for the most part of the day. Even if they themselves do not do so, any child's play was usually sacrificed in fetching water at the bidding of the womenfolk in the house.

Role in policy decisions relating to state-made provisions for water both through traditional and formal methods

It is an accepted fact that women are excluded from policymaking as well as involvement in the management of water in India in general. However, as discussed in the coming sections, in issues involving the mobilisation of access to water at the village level as well as their active involvement in ensuring better drinking water facilities, their presence is almost absent. Even in mountain villages, studies have revealed that fetching water from natural sources has been the prerogative of women too but their exclusion is apparent in the modern policymaking. Also, since the setting up of any *dhara* as well as the use of pipes and other means of water supply involves manual labour, it is the men who are primarily involved and thus, the women have traditionally been 'fetchers' while men the 'finders' or 'resourcers' of any water supply system, including the traditional *dhara* and *kua*.

Women have always had access to water as a resource in the two villages and in fact, their role as the primary preservers has been defined in a very cultural way. Within the framework of traditional methods of access to water, women have always been actively involved. Although in the villages, the natural sources of drinking water have been in existence since a long period of time with the villages having evolved around them, women have been actively participating in ensuring their sustenance.

These women have been most instrumental in the preservation and mitigating pollution of these sources through the observance of festivals like the Nag Panchami, Sansari Puja, Indra Puja etc., keeping intact the traditional observance of sacredness of water as a resource, even in the historical absence of positive water laws.[23] Their belief in the sacredness of these water sources is quantified by the fact that women themselves have not challenged the practise to stay away from the collection and use of water and being dependant on other female members or children to provide them water when they have their monthly menstrual cycles.

Recently, state monopoly in water facilitation has excluded these women to a huge extent because representation of women in policymaking through panchayat and district level bodies, involved in water-related issues, is non-formal. In fact, these villages lack any formal water management bodies and any representation in water issues to government officials is made by male members. In village level meetings regarding water, women do attend meetings but it is apparent that their voices are not taken into consideration.

For example, the rainwater harvesting tanks are set up by male *mistris* (masons) and any breakage or maintenance work is difficult for women to undertake in case of any damage. Hence, there is a dependence on male labour for the same creating a chain of exclusion.

Although women and men in the two villages equally understand the significance of a constant source of drinking water, state provisions in ensuring the supply should include women in policymaking.

4.   Narratives in India with respect to gender and water access

Sarah Ahmed writes that in India, '[s]tories abound about the relationship between water and the feminine principle, connecting the life-bestowing power of water with the sacrifices women make during times of water scarcity' (Ahmed 2005: 1). According to the eco-feminist narrative Bina Agarwal, women have been bestowed with the feminine principle which further propagates the idea of women as being closer to nature and men being closer to culture (Agarwal 1992: 119–158). Feminist environmentalist Vandana Shiva has written that third world women have a special knowledge of nature and a dependence on nature and this knowledge has been systematically marginalised under the impact of modern science. She writes that

> Modern reductionist science, like development, turns out to be a patriarchal project, which has excluded women as experts, and

has simultaneously excluded ecology and holistic ways of knowing which understand and respect nature's processes and interconnectedness as science.

(Shiva 1998: 14, 15)

On the other hand, Agarwal propagates 'feminist environmentalism' (Agarwal 1992: 149) as opposed to 'eco-feminism'. She writes this in critique of Indian eco-feminists like Shiva stating the idea as being Hindu centric and not extending to non-Hindu women which again creates another exclusion of women as even non-Hindu women in India have close relations with nature and its conservation. In promoting her idea of feminist environmentalism through studies where she has focused on rural women, Agarwal states that there are other structural divisions like gender, class, race, caste, organisation of production, reproduction and distribution. These structures define women's interactions with nature, the approach of people with the environment in general and their attitude towards climate change. Hence, she states that cultural and other constructs need to be taken into consideration.

Women's relationship with nature has also been projected through the management of the village commons of which water sources are the main area where they have a semblance of control. This, feminists argue, is because they are the main managers and preservers of water sources in India but their lack of proprietary rights over land has disadvantaged them. In fact, this seems to form the crux of most feminist narratives relating to women and water. Kuntala Lahiri-Dutt writes that 'Feminist researchers have shown that the lack of women's rights to land lie at the core of disenfranchisement of women, an observation that is also true for women's access to water' (Lahiri-Dutt 2009: 276).

Land and property define social positions and loss of farming lands and agricultural livelihoods increase feminisation of poverty, regardless of the topography. Also, land is usually seen as a joint property by both men and women in a household and so is its use and control. However, the title rests with the man and in case a female's position in the household is threatened, e.g. with the breakdown of marriage, then her right to the perceived joint ownership and control is too (Rao 2005: 4702). Undoubtedly, women's access to natural resources including water is most affected when their rights to land are absent, minimised or lost.

Feminists also write of the lack of women's participation in water resources management and this is further perpetuated by their lack of ownership and proprietary rights on land. As a result, it affects women's right to equal citizenship as envisaged in the constitution by ignoring their water citizenship.

Exclusion of women from water resource management and developmental projects is also another issue that gender discourses on water have focused on. They state that modern water projects exclude the participation of women in the real sense. Sarah Ahmed writes that

> The concept of participation is not new, neither is participation in itself a panacea for achieving project or programme objectives. Participation is often seen as synonymous with empowerment, but participatory processes do not necessary challenge internalised oppression or lead to self-efficacy.
>
> (Ahmed 2005: 41)

These disadvantages are further perpetuated when 'statization' of natural resources takes place. Agarwal writes that '[s]tatization and privatisation of communal resources have, in turn systematically undermined traditional institutional arrangements of resource use and managements' (Agarwal 1992: 129). She further writes that introduction of new techniques of environment management means that women have to forgo their role of being keepers of traditional conservation knowledge and could enhance their gendered alienation within the patriarchal set-up (ibid.: 133).

5.   Contextualising these gender narratives in respect of mountain women

'Mountain inhabitants are subject to place sensitivity, but also to social sensitivity, finding themselves isolated as well as politically and economically marginalized more than populations elsewhere' (Zurick and Karan 1999: 510). On the man–environment relationship in the Himalayan ecosystem, Kumar and Singhal write that there is a symbiotic relationship between man, animal, land and forests in the Hill Districts since in a fragile ecosystem, each is dependent on the other. Also that '[t]he human (*mostly by women*) activities such as wood and grass cutting, grazing, lopping and agricultural cropping on mountain slopes is not rationalised' (Kumar and Singhal 1996: 28, emphasis added). Susanne Wymann von Dach writes that

> Numerous studies have shown that mountain women have heavier workloads than men have. Men and women share agricultural and livestock tasks quite evenly, but women have additional domestic responsibilities, such as preparation of food, collection of water and wood for fuel, child-care, and maintenance of family health.

Steep slopes, great distances, and especially the absence of men due to increasing outmigration intensify the workload of mountain women.

(Wymann von Dach 2002: 237)

Mountain women and their proximity to nature has not only been in the physical sense but also on the psychological and emotional which can be seen by the fact that most of the community's environmental movements in India started in the mountains and hills and also involved women or were started by women.[24] Also tribal communities are also in the forefront when it came to these environmental movements.[25] Bridgette Leduc *et al.* write that although

The Himalayas are home to people from a variety of ethnic groups with different cultures, religions and social structures . . . [t]he common denominations for mountain women are the hardships of their life and the multitude of gender discriminations they face.

(Leduc 2008: 7, 8)

Lynch and Maggio write that

In contrast to their lowland counterparts, in traditional mountain cultures, women often retain a high level of responsibility and control over natural resources and over finances derived from the exchange or sale of goods and services. In many traditional mountain communities, women are also the primary stewards of indigenous knowledge and natural resource management.

(Lynch and Maggio 1997: 14).

Leduc *et al.* also state that 'they are considered social assets in terms of their indigenous knowledge on natural resource management' (Leduc 2008: 7, 8). And Wymann von Dach says, 'Failure to recognize the gendered nature of knowledge and integrate women in development processes means losing half this knowledge'[26] (Wymann von Dach 2002: 237).

Pradyumna P. Karan writes:

The cultural barriers to the flow of information to women are real. Women in the Hindu Nepalese communities may be considered loose or immoral if they talk with unfamiliar men . . . [o]pportunities for women to obtain agricultural, natural resource, and conservation related skills are limited by culturally influenced beliefs and social practices. For environmental conservation and planning, it is important to incorporate women.

(Karan 1989: 270)

These 'cultural barriers' permeate through all mountain communities. Although there is a substantial change in the involvement of women in community activities in today's context, the general observations with respect to state policies not being gender neutral and lacking in involvement of women still seems relevant and true in the context of water policies and needs to be changed. In fact, the historical 'gender discrimination, gender exploitation, and disenfranchisement of women are mentioned as persisting in mountain regions within development contexts over a decade ago' still exists and have been aggravated by the socio-economic inequalities at the level of the community as well as the sexes in today's context (Verma 2014: 188, 189).

Women of the mountain have had very little control over the natural resources that they nurture, preserve and manage on a daily basis. While this responsibility is thrust upon them by culture and community norms, the same deprives them of ownership over these resources. In addition, the gendered nature of the modern development process and the consequent social changes have reinforced this discrimination or introduced gender discrimination by selective intervention in favour of men (Gurung 1999: 515, 516). Developmental initiatives based on Western ideas of a society, their intellectual isolation from global changes due to topography and 'male bias in technology'[27] Acharya (2000: 515–540) has permeated to all areas of their daily life including natural resources management.[28]

6. Conclusion

These narratives are so very apt in the case of villages where the field study for this chapter was undertaken. The most glaring instance of the gradual seclusion of women was with the introduction of modern techniques of water management, leaving gender-sensitive issues outside the new frameworks. This might appear to make water more accessible, but it is not conducive to their traditional role as primary water managers. In fact, introduction of patriarchal technologies only seems to have increased their problems as was seen in the case of maintenance of water harvesting tanks.

With changes in rural economic set-up of mountain areas, abandonment of farming as a source of livelihood and increasing migration of men to urban mountain towns as well as the plain areas like Siliguri, women become primary caretakers of both land and sustenance in these households. As was observed earlier, however, they are merely 'caretakers' or 'unpaid labour' in absence of men as they do not have ownership rights.[29]

The field study revealed a move away from the traditional roles of women in Hindu families, which can be attributed to the need for and necessity of women in active involvement of daily activities in both laborious and non-laborious activities of a mountain village. This is not a surprising trend since mountain women have customarily and by social norms, been given an enhanced status comparatively influenced by environmental factors although the degrees may vary in various regions (Wymann von Dach 2002: 236–239).

Many women in the villages are formal village level State employees and some are actively involved informally in economical and developmental activities that are taking place around the villages in the form of constructions of road, public buildings etc. Some women even mentioned the active participation of men in traditional roles of cooking and cleaning the house and hence, meaning that men do have a very clear idea and are more sensitised about the impact of water scarcity in daily running of the household.

Hence, conscious and active participation of both men and women in implementation of water policies and mobilisation of their common intellectual resources should not be a problem even if these policies are projected as gender sensitive.[30]

Water conflicts in these two villages have been historical and unique to each village. In the village of Dumi Gaon Ward, the conflict has been not in the procurement of water from the *Dumi Kua* but in the sharing of water from the upstream *Bar Kua*. The single water navigation system facilitated by the villagers through the use of PVC pipes and water tanks and taps provided means that upstream water users have a monopoly and power in the release of water for downstream consumption. Even women play an important role in this village-level water politics where they are equally responsible for monopolising and polarising water accessibility.

However, this is not prevalent in the village of Ahley Ward, as access to water is difficult for all because of the downhill location of the main natural source. Hence, in the former, village-level water management committees could be incorporated outside the panchayat and local governance set-up with significant involvement of women from upstream and downstream households for fair allocation of the water.[31]

Since both villages face acute water shortage during a part of the year, not only drinking but sanitation and hygiene also become an issue.

Interestingly, some of the villagers mentioned that in the past few years, men and women have driven around in taxis in search of water and even visited the downstream Rangit River embankments nearby Jorethang to wash clothes and bathe. They mentioned that for them, in those times, it was as if petrol was cheaper than water, but they were forced to make the economic compromise for the sake of sanitation and hygiene.

Also, due to lack of proper use of water harvesting tanks and scarcity of flowing water for bathing purposes, women, especially in Ahley Gaon Ward, visit the *dhara* to bathe in the open. This, the women mentioned, was an extremely awkward decision, but one borne out of desperation, and has been continuing for a long period of time but which they wished would change with proper supply of running water to bathrooms which have been constructed with the help of state funding. Not to mention, poor hygiene due to water scarcity is an issue with men and children too in both the villages. Hence, involving women in water-related decisions by the policymaking bodies is not only about how to supply but also why to supply and the main reason is to ensure a secure and private atmosphere for women vis-à-vis water use.

Also, there is water swapping and 'stealing' from water supplies provided to nearby villages which are both consensual as well as thorough stealth. These result in not only loss of revenue to the state in the form of water taxes but also possibilities of conflicts in the village.

Hence, community tanks fed by state-provided drinking water supplies, community rain harvesting tanks specifically for collecting drinking water, water treatment facilities in these community tanks, education and mobilisation of both men and women in sanitisation of harvested water could ease the water crisis in these two villages. Economical use of water during monsoon when both the natural sources as well as harvesting tanks provide abundant water and sharing of water in the community during harsh seasons needs to be encouraged. This can be effectively managed by setting up rules and regulations of water use, both of natural sources as well as harvested.[32]

The villagers, both women and men, seem to be aware of the impact of climate change on water availability both through the print and electronic media as well as their inherent ability to watch weather changes, borne out of their farming background.[33] However, intensive education and mobilisation in efficient water use and conservation through modern techniques for times of scarcity was much seen. The conclusion in this aspect is that women in these villages are more privileged in that they do not need to fight gender defined roles to become involved in water management at the community level, like their counterparts in the plains of India. Their main barrier at present is in technological and modern water management techniques for which they need to be educated at the same level and alongside men as equal partners to gain access to water.

In *Beyond the Nature/Society Divide: Learning to Think About a Mountain*, William Freudenburg, Scott Frickel and Robert Gramling write:

> When the nature of human interaction with the environment is understood more clearly, it is possible to see that the greater need may be to resist the temptation to separate the social and the environmental and to realize that the interpenetrating influences are often so extensive that the relevant factors can be considered 'socioenvironmental'.
>
> (Fraeudenbeurg *et al.* 1995: 38)

Notes

1 Dublin Statement on Water and Sustainable Development 1992, as adopted in the International Conference on Water and the Environment (ICWE), Dublin, Ireland, organised on 26–31 January 1992.

2 Archana Tiwari writes that '[o]nly 29% of the respondents were aware of water conservation and rainwater harvesting techniques'. She also writes that apart from women, children are also involved actively in the collection and management of water sourced from running sources and that boiling of water is common (Tiwari 2012: 41).

3 Literacy rates of male–female in the South District are 87.06 and 79.58 as per the 2011 census. On a state level, the male literacy in Sikkim stands at 87.29 per cent, while female literacy is at 76.43 per cent. In actual numbers, total literates in Sikkim stands at 449,294 of which males were 253,364 and females were 195,930. Provisional Population Totals, Paper 1 of 2011, Sikkim Series 12, Census of India 2011.

4 Sandeep Tambe *et al.* (2009) conceptualised the Dhara Vikas programme which focused on revival of springs of Sikkim. The project was undertaken from the years 2008 to 2010 under the aegis of the Department of Science and Technology, Govt. of Sikkim. Figure 3 at page 15 of the article shows South Sikkim, including Namchi as the most drought prone areas of Sikkim.

5 Hinduism is a religion that was adapted in the two villages during the early 1900s before which the Magars and the Rais (kirantas) were animists and followed Shamanism. Hence, the current population is mostly third- and fourth-generation Hindus.

6 It would be important to mention here that the Magars and Rais of Sikkim have been demanding for a scheduled tribe status and this has meant that they are going back to their indigenous practices, beliefs and culture

through a concerted effort at de-*sanscritisation* and abandoning the practices of the Hindu religion.

7 The families with at least one member employed in the government have a relatively higher standard of living and this has meant that government jobs are highly coveted. With diminishing agricultural returns, most of the current generations of youngsters are moving away from learning agricultural practices to attaining an 'English education' to increase their employability in the government and other service sectors. Hence 'English schools' have cropped up in villages across Sikkim where the Montessori system of education at the entry level prepares the village children to gain entry into the higher-ranking state- and central-aided schools like the Kendriya Vidyalaya Schools. The state primary, secondary, senior secondary as well as college education is entirely in English and hence, the thrust of parents in pushing their children towards an 'English education' is very high, sometimes taking them away from the rural areas to the urban setting where the environment is considered more cosmopolitan and modern or 'English'.

8 The *khetala* system is a type of community farming where labour is offered in exchange for wages (*rojkari*) or labour (*parma*) in the villages of Sikkim during the sowing and harvesting seasons. The *parma khetala* operates on a rotational system, based on mutual understanding and respect between the members of a village with the absence of any exchange of cash or kind except food during the day. This is especially prevalent amongst the Hindu communities all over Sikkim. The *rojkari khetala* farm labour is another wherein there is an exchange of cash or kind (in the form of a meal and grains) and labourers from the neighbouring villages and Nepal are the main contributors. The in-migration of wage-based *khetala* from Nepal is a very recent trend in Sikkim and prevalent in those places where landholdings and agriculture production are huge in area and involves cash crops like ginger, orange, rice and cardamom. *Parma khetala* is the prevalent form of *khetala* in the two subject villages of this chapter.

9 The region has historically had high yield of cash crops like ginger which has made it possible for farmers to subsist on income from agriculture. Seasonal vegetables also find market in the nearby towns of Namchi and Jorethang. Dairy farming is also a good source of income with an average of 10–15 L of milk sold at Rs 20 leading to a regular source of income.

10 Cattle rearing for milk and sale are also a regular feature, but the animals are rarely sold for meat production as most of the villagers are Pranami Sadhus who belong to a branch of Vaishnavism which entails that the followers abstain from eating meat, consuming alcohol, smoking etc. This could also explain the absence in the rearing of chickens and pigs by the families of the two villages which is a usually a very common feature in the households of Sikkim.

11 Figure 3 at page 15 of Sandeep Tambe *et al.* (2009) shows South Sikkim, including Namchi, as the most drought prone areas of Sikkim. Also see infra note NO in Tambe *et al.* (2012a: 65).

12 Scientists involved in the Dhara Vikas project which is a pioneering spring shed development programme undertaken by the Rural Management and Development Department, Govt. of Sikkim have attributed the

drought-like conditions in the lower parts of the West and South Districts to the following:

1 It is located in the rain shadow of the Darjeeling Himalaya and receives about 150 cm of annual rainfall, which is much less than the 250 cm received in other parts of the state.
2 The annual rainfall is received in a concentrated spell of 4–5 months (June–September), with drought-like conditions for 3–4 months (January–April).
3 The steep physical terrain of the Rangit and Teesta river gorges results in high surface runoff and limited natural infiltration.
4 Most of the villages are situated in the upper catchments, while the reserve forests are situated in the valley along the river bank, thereby reducing their rainwater harvesting potential.

See Sandeep Tambe *et al.* (2012a: 65).

13 'In Sikkim, sacred groves have been reported from all the four districts. All the sacred groves are attached to the local monasteries (Gumpas), dedicated to the deities and managed by the Gumpa authority or Lamas, or often by the village community. Out of 35 sacred groves found in Sikkim, 24 are terrestrial and 11 are aquatic sacred lakes or water bodies. The Kabi sacred grove of North Sikkim is the largest and has special historic importance' (Dash 2005: 427). Though, Spafford Ackerly (2013) wrote that till date 56 sacred groves have been recognised in Sikkim. For more information on the sacred groves in Sikkim, see generally Avasthe *et al.* (2004).

14 See note 4.

15 Wild roses bloom in the *ahal* during the spring and the water level raises up and down according to the changes in the season. The villagers have observed that the water levels have gone down immensely in the last decade and they blame it on the low rainfall and changing weather patterns. Being an agrarian community, listening to nature and its whispers of impending dangers have always been a part and parcel of the lives of these villagers, as is the case in any parts of Sikkim.

16 A local beer made of fermented millet.

17 The majority population belonging to the Rai and Magar communities has inculcated the practices of the Hindu varna system after their 'sanscritisation' although they were never considered a part of the varna system. Such sanscritisation have seeped in all practices including their attitude towards the purity of water.

18 There is an interesting phenomenon going on in the village of Dumi Gaon which also has historically followed untouchability as sanctioned by the Vaishnavite beliefs. A large number of scheduled caste families live near the main water source uphill and they exercise a lot of control over the amount of water that flows downhill. Although they are still marginalised socially, their control over the water flow seems to have given them a semblance of superiority over their historic ostrasisation. Their recent conversions to Christianity seems to have emboldened them to defy the social dictates and divert much of the water to their homes where they use huge Sintex water storage tanks, something unthinkable in olden times, where

monopolisation over community water sources were considered a social wrong.

19 Harvested rainwater, which lies stagnant for months, is considered impure for drinking and even boiling or filtering. It is not considered good enough to make it fit for consumption. The attitude towards collected/stagnant water is such that day-old water is not considered pure enough for the daily 'puja' rituals when water is offered in small brass tumblers. Only 'new' water is offered which is freshly collected from a stream or a flowing water source. This is mostly done by the children or a female who is not undergoing her menstruation.

20 *Dhara*s are mountains springs that 'are the natural discharges of groundwater from various aquifers and in most cases unconfined. In Sikkim, 80% of the rural households depend on spring water for their rural water security . . . [s]ome of the springs are considered scared, are revered as *Devithas* and are protected from biotic interferences' (Tambe *et al.* 2012a: 62).

21 Collection of water in the night to avoid traffic and quarrels is a norm where men mostly do the task. Negi and Joshi writes of this practice even in the Uttarakhand mountains. See G. C. S. Negi and Varun Joshi (2012), 'A Simple Eco-Technology to Address Drinking Water Crisis in the Western Himalayan Mountains, Gangtok', *IMI-SMDS (Sikkim, 2012), Compendium of Papers*, Vol. 44–48, p. 45.

22 Villagers of Ahley Gaon recounted the difficulties faced by them during the previous winter where the *dhara* stream dried up to a trickle. The village, which becomes dusty and arid during the dry season, faced such problems that they had to buy water loaded and supplied in trucks. They even mentioned that they, on many occasions, went down to the Rangit to wash their clothes and bathe properly, quipping that for them water became more expensive than petrol.

23 See Jain *et al.* (2004) write about the traditional practice of attributing sacredness to water bodies and which have been passed down through generations. This sacredness of water bodies have been able to act as very important conservation tools in the absence of any positive laws for environment management and conservation, which only started after the merger in the early 1980s in Sikkim.

24 The Chipko Movement for instance. See Agarwal (1992: 126, 150).

25 In Sikkim for instance, the Lepchas and the Bhutia communities have been active in the anti-dams movements where the perceived threat is not only to the environment but also to their community and indigenous characteristics.

26 'The lack of ownership limits women's access to other resources and information. They cannot use land as security to obtain the loans they need to invest in their farms or develop small, innovative businesses. Extension programs and training courses are still designed for male farmers, even where men are absent because of off-farm activities. Despite the increasing number of initiatives by NGOs and governments to improve sanitation and access to medical services and modern communication networks in mountain areas, restrictive patriarchal systems often limit the benefits of such improvements for women' (Wymann von Dach 2002: 237).

27 Writing on the mountain women of Nepal – India Himalayas, Meena Acharya (2000: 535) observes that 'Experience from Nepal and other areas of the region . . . indicate that, in societies with existing gender discrimination in access to land and other resources, the commercialisation process further marginalises women from the development process, in both agriculture and industry. . . . Further, even in areas where women may inherit land, access to and control over new technology are exclusively male. As soon as a new technology arrives, men take over the task. . . . This can be attributed to the male bias in technology and differential male/female access to education. Gender issues in development cannot be perceived only as an efficiency issue to be dealt with in the poverty alleviation programmes.'

28 Orem Declaration and the Bhutan+10 are some international initiatives that have focused on mountain women and their empowerment.

29 This is an increasingly frequent phenomenon in the recent years along the Greater Himalayan region of Sikkim, Nepal etc. influenced both by shortage of water for agricultural and domestic purposes as well as fuelling neglect of the sustenance of traditional modes of water management. See generally Soumyadeep Banerjee *et al.* (2012).

30 See Nitya Rao (2005: 4704), where non-recognition of conscious gendered differences in development projects leads to lack of initiative on the part of women to express continued involvement in the projects. Hence, their involvement must be structured within the plans of the projects. Also see Susanne Wymann von Dach (2002: 237, 238).

31 International Centre for Integrated Mountain Development reports the active involvement of mountain women in ensuring effective management of water resources in its report titled *Local Responses to Too Much and Too Little Water in the Greater Himalayan Region* (2009) in a study conducted in some mountain areas of Pakistan, India, China and Nepal.

32 'The main challenges for ensuring rural drinking water security include long term upspring-downspring arrangements with institutional arrangements for water user group, technical know-how at the local level to prepare scientific spring-shed development plans by understanding the geohydrology and identifying the recharge zone, standardization of spring-shed development technology, reducing cost of construction of water storage tanks, dissemination and acceptance of these new technologies, building on existing cultural religious beliefs, effective people's participation and sourcing public financing for funding these new initiatives' (Tambe *et al.* 2012b: 14).
 'It is an important challenge to combine modern methods and techniques with indigenous knowledge and traditional institutions for local water management' (Chalise 2005: 93).

33 In the report, the managing director of SIMFED writes that in analysing '[t]he Climate-related agriculture sector vulnerability . . . has pronounced impact on the rain-shadow/drought prone areas of South and West Sikkim. These Gram Panchayats are mainly in subtropical zone or in the middle hills of South and West Sikkim. Mainly vulnerable Gram Panchayats are in Sikkip, Melli, *Namchi*, Jorethang, Soreng and Kaluk Blocks of South and West Sikkim. These villages face highest exposure with low adaptive capacity coupled with high level of sensitivity regarding agriculture sector.

In case of district wise analysis of results, it was observed that South Sikkim has maximum vulnerability followed by West District' (Swaroop [undated]: 7, 8, emphasis added).

The Sikkim State Action Plan on Climate Change published by the Government of Sikkim identifies the 'water sector' as an area of concern due to climate change vulnerability and states the adaptation strategies to meet the challenges. The strategies are not gendered and presume a blanket community-level participation.

References

Acharya, M. 2000. 'Economic opportunities for mountain women of South Asia: The poverty context', in M. Banskota *et al.* (eds.), *Growth, Poverty Alleviation and Sustainable Resource Management in the Mountain Areas of South Asia*. Kathmandu: ICIMOD-Deutsche Stiftung fur internationale Entwicklung (ZEL), pp. 515–540.

Ackerly, S. 2013. 'Sacred groves, ecological saviours? The story from Sikkim-India', *Sacred Geography*, Retrieved from: www.himalayanconnections.org [Accessed 12 November 2014].

Agarwal, B. 1992. 'The gender and the environment debate: Lessons from India', *Feminist Studies*, 18 (1) (Spring): 119–158.

Ahmed, S. 2005. 'Why is gender equity a concern for water management?', in *Water Flowing Upstream: Empowering Women through Water Management Initiatives in India*. New Delhi: Fortune Books, pp. 1–50.

Avasthe, R. K., P. C. Rai and L. K. Rai. 2004. 'Sacred groves as repositories of genetic diversity: A case study from Kabi-Longchuk, North Sikkim', *ENVIS Bulletin: Himalayan Ecology*, 12 (1): 25–29.

Banerjee, S., J. Y. Gerlitz and B. Hoermann. 2012. 'Labour migration as an adaptation to water hazards: Cases in China, India, Nepal, and Pakistan', in N. S. Pradhan *et al.* (eds.), *Role of Policy and Institutions in Local Adaptation to Climate Change Case Studies on Responses to Too Much and Too Little Water in the Hindu Kush Himalayas*. Kathmandu: ICIMOD, pp. 57–73.

Chalise, S. R. 2005. 'Water resources management in the Hindu Kush Himalayas: An overview', in *Large Dams for Hydropower in Northeast India: A Dossier,* compiled by Manju Menon and Kanchi Kohli. New Delhi: Kalpavriksh and South Asia Network on Dams, Rivers and People, pp. 89–97.

Dash, S. S. 2005. 'Kabi sacred grove of North Sikkim', *Current Science*, 89 (3): 427, 428.

Freudenburg, W. R., S. Frickel, R. Gramling. 1995. 'Beyond the nature/society divide: Learning to think about a mountain', *Sociological Forum*, 10 (3) (Springer): 361–392.

Gurung, J. D. 1999. *Searching for Women's Voices in the Hindu Kush-Himalayas*. Kathmandu: ICIMOD, pp. 515, 516.

Jain, A., H. Birkumar Singh, S. C. Rai and E. Sharma. 2004. 'Folklores of sacred Khecheopalri Lake in the Sikkim Himalaya of India: A plea for conservation', *Asian Folklore Studies*, 63 (2): 291–302.

Karan, P. P. 1989. 'Environment and development in Sikkim Himalaya: A review', *Human Ecology*, 17 (2) (June): 257–271.

Khawas, V. 2004. *Sustainable Development and Management of Water Resource in Mountain Ecosystem: Some Examples from Sikkim Himalaya*, Retrieved from: www.mtnforum.org/sites/default/files/publication/files/26. pdf [Accessed 22 October 2014].

Kumar, P. and R. M. Singhal. 1996. 'Role of women in sustainable development of the degraded lands of the Himalayan eco-system (Darjeeling)', *Himalayan Paryavaran*, 4 (1): 28–30.

Lahiri-Dutt, K. 2009. 'Water, women and rights', in R. I. Ramaswamy (ed.), *Water and the Laws in India*. New Delhi: Sage Publications, pp. 275–308.

Leduc, B. *et al.* 2008. *Case Study: Gender and Climate Change in the Hindu Kush Himalayas of Nepal*. Kathmandu: ICIMOD, pp. 7, 8.

Lynch, O. J. and G. F. Maggio. 1997. *Mountain Laws and Peoples: Moving Towards Sustainable Development and Recognition of Community-Based Property Rights: A General Overview of Mountain Laws and Policies with Insights from the Mountain Forum's Electronic Conference on Mountain Policy and Law*, at Mountain Forum in conjunction with Center for International Environmental Law, Washington, DC, USA. Retrieved from: www. mtnforum.org/ [Accessed 25 August 2013].

Rao, N. 2005. 'Women's right to land and assets: Experience of mainstreaming gender in development projects', *Economic and Political Weekly*, 40 (44/45): 4701–4708.

Shiva, V. 1998. *Staying Alive: Women, Ecology and Survival*. London: Zed Books, pp. 14, 15.

Swaroop, B. (Undated). *Agricultural Sector Climate Change Related Vulnerability Assessment of Rural Communities of Sikkim Himalaya, India*. Gangtok: Sikkim State Cooperative Supply and Marketing Federation (SIMFED).

Tambe, S., M. L. Arrawatia, R. Kumar, H. Bharti and P. Shrestha. 2009. *Conceptualizing Strategies to Enhance Rural Water Security in Sikkim, Eastern Himalaya, India*. Selected Technical Papers from the Proceedings of the Workshop on Integrated Water Resource Management Held on 27th November 2009. Salt Lake, Kolkata, India: Central Ground Water Board, Eastern Region, Ministry of Water Resources, Government of India, pp. 5–8. Available at www.sikkimsprings.org/dv/research/Sikkim%20Strategy%20for%20Rural%20Water%20Security.pdf.

Tambe, S., G. Kharel, M. L. Arrawatia, H. Kulkarni, K. Mahamuni and A. K. Ganeriwala. 2012a. 'Reviving dying springs: Climate change adaptation experiments from the Sikkim Himalaya', *Mountain Research and Development*, 32 (1): 62–72. Available at www.mrd-journal.org [Accessed 29 October 2014].

Tambe, S., *et al.* 2012b. 'Climate change, water security and adaptation initiatives in the Sikkim Himalaya (Gangtok)', *IMI-SMDS2 (Sikkim 2012), Compendium of Papers*, pp. 12–15.

Tiwari, A. 2012. 'Water quality and quantity analysis in Sikkim, North Eastern Himalaya', *Current Science*, 103 (July): 41–45.

Verma, R. 2014. 'Business as *Un*usual: The potential for gender transformative change in development and mountain contexts', *Mountain Research and Development*, 34 (3): 188–196.

Wymann von Dach, S. 2002. 'Integrated mountain development: A question of gender mainstreaming', *Mountain Research and Development*, 22 (3) (August): 236–239, Retrieved from: www.k-state.edu/geography/people/ rmarston/Papers/Marston%20AAG%202007%20Pres%20Address.pdf [Accessed 20 February 2014].

Zurick, D. and P. P. Karan. 1999. '*Himalaya: Life on the Edge of the World*, Baltimore, John Hopkins University Press in Marston, Richard A. "Land, Life, and Environmental Change in Mountains"', *Annals of the Association of American Geographers*, 98 (3): 507–520.

3 Challenges to women as food and risk managers in the context of floods

A case study from Tinsukia[1]

Sarah Marie Nischalke and Suman Bisht

1. Introduction – setting the scene

> I am a single woman. I could not save my animals in the floods because it was just me. I could not save my goats and had to keep the cows in the stable. Two of them chocked on silt in the stable.
>
> (Nepali farmer, F, 60, Lower Lawpani, Assam)

The state of Assam, located in Northeast India, consists of the Brahmaputra and Barak river valleys. Both these valleys are characterised by regular floods. In fact, Brahmaputra is one of the most flood prone rivers in India with its more than thirty tributaries throughout its length. Periodic flooding is ecologically important because it deposits fresh alluvium and replenishes the fertile soil, so that flooding, agriculture, and agricultural practices are closely connected.

However, massive floods also cause serious erosion, loss of life and livestock and heavy damage to infrastructure, communication and property. Unpredictable floods in Assam have over the years led to decrease in agricultural productivity on account of risk avoidance (low inputs into agriculture due to high probability of floods that may wash away costly inputs) and sand-casting.

Socio-economic systems, characterised by agricultural and natural resource-dependence, are inherently more sensitive to climate-related environmental changes. Given the tenuous link between floods and agriculture, any climate-related environmental change not only transforms smallholder farms but also restructures the whole farming systems.

2. The need for gender-disaggregated farming system analyses

This chapter is based on a farming system analysis approach, which not only considers production aspects of farming but also investigates the socio-political environment that includes biophysical conditions, natural capital portfolio and assets like land, animals, buildings, machines, liquidity and natural conditions as well as the history, knowledge and perceptions of the farm family along with overall environment, which extends to the village, district or state level, covering markets, policies, networks and location (Darnhofer *et al.* 2008). This approach not only helps us understand what a farmer is doing but also why and how he or she is doing it. It enables the researcher to draw 'interactions between farms and their natural, social and economic context' (Darnhofer *et al.* 2012: 2).

The inclusiveness of this systems perspective (Norman 2002) enables researchers to incorporate women farmers and gender perspectives (Schiere *et al.* 2004) as part of the systems thinking. While in the last two decades, many researchers have incorporated participatory approaches and gender analysis within this approach, agricultural scientists and economists who dominate this field often retreat to reductionist approaches that tend to factor out women (Norman 2002). In the context of restructuring of farming systems given climate and social change conditions, exclusion of women who are part of the group of resource-poor farmers in heterogeneous production environments that shape central elements of the farming system can be a grave mistake (Darnhofer *et al.* 2012).

The 'ongoing adaptation to an ever-changing environment' has become the base in the shift of understanding farming systems (Darnhofer *et al.* 2008: 339). This calls for careful investigations of gender roles and the role of women farmers in these systems. Farmers are moving towards an unforeseeable direction and their attitudes, structures and activities build and sustain the ability to cope with change (ibid.).

An emerging body of literature provides empirical evidence of the ways, in which crisis situations (including climate change) exacerbate already existing inequalities (including gender inequalities), vulnerabilities and poverty. Gender-differentiated roles and responsibilities, rights, access, knowledge and priorities shape vulnerabilities, often resulting in women suffering disproportionally because of socio-economic constraints and inequalities (Brody *et al.* 2008; Parikh 2007).

The system approach needs to embrace gender-disaggregated transition capabilities and differences in the room to manoeuvre between the sexes to increase adaptive capacity of the farm households as a whole. Depending on the circumstances, gender-focused work on female spaces of opportunities within the farming systems makes sense, especially if women become the centre point of the farm household and replace the male family members. In the case of Assam, the changes that affect the women farmer's realm the most are climate-related environmental change in the form of flooding and markets in the form of labour markets that deduct the male labour force from the farms as well as new market potentials (cash crops, fish ponds, fowl etc.) that both potentially increase liquidity through outside income or cash crop earnings and widen the women's and farm households space of opportunity. An increased liquidity can also increase adaptive capacity and room for innovation, because money can be reinvested in the farm household system. Lastly, new preferences and priorities of farm households also play a role and shape their activities. The high priority of education for children as a way out of agriculture and conspicuous consumption influence decision-making on the farm. The most critical aspects that were identified for the female farmers, in our case study, to cope with change were the lack of social and market networks, including extension services to make effective investments in agriculture or adaptive practices as well as the lack of knowledge on external inputs to agriculture and access to resources (economic, political and social), which disable them to fulfill the task of a farm manager.

3. Introduction to study area and predominant features of the farming system

The district of Tinsukia, eastern Assam, with 100,000 population is characterized by three economic trends: coal mining, oil industry and tea plantations. There are examples of agricultural subsistence land being taken over by craters of coal and large tea plantations. As big tea companies gain more and more influence, small-scale farmers too dream of transforming their fields into tea estates and experiment with tea plants on their lands. In at least three out of the five villages,[2] which formed part of the scoping visit to identify the field site for the case study, it was found that there were cases of farmers converting paddy fields into tea gardens. However, not all land is suitable for tea and this was one of the important factors that prevented farmers in these villages to take to tea plantation. Agricultural land at low elevations, threatened by floods, is not good for cultivating tea but does benefit subsistence cultivation through fertile silt deposits brought by 'good' floods.

Lower Lawpani, where qualitative fieldwork was conducted, is situated in Saikhuwa block in eastern Tinsukia, close to the river Lohit. The village is unique to Assam as it consists mostly of communities that settled in Assam at least two to three generations back. Out of a total number of 164 households, 110 households belonged to families that traced their origin to Nepal, about 40 households belonged to the Adivasi community (a tribal community, commonly known as 'tea tribe' as many of them used to work on tea plantations in the past) and 10 households belonged to families with roots in Bihar (northern state in India, which is geographically close to Assam). In the village, there were only 4 Assamese households. Even though many households had working knowledge of the Assamese language to get through daily routines, most of them used their ethnic language to communicate with their own community members (Nepali, Bihari and Adivasi).

This ethnically mixed village is dependent on subsistence agriculture for their livelihood with paddy and mustard as the two major crops. Even though the farmers describe themselves as paddy cultivators, livestock, especially cows, bulls and buffaloes, play an important role in the agricultural system for ploughing and fertilising the fields, as an income source through milk production and as social safety net (selling of livestock for post-flood recovery is common and livestock meat is also an important source of food during shortage of staple crops).

The farm size varies in the village with some households having almost no cultivable land to a few households with large farms. In our sample size, there were no households without land. The size of the landholdings ranged from 1 to 25 bigha[3] with an average of cultivable land of around 10.4 bigha. There was not much variation in the range of the size of the landholding in different communities; however, there were visible differences in productivity from the land with Adivasi households faring the worst.[4]

Annual floods are a defining feature in this area with regular damage to agricultural crops. The farming system in the village benefits from good floods[5] (river-borne nutrients) and suffers from bad floods (sand deposits), but the farmers have learnt to live and adapt to the floods. Paddy and livestock are lost almost every year to floods, depending on the intensity of flooding. This led the farmers to experiment with winter vegetables as cash crop in the last six to eight years, like tomato, eggplant, cauliflower and peas. While earlier most of these vegetables were grown for self-consumption, farmers increased the scale of production for sale in the market to compensate for the loss of paddy to floods. The sale of these vegetables in the market town of Dholla (about 6–7 km from the village) and Dum Duma (about 20 km from the village) brings in much required cash to the villagers. Selling of vegetables in the market is done mostly by men. The road from Dholla to Lawpani is a stretch of unpaved road, which was built two years back. Public transport on this road is very limited. Men transport vegetables to the market on bicycle. The road is cut off for about three to four months during monsoon. This lack of connectivity to the market is a hindrance for women to exploit the potential of winter vegetables as cash crops.

Only a few households are able to produce sufficient quantity of paddy for year-round consumption. Most of the families purchase food from the market and receive some stocks through the public distribution system to fill the gap.

4. Women as farmers and food managers in times of flood

Food and nutritional security embraces the three aspects of availability (food production), access to food and utilisation (a fourth aspect of stability is treated here as an integral part of each of the three as it can refer to availability, access and utilisation dimensions of food security; FAO 2006). To be food secure, a population, household or individual must have access to adequate food 'at all times' (ibid.). It implies that there should not be a risk of losing access to food as a consequence of sudden shocks (e.g. an economic or climatic crisis) or cyclical events (e.g. seasonal food insecurity). Especially child nutrition but also general food practices need continuity to assure healthy growth and life (ibid.).

In short, food security in its broader connotation, results from the availability and access of adequate and nutritious food at country, household and individual levels with effective consumption and adequate nutrition outcomes – all in a sustained manner. As such, it is intricately linked with a woman's multiple roles, expressed in her productive, reproductive and caring functions (Rao 2005).

Rural women in Lower Lawpani are active farmers (producers) and traditionally the food managers of the farm households; therefore, they are mostly involved in making sure that food is available for home consumption (availability) and deciding what and how food is utilised in the kitchen and how feeding practices especially of small children are maintained (utilisation). However, in disaster situations and under circumstances of change, the research showed an increased challenge for women in all three aspects of food security, especially access to food. The research also revealed women's limitations in space to manoeuvre under circumstances of change.

Women's role as producers

Bina Agarwal (1997) has argued that in developing countries, the gender division of labour within and outside households is quite evident with women mostly performing the tasks of transplanting, weeding, and harvesting within agriculture. Similar patterns of division of labour based on conservative gender roles are evident across all three communities in Lower Lawpani.

Women's role in farming revolves around developing paddy nursery, transplanting paddy, harvesting and weeding. Milking, threshing and collecting firewood is done by men and women both, whereas ploughing, irrigation and herding are considered male activities. Agarwal (1997) also argues that given the task specificity of agricultural work, women also face sharper seasonal fluctuations in employment and earnings than men. Due to the basic nature of work, performed by women in rural areas, it is considered a non-market economic activity (Choudhary and Parthasarathy 2007) and remains unrecognised (Sidh and Basu 2011) and excluded from analysis (Shelton and John 1996).

The interviews with women farmers showed that they lack detailed knowledge of external inputs into agriculture, including crop varieties, applied fertilizer and pesticides, financial aspects and agricultural costs. Women have very limited power to make decisions within the system. Almost all decisions around major cereals, animals and cash crops as well as the use of pesticides or fertilizers are taken by men. Even if husbands or other male family members migrate, they continue to be the decision makers:

> My husband only does ploughing, everything else I do. I can manage the fields if the husband is not there by hiring men but he cannot do that. He cannot manage the house and the field together. But he brings in cash income so he dominates.
>
> (Bihari farmer, F, 36, Lower Lawpani, Assam)

Women's limited access to information and resources such as land and credit, their inability to plough the land and lack of access to cash income further prevents them from developing their capacities as producers in agriculture, even though they play a crucial role in food security.

Vegetables are usually the domain of women. Women focus on vegetables because it requires low external input, it provides a variety of food for the family and the production does not depend on the availability of larger amounts of money. In comparison, for field crop production, they are dependent on men for ploughing and it is more labour intensive. As a result, women favour horticultural crop cultivation over staples and livestock. While men clean the patch of land for vegetables, the women plant them and take care:

> Growing vegetables is not so difficult. I can grow vegetables even if there is no one to plough. It does not require intense ploughing

and unlike paddy we do not have to replant it or take out the weeds all the time.

(Bihari farmer, F, 70, Lower Lawpani, Assam)

While women have very little decision-making power in regard to production of food, they have full responsibility for food preparation and utilisation of food. However, decisions around changes in production patterns (e.g. what to grow and in what quantity) or restructuring of agricultural system (e.g. shifting from subsistence agriculture to horticultural crops or tea) is rarely based on nutritional value of food items (diversity, nutritional value of variety etc.), food security considerations (stability of production, flood resistance of crops etc.) or labour intensity, with no consideration of women's work burden, but mostly based on market value and economic considerations.

Women's role in access to food and food distribution

Women in Lawpani are traditionally responsible for managing the food stocks and feeding of their families along with household work such as cooking, cleaning and taking care of children and small livestock. Even before the floods in 2012, most households had to purchase food supplies for at least two to four months from the market. However, in more than 30 per cent of households, the reliance on the market increased immensely after the floods and threatened food security. Many households had to purchase even the standard staple items such as rice and mustard from the market under a very constrained financial situation. As most people lacked seed stocks and were still very reluctant to start cultivation in 2013, in anticipation of possible floods, they concentrated on a few vegetables for home consumption. Despite purchasing food from the market (with income earned from off-farm activities by the male members of the family), women's involvement in providing access to food after the floods in 2012 was defined by growing a few horticultural crops (e.g. different kinds of gourd, eggplant and ladyfingers) on the farm for home consumption, bartering and exchanging food, and collecting wild vegetables, fruits and mushrooms from the forest. Several Adivasi families reported that they majorly increased their fishing activities to fill their plates.

Even though more than 60 per cent of households owned a ration card to purchase subsidised food items through the Indian public distribution system, the families did not consider these as an important safety net or support system due to the negligible amount distributed through this system (20 kg rice, 1.5 kg sugar and 3 L kerosene per month depending on availability). For an average household of five people, 20 kg rice, cooked twice a day, is barely enough for a week. Therefore, women as the ones responsible for feeding the families faced enormous pressure after the floods. The limited emergency stocks distributed by the government were of little help. To cope with the situation, women pushed the alternative economy (explained later in the chapter) and intensified the collection of wild vegetables and fruits from the forest to outbalance the missing variety in diet. While the portions and frequency in food were not compromised, variety and diversity were. Therefore, women farmers who usually went to the forest on a weekly basis before the floods, increased the frequency to twice or thrice a week after the floods to collect green leafy vegetables such as *kukurdaina* (rough birdweed), canes/roots such as *toragojali* or *bet* or fruits such as *autenga* (elephant apple). In winter, only fruits and canes were available in the forest.

Women used their social networks within their ethnic community and made them an important part of the food distribution system. Whereas they provided more informal access to food, men were more responsible for the provision of formal access to food by selling agricultural products in the market and by earning cash through off-farm employment.

Women's role in food utilisation and consumption

Nutritional security is mostly in the hands of women as food preparation is their responsibility and they exhibited much higher interest in food knowledge than men. Despite the critical financial situation of many households and constrained agricultural production, diet diversity was relatively well maintained one year after the floods, which was also followed by a period of drought (though the nutritional level was yet at par with that before 2012). Families consumed not only a staple-based diet but also between five and seven different food groups per day (Household Dietary Diversity Score), including rooty vegetables, green leafy vegetables, vitamin-A rich fruits and animal products. Even though the women in Lawpani lack the knowledge on properties of food items, they have a good sense of the importance of diversity, especially in case of small children. They enrich their diets through the frequent collection of wild plants, seasonal fruits and the rotation of vegetables and keep processed food items to a minimum.

However, 10–15 per cent of the investigated households showed low diet diversity and could only manage to consume three to four food groups per day, which endangers their nutritional security and threatens the growth of their children. The responsible health workers for the village (the ASHA[6] worker and the multi-purpose worker from the Saikhowa State Dispensary) confirmed that malnutrition among children is rare in the village because feeding practices are relatively well established. According to their village health records, out of eighty children in the primary school in the village, only five to seven were found malnourished. One year after the floods, most families were yet to reach the nutritional level from before 2012. However, interviews with young mothers showed satisfying feeding and hygiene practices as breastfeeding is done up to two years of age of the child, which is crucial for its growth and development and women exhibited basic knowledge on hygiene as well. Unfortunately, misconceptions and traditions encourage women to start complementary feeding too early, which negatively interferes with breastfeeding and bears an unnecessary risk of exposing children to contaminated water and food.

The examples show the important role women play as food and food risk managers and also reveal limitations that woman face in their room to manoeuvre either due to knowledge gaps or limited decision-making power.

5. The flood of 2012: women as risk and disaster managers

Like other parts in Assam, regular floods have been a feature of Lower Lawpani for generations. However, villagers could recall only two incidents of 'bad floods' in the last thirty to forty years. In fact, in the ten years before 2012, the farmers felt that the floods had actually helped their agriculture and they described these years as the best in agricultural production.

In 2012, the villagers recalled having heavy rainfall from mid-April to mid-June, leading to moderate floods in early July that according to the villagers 'brought in right amount of silt that benefitted the crops and promised good production' (FGD with male farmers). In the first week of September, villagers faced seven days of continuous but light rainfall, which then turned into heavy rain, lasting for another eight days, finally resulting in a devastating flood. The water continued to rise for a week, covering fields and houses and taking away the lives of three people. The occurrence of this destructive off-season flood destroyed paddy and vegetable crops in the fields, food and seed stocks in the houses and killed hundreds of cows, goats and other livestock that used to serve as a social safety net and food source.

Only a few households had the facilities like *changghar* (platforms on stilts) or boats to protect themselves and their livestock. Most people felt helpless and could not cope well with the disaster. Especially single women or women in migrant households lamented the absence of males during this time of disaster.

In the investigated fifty-one farm households, up to three-quarters of land was lost for the next two to three seasons due to sand-casting, reducing the average cultivable land size from 10.2 to 5.5 bigha. In addition, the floods reduced the number of livestock from 2,371 to 977 animals, which were used as an income source or engaged in farm activities. In total 1,394 animals and 222.5 bigha of land were lost. In particular, the loss of ox or buffaloes restricted the ability of farmers to plough the remaining cultivable land. Many farmers also lost water pumps and pipes that were used for irrigation for off-season farming. This devastating flood drastically changed the space of opportunity for men and women. All in all, only 64 per cent households could be ranked as food self-sufficient after the floods as compared to 92 per cent before the floods. Families with established farm and livelihood systems went down the wealth spiral and described themselves as 'now we are poor'. Most of the families managed to survive the flood due to food stock from earlier seasons and by selling some of the remaining livestock.

Search for alternative livelihood sources and migration

Before the devastating floods of 2012, the farmers managed to adapt to annual floods with diversification in crops and livestock. However, the colossal damage caused by it in terms of infrastructure, loss of livestock and crop and sand/silt deposition on agricultural land further raised the level of risk associated with agriculture. Many of the households that reported sand- and silt-casting assessed that they would not be able to cultivate the affected land for the next two to five years. The reduction in the available cultivable land forced the families to look for alternative livelihood sources. Men from at least 35 per cent of the interviewed households in Lower Lawpani sought alternate employment as daily wager in a nearby bridge construction company. This provided an accessible source of income close to the village, in the absence of the farming option. Most of the men worked at night as security guards for the construction material. Others were involved in loading and unloading of material, operating small cargo boats and cooking. In addition, the Adivasi and Bihari families also depended on fishing besides farming as an alternate income source.

Besides daily wage work, about 28 per cent of the interviewed households reported at least one male member living and working outside the village. While some worked in other states like Tamil Nadu, Andhra Pradesh, Bihar and Goa, others worked outside the village but within the district or within Assam. In case of 50 per cent of the migrant households, migration was 'flood-induced': i.e. the households reported that the male member moved out to work after the floods of 2012 as farming became impossible due to sand deposition. The men mostly worked as security guards, drivers or mechanics. Many interviewees expressed the desire to migrate: 'Sometimes I think of going to Chennai. I think it will be easier to earn money there' (Nepali farmer, M, Lower Lawpani, Assam).

Often the adaptive outmigration of men increases workload of women, which negatively affects agricultural outputs, time allocation for food preparation and caring of children and livestock. In cases where migrant males are in poorly paid employment, the remittances are not enough to replace the missing male workforce with hired labour. Hence, the families face the risk of being less food secure than before (Kurvits *et al.* 2013). In Lower Lawpani, the devastation by flood was so extreme that even after nine months, farming as an activity was very limited. Hence, it was too early to assess the impact of outmigration of men on women's workload and the role that remittances and outside income played in the recovery of the farm households (resilience) and for ensuring food security.

Compared to men, women had very limited alternatives and often lamented the lack of opportunities during interviews. Some of them sold vegetables near the construction site to supplement family income, while a few others worked as daily wager on farms in the neighbouring villages. The MGNREG (Mahatma Gandhi National Rural Employment Guarantee Scheme) scheme offered very little opportunities to this village, but the few options that were available collided with the workload of the women and were located too far away, so that all the women declined.

Coping with change

Despite being traditionally the food managers of the households, women also become more and more responsible for risk and disaster management as well as farm management without the opportunity to develop appropriate skills and knowledge. Several women reported overstrained capabilities in the context of flood: for example, they were unable to save their resources because they lacked labour to put animals on the *changghar* (platforms on stilts). After the flood, very few managed to push the family to change the structure of the farm, leasing out land (sharing the outputs), reducing the number of livestock or shifting to less labour-intensive crops, so that they could handle the workload better and prevent negative effects on agro-outputs and time allocation. This is also one explanation why women pushed alternative economies in the village as part of flood recovery. The *bhagi* system (sharing) became more and more prevalent. Besides sharing arrangements of land, women initiated the sharing of fowl and goats and practiced other forms of bartering, e.g. sharing their weaving skills in exchange for material. For example, one family borrowed a pair of chicken from their neighbours and took the responsibility of their daily care on the condition that when the chicks are born, they will be divided equally between the lending and borrowing families. In this way, women relieved themselves of some responsibility and workload and still ensured good care of their families. In migrant households, where remittances are not enough to compensate the lack of labour on the farm, such arrangements become extremely important.

Despite the traditional gender roles, the research found a few women who tried to exploit new rooms to manoeuvre and to improve the livelihood situation of the farm household. One woman tried to convince her husband of focusing on pumpkin as a more sustainable investment and stable income source than current fishing activities:

> I tell my husband that if we put little effort in the field and grow pumpkin then we can sell something. I feel that the land will give us more than the river. If we are able to grow then we can store and sell whenever we need. The river has no guarantee. Today there is fish tomorrow nothing. He said this year he will spend more time tilling the land. Let's see.
>
> (Bihari farmer, F, 35, Lower Lawpani, Assam,
> nuclear family with young children)

Two other women pushed their families towards fruit (banana and jackfruit) and beetle nut tree cultivation, because it provided a stable income source (during the season), it required little labour input and contributed to their nutritional security. In two other cases, women with migrant husbands took the initiative themselves and started planting new crops (tea) or crop varieties:

> I sowed 50 kg of tea seeds couple of years back. I developed the nursery but I could not manage after that. The land here has too much grass and it requires a lot of weeding. I could not do the weeding properly. I would have managed it if I had the resources to hire 3–4 labour, but on my own it was difficult to do and the

nursery was destroyed. I have been interested in tea for a long time. My husband's brother lives in Philobari near Dum Duma and has been doing Tea Plantation for many years and earning well. I thought I should also try it and maybe I can also earn money. So I asked him for the seeds. Last year we had floods so I cannot try it again this year. I will definitely try it in future.

(Nepali farmer, F, 36, Lower Lawpani, Assam, with husband working in Arunachal Pradesh)

This year I decided that we should try ranjit dhan [a special rice variety] so I went and got seeds from the Pradhan.

(Bihari farmer, F, 36, Lower Lawpani, Assam)

Looking at these examples, it becomes clear that gender roles are changing as part of the social transformation; however, these were exceptions in the described village environment. Mostly, women start experimenting and try out new ways of farming, when pushed to the wall in the context of flood devastation. What is described above are generally coping strategies and not adaptation strategies, as the women are reacting to changes as best they can. Adaptation strategies, however, require an additional thinking ahead and planning of measures to improve the adaptive capacity of women based on already existing capacities.

The restructuring of the farming systems (reduced cultivable land, loss of water pumps and pipes for off-season irrigation, loss of seeds, outmigration of men etc.) and the extended role of women as care-givers and farm household managers requires an upgrade in women's knowledge on disaster management and preparedness as well as how to make the best use of remittances in the form of investment in family food security and the farm system. For that, they need more equal access to economic capital (insurance, credit etc.), political resources, social resources and time resources.

Women are widely disadvantaged in their rights, knowledge, time and resources, so that they are highly vulnerable and at high risk to suffer more from disaster than males (Cannon 2002; Verma *et al.* 2011).

6. Conclusion: changing farm-scapes – livelihoods beyond economics

Climate-related environmental change in the form of flooding and social change in the form of migration and transformations in gender roles, perception and preferences in the village are parallel trends that affect each other.

Amartya Sen (1981) has argued that food security is not just linked to food production but also depends on a range of entitlements including ownership (through trade, production, own-labour or inheritance), exchange (through market-based trade or transfers from the state, such as public works, social security and food subsidies) and legal entitlements. So, starvation can result from a fall in endowments (such as land alienation), unfavourable shifts in exchange entitlements (as seen in food price and wage fluctuations) and the difficulties of implementing legal rights, rather than just the result of production constraints. In the case of Lower Lawpani, we find that women's access to the above-mentioned range of entitlements is very limited.

There are many constraints for the women in Lower Lawpani, which also affects their right to entitlement: the traditional labour division (inability to plough the fields), their lack of access to cash income and ownership of land, limited mobility and low decision-making power as part of cultural restrictions, which limits their participation in the markets as well as use of cash income or decisions around restructuring of the farm economy. Women's needs (less labour intensity) and ideas (stability of income sources) are often not taken seriously or put into practice. They also have little access to alternate livelihood sources and lack the networks, the knowledge on prices, new technologies, market processes and dynamics to sell and make use of the market as an income source.

Women have very little alternative livelihood options, while men had access to off-farm employment even before the floods, in the areas of manufacturing, wholesale/retail, bamboo cutting or agricultural work. In contrast, only 3 per cent of women (after floods 5%) worked in outside employment. Their options are limited to agricultural labour – which is mostly seasonal and involves rice replanting, which comes at a time when their own fields need to be worked on – or working as a cook in public schools or a helper in households. Only 1 per cent of women in the village have a business compared to 19 per cent of men who had their own shop, workshop etc. Migration rates also reflect the constraints that women face. Only 2 per cent work as household help in private households outside the district or abroad versus 12 per cent males, who mostly work in security or the service sector.

However, the transformative situation of women within the village farming system shows the importance to reflect on the term of 'livelihood'. 'Livelihood' usually refers to a minimum of economic security, 'a means of gaining a living' (Chambers and Conway 1991) and securing basic necessities such as food and shelter, and is usually measured only as a monetary value. Looking at the situation of women in the village, it seems most important that livelihoods are not only valued in economic terms such as how much one vegetable variety fetches in the market versus another one, but life quality. The way of life or well-being of farmers is not really reflected in the economic situation. The right to life and the right to choice should not be limited to the wealthy. Especially the well-being of women farmers is as important to the farm household's capabilities as economic stability, because health is the most important asset that a farmer has. Also the high aspirations of the youth should be met and not restricted to the (non-) choice between agriculture and a 'good' life. Hence, labour intensity and environmental impact, as two examples, represent values in themselves, especially after looking at the increasing work burden of women and decreasing productivity trends in South Asia due to environmental degradation. The current mentality in Lower Lawpani is not profit oriented. Instead, subsistence production and independence are perceived as important and people are reluctant in investing more energy into market production than required for good caretaking of the family. This kind of thinking can provide a good base for integrating non-economic values into decision-making processes of farmers.

7. Way forward

Due to the extensive discussions on climate change, many agricultural policies and strategies are in a process of being revised and rearranged in regard to climate smartness. A substantial part should be the inclusion of gender-sensitive approaches to agriculture, because women are known to suffer the most from adverse impacts of climate change (Verma *et al.* 2011). It is not enough to set up women groups or self-help groups (SHGs), but it is an essential part to develop agricultural strategies together with female farmers/workers according to their observations and needs to make activities sustainable and farm household systems more resilient. There is no point in introducing flood-resistant rice varieties, if no labour is available on the farm to prepare the land and take care of the rice. The new situation and change in distribution of human resources and availability need to be included in recommendations for farmers.

In many villages, technological and financial support is needed for male and female farmers. Remittances and outside income is limited, losses after the flood situation and fear to continue in farming immense. Approaches on how to withstand the floods or to invest in different agricultural sectors (winter vegetables, livestock etc.) need to be reevaluated based on climate smartness and gender sensitivity, and especially women farmers need trainings to upgrade their skills and knowledge as farm and disaster managers. The emerging spaces of opportunities for both sexes need to be used as the base for such recommendations. If migration rates are as high as in this area, market value is not the most important aspect but labour intensity along with water and input intensity, and climate sensitivity (floods) are as relevant. The flood situation also showed how important diversity of ecosystems, agriculture and livelihoods was for coping, survival and food and nutritional security in the affected villages. Biodiversity helps to maintain resilience of ecosystems to floods, economic independence through crop diversity and a healthy life of farmers through diet diversity. However, it needs official support to counterbalance the current economic trends in Assam, which result in disappearance of forest and agricultural subsistence land. Therefore, climate-smart approaches need to include diversity and provide incentives for farmers to maintain their surroundings and agricultural diversity in the farming system.

Finally, there is an obvious need to support women groups in these villages. According to the authorities in charge in the BDO (Block Development Office), the area of Lower Lawpani and its surrounding villages were to be tackled by government initiatives for SHGs in 2014. This could help to increase women's financial independence and their influence and decision-making capability. However, it seems as important that their role as farmers need to be recognised, supported and their capabilities upgraded. One step could be that new agricultural livelihood options (pumpkin, tea, fowl, fish etc.) could be explored and market linkages improved. Until two or three years ago, the village was only accessible by water (monsoon) and bicycle, which made it impossible for women to use the market. Now that a road has been built to enable the bridge construction, the space of opportunities for women has widened and they can make much better use of the market than before. The base for developing strategies and project activities, however, needs to be provided by substantial research (e.g. gender-disaggregated farming system analyses) which can generate data on spaces of opportunities, needs and capabilities of women farmers along with gender-focused work, especially where the farm household systems are dominated by women.

Notes

1 This chapter is based on the fieldwork conducted as part of the place-based studies under the Himalayan Climate Change Adaptation Programme (HICAP). HICAP is implemented jointly by ICIMOD, CICERO and Grid-Arendal in

collaboration with local partners and is funded by the Ministry of Foreign Affairs, Norway and Swedish International Development Agency (Sida). The place-based studies approach, designed by Prof. Tor Aase from CICERO, investigates the flexibility of farming systems in different sites across Hindu Kush Himalayas. We would like to acknowledge the support of Partha J. Das from AARANYAK (Assam-based organization), Earnest Lotha, Dhruba Chetri and Dibya G. in facilitating the fieldwork for the site in Assam. Finally, we would like to thank the villagers of Lower Lawpani for allowing us access to their homes and sharing their experiences with us despite the challenges they were facing.

2 Kopatali No 1 and Lawpani (Saikhuwa block), Namtok – Tongsa, Sonali Janjati and Ulup (Margherita block).

3 Bigha is the common unit of land area measurement in Assam, 1 bigha equals 1,337.8 m^2.

4 The reasons for the differences in productivity were not the focus of this case study; but based on observation and discussions with the community, links can be drawn to differences in family size, lack of resources and knowledge for external inputs into agriculture as well as lack of market networks.

5 A 'good' flood was described by the farmers during a focus group discussion as one which is of low intensity, speed and water level; lasts for few hours to few days; and brings in *pallock* (i.e. silt) and river-borne nutrients. Even though it damages a small percentage of the crops, overall it results in improved yield. A 'bad' flood not only destroys the standing crops but also brings in *balu* or sand, which can leave the land uncultivable for several seasons.

6 Accredited Social Health Activist.

References

Agarwal, B. 1997. 'Environmental action, gender equity and women's participation', *Development and Change*, 28: 1–41.

Brody, A., J. Demtriades and E. Esplen. 2008. 'Gender and climate change: Mapping the linkages – a scoping study on knowledge and gaps', *Unpublished paper, prepared by BRIDGE*, Institute of Development Studies (IDS), UK for the UK Department for International Development, Retrieved from: www.bridge.ids.ac.uk/reports/Climate_Change_DFID_draft.pdf [Accessed 24 June 2014].

Cannon, T. 2002. 'Gender and climate hazards in Bangladesh', in R. Masika (ed.), *Gender, Development and Climate Change*. Oxford: Oxfam Publishing pp. 45-50.

Chambers, R. and G. R. Conway. 1991. 'Sustainable rural livelihoods: Practical concepts for the 21st century'. *IDS Discussion Paper 296*. Brighton: University of Sussex.

Choudhary, N. and D. Parthasarathy. 2007. 'Gender, work and household food security', *Economic and Political Weekly*, 42 (6): 523–531.

Darnhofer, I., S. Bellon, B. Dedieu and R. Milestad. 2008. 'Adaptive farming systems – a position paper', *Presented at the 8th European IFSA Symposium*, 6–10 July, Clermont-Ferrand, France.

Darnhofer, I., D. Gibbon and B. Dedieu. 2012. 'Farming systems research into the 21st century: The new dynamic', *Springer Science and Business Media Dordrecht*, p. 2.

FAO. 2006. 'Food Security'. *Policy Brief*. June Issue 2. Rome.

Kurvits, T., B. Kaltenborn, S. Nischalke, B. Karky, M. Jurek and T. Aase. 2013. *The Last Straw – Food Security in the Himalaya and the Additional Burden of Climate Change*. Arendal: UNEP GRID.

Norman, D. W. 2002. 'The farming systems approach: A historical perspective', *Paper presented at the 17th Symposium of the International Farming Systems Association*, 17–20 November, Buena Vista, FL.

Parikh, J. 2007. *Gender and Climate Change – Framework for Analysis, Policy and Action*. India: UNDP, Retrieved from: www.data.undp.org.in/Gnder_CC.pdf [Accessed 24 June 2014].

Rao, N. 2005. 'Land rights, gender equality and household food security: Exploring the conceptual links in the case of India', *Food Policy*, 31: 180–193.

Schiere, J. B., R. Groenland, A. Vlug and H. Van Keulen. 2004. 'System thinking in agriculture: An overview', in K. Rickert (ed.), *Emerging Challenges for Farming Systems – Lessons from Australian and Dutch Agriculture*. Rural Industries Research and Development Corporation 03/053.

Sen, A. 1981. *Poverty and Famines: An Essay on Entitlement and Deprivation*. Oxford: Clarendon Press.

Shelton, B. A. and D. John. 1996. 'The division of household labor', *Annual Review of Sociology*, 22: 299–322.

Sidh, S. N. and S. Basu. 2011. 'Women's contribution to household food and economic security: A study in the Garhwal Himalayas, India', *Mountain Research and Development*, 31 (2): 102–111.

Verma, R., M. Khadka, R. Badola and C. Wangdi. 2011. *Gender Experiences and Responses to Climate Change in the Himalayas*. Kathmandu: ICIMOD.

4 'Constructed' images of gender and gender roles in the Northeastern Himalayas

Virtual and actual

Subhadra Mitra Channa

1. Introduction

Socially recognized gender roles across the world are deeply embedded and informed by the manner in which gender as a relational attribute is rooted in the political/historical context, the cosmological world and also the ground realities of environment and resources. Gender informs relations within a particular social entity but also relates a unit, a tribe, a village, a region or a community to the rest of its socially interactive world. Relations of hierarchy are often built up around and justified by the way in which the gender relations of a society are constructed and viewed by others. Thus, stereotypical images of sexual laxity, negative traits evaluated in terms of the values of the social segment that is more powerful, are often attributed to the women of the marginalized segment. For example, the northeastern part of India has been at the receiving end of stigmatized gender constructs and negative images and in particular of its women. I would like to argue that the relative isolation of the Northeast from the caste-based patriarchal norms of mainland India – in spite of the spread of Hinduism in some of its parts, its historical association with East Asia (including physical similarities) and political isolation – have had a cumulative impact on the virtual images of the 'northeastern women'. Such negative images are particularly strong in the northern Hindi belt because of its inherently patriarchal and hierarchical society even as compared to other parts of India. The dominance of Christianity and of Western values among the tribes of Northeast has added to the fiction about the Northeast women. Although such images are 'virtual',[1] they are real in their social impact especially as expressed in the form of sexual harassment and negative social behaviour experienced by the northeastern women (and men[2]) on the streets of the cities such as Delhi.

This chapter focuses on some of the historical and political background and context of such constructs that are both stereotypical and hierarchical. At the same time, it needs to be pointed out that the construct of Northeast is also essentialised and fictional and follows more of a mythical image than being a description of reality. Quite necessarily, the image of the so-called northeastern woman is equally reductionist and monochromatic, far away from the rich diversity of this region.

The Northeast of India is composed of seven or eight states (if one includes Sikkim) and has a diversity of population that is differentiated on the basis of ethnicity, religion, culture and social organisation. In a state like Manipur for example, the upper caste Hindu Meiteis are quite different from the tribal, mostly Christian Tangkhul Nagas, and these are different from the lower castes of Hindus. As Brara (1998: 83) has described, 'Manipuri society consists of seven *salais* (Meiteis), the Brahmins, and the hill people (belonging mainly to the Naga and Kuki-clan groups). Besides these groups, there are exclusive pockets of Muslims (called *Pangals*) and the Mayangs (term used for outsiders).' The Nagas and Kukis have always asserted their different identities and the people of Arunachal would not like to be confused with the Mizos. The patriarchal Naga society is quite different from the matrilineal Khasis. The Hindu Assamese are closer to mainland Indians in their culture, religion and way of life than they are to the rest of the Northeast. The people of Tripura are likewise dominated by Bengali culture, although they too have sizeable tribal population. 'North-east India is emblematic of the regions where it is not only the extent of diversity that seems immeasurable, but also its irregularity' (Ramirez 2014: xviii).

So another question that needs to be raised in the beginning is about the process, both political and cultural 'construction' of the 'imaginary' Northeast, the one that is present in the collective imagination of the majority people of India. At the mention of the word 'Northeast', a typified image is conjured up, that of a mongoloid looking person in fashionable Western attire. It is a racialized and culturally exoticized image. Obviously, no North Indian would identify a *saree* clad woman from Tripura sporting all the paraphernalia of a Bengali married woman as northeastern and a similar situation exists for the Assamese women as well although they have a different dress. Thus, the Northeast has become more than a geographical zone; it has become a cultural construct, an imaginary space of specified imagery that has more to do with the gaze of the people of peninsular India than the actual situation. In this sense, the Northeast perhaps has something in common with all the similarly marginally situated places of India, where the marginality is more with respect to what may be called as the 'mainstream' (Channa 2008: 71) of Indian population than mere geography, although the latter too plays a significant role. For example,

Klenk (2010: 198, 199) writes with respect to Uttarakhand of the Central Himalayan region, 'Uttarakhand figures as a marginal, contradictory place in the north Indian social imaginary, simultaneously romanticized and scorned by urban middle classes and elites'.

Another aspect that needs to be taken into account is the self-image of the people, including both men and women, from the Northeast. Like all people in a situation of dominance and subordination, the people of Northeast are pushed into constructing selves, not only by their own self-image but also by the expectations of the gaze turned on them by the dominant people of the subcontinent. When they come to cities like Delhi, they are forced to conduct themselves in a manner that often fulfills the expectations of the local people, either voluntarily or involuntarily. In my observation as a teacher in Delhi University with many students and also colleagues from the Northeast, this dual self-image often takes the form of extreme shyness and withdrawal on part of the women and a rather defensive attitude on the part of the men.

Thus, when we are discussing the perceived gender imageries of the people from the Northeast by the people of mainland of India, a number of factors come into play. These include as we have just discussed, the construction of the 'Northeast' as an image born out of the historical, political and situational factors that have influenced the way 'Northeast' is generally perceived by the rest of India. The real differentiations and ground realities are often ignored in favour of the 'construct' born out of a collective hallucination about a region that most Indians feel alienated from. The people of the Northeast too are caught in a situation of duality, where what they are and what they are expected to be often gets them into a fuzzy self-image.

Lastly, I would also like to analyse to some extent the gender differences internal to the people of the Northeast, giving examples from some of their own narratives. The data for this chapter is based on my long-term engagement with people of the Northeast, especially with the women whom I have known as students, as colleagues and through my many visits to this region.

2.   The constructed and the real

The imaginary reconstruction of women from the Northeast, in the popular consciousness of people from mainland India, is that they are 'modern' (read Westernised) that again means that they are not restricted by the so-called inhibitions under which upper class/caste women in most of India are restrained. Such fictions of modernity also translate into expectations of unlimited freedom. There is nothing that can be far from the truth.

Before we understand why such an image exists, it is essential to understand how most people in India, especially those belonging to the majority caste-based Hindu society, classify and understand gender roles and hierarchies. In an earlier work (Channa 2013b: 32, 33), I have discussed how caste norms and values are primarily the reference point for classifying men and women, the gender roles they are expected to perform and the manner in which society in general should approach them. Upper caste Hindu women were normally treated as *devi* (goddess) and generally approached with deference and respect. Women in high political positions are also treated with great respect; since Hindu society accepts a goddess with power, a powerful woman becomes automatically a 'goddess' and may be even worshipped, like Mrs Indira Gandhi and more recently Jayalalitha.

However, a very different attitude prevails for the woman from a lower rung of society, the lower caste/class woman, the *dasi* or the menial worker. Another category not worthy of deference is the 'foreign' or the *mleccha*, the non-Hindu. Interestingly enough, in most of peninsular India, even Muslims and Christians follow the caste norms and are treated more according to their caste status than their religious status. Those familiar with the ethnographies of Kerala, for example, know that Syrian Christians are treated quite like upper caste Brahmins, while Christian converts from lower castes are treated exactly like 'untouchables'. The Hindus are deferential towards upper classes of people of other religions including foreigners as they are regarded as the upper castes of their respective societies.

But the respect and reverence shown to upper caste/class women are conditioned by their lifestyle and appearance and not simply by their caste status. Thus, a well-dressed woman in a *saree* getting down from a chauffeur-driven car is automatically treated with reverence, while a woman dressed 'inappropriately' and travelling in a public transport is harassed and humiliated. With deep roots of feudalism and caste, Indian society in general is hierarchical to the extreme.

Following these socially derived prescriptions, the imagery of the woman from the Northeast is racially and culturally informed. The racial component comes from their allegedly 'Mongoloid' looks that put them in the category of 'foreigners'. The assumptions that they are all Christians and therefore casteless, that they all eat 'exotic' and forbidden (polluted) foods, and that they wear 'Western' clothes add to their cultural marginalisation. This deadly combination, racial and cultural, puts them in the category of 'exploitable' bodies, a category of women who need not be respected. They have neither caste nor class.

A majority of persons from the Northeast, who come to a city (like Delhi), come as students. They are young and they do not have much money. They travel by public transport and live in rented apartments. They come from places that are usually small and have character of a 'Gemeinschaft'.[3] They are frightened, feel vulnerable and alienated. They wear Western clothes as that is their normal attire. Significantly, this mode of dressing had initially attracted the attention of local men, who equated 'respectability' with the kind of clothes the women in their own families wore. However, over the decades, the local women of all classes have adopted the Western dress in large number, but still the girls from Northeast remain targeted, as they appear to be more attractive because of their lighter skins and generally 'modern' appearance. Most importantly, as the men who harass them will tell you, 'They do not look like our mothers or sisters'.

3. The Northeast in the 'Indian' imagination

The Northeast as a whole is also projected by media and popular culture as a place of insurgency, a place that is not comfortable with its association with India, and overall the Northeast remains in the collective imagery as an essentialised 'Other'. Most Indians do not recognise them as 'like us'. Like all forms of otherness, these differences are both highlighted and emphasized through the creation of various myths. Undoubtedly, there are overt and striking differences. Food habits is a major issue, as predominantly vegetarian upper castes of northern India look with aversion on the non-vegetarian lifestyle of these people. More importantly, they eat 'forbidden' meats like those of cows and pigs and allegedly dogs as well. While the former kinds may still be accepted as they are on the menu of many Indians, but the last named remains a matter of much apprehension. But what is ignored is that these people like the rest of India also eat vegetables, rice and pulses that is the staple diet of many local people in northern India. The point that I wish to make is that it is always the 'differences' that are emphasized and not the similarities. For example, a vegetarian person could find much to eat in a traditional Naga cuisine but few would believe that.

Because of this alienation, the bodies of the Naga women and also from other places of Northeast are treated as 'exploitable'. Like all other similar situations, this exploitation is rationalised by the image of the 'liberated' and modern tribal woman, who is equated with the foreign tourist, as 'women who like to have some fun'. The North Indian men are much taken up by the fact that these women move unescorted by elderly family members and have no inhibition for drinking alcohol or smoking (this is an image and not a reality). Many myths are floated as to how 'tribal' society is promiscuous and free sex is permissible. For any anthropologist or anyone even remotely familiar with Nagaland, Manipur or any of the other regions of the Northeast, these myths are known to be completely imaginary.

Such has always been the situation when one group comes in conflict with another or when one is dominated by the other. Khan (2006: 111) writes referring to the situation of Partition of the Indian subcontinent in 1947, 'The injuries that seemed to crystallise Partition's violence were mostly inflicted on women of "Other" groups. For it was through their bodies that "Self" and "Other" were defined as diametrically opposed notions of differentiation.'

While the unlettered masses use only their visual impressions like physical looks and dress to create the 'otherness', the educated people use even more subtle but insidious constructs. For example, in a seminar, I was taken aback and aghast to hear from a highly placed government official, 'Why should we accept the people of Northeast like ourselves? Did they take part in the freedom struggle?' Such comments are born out of both prejudices and ignorance. First, The gentleman in question was not informed that many parts of Northeast, including Nagaland and Manipur, did take part in the freedom struggle and they did fight the British, but not in the name of Indian nationalism but for the sake of their own freedom. Second, the people of Northeast, except for places like Assam, Tripura and Manipur, were fairly isolated from peninsular India. The idea of an 'Indian nation' was not created in this region as it was in the rest of India. Thus, those who intellectualise the differences are even more prejudiced and ignorant in their constructs than the ordinary people who respond to the face value of how they see things and not how they interpret them. Thus, an ordinary citizen may respond to the difference in appearance alone, while the so-called enlightened citizen will bring in issues of insurgency, their own version of 'Indian nationalism' etc.

Let us also take a look at how the Northeast has constructed its own version of 'India' and although it is part of the same historical and political process, to examine the views of the people of the Northeast is to take the point of view of the dominated as compared to that of the dominant section of the larger political entity.

4.   'India' in the imagination of the Northeast

It has already been mentioned that Northeast is a diverse and culturally heterogeneous region. Likewise, the relations of its different segments vary according to their historical/cultural relationship with the mainland. To take the case of the Nagas would be to take a community that is stereotypically northeastern as per the image that is held in the minds of the dominant majority. This is not to say that people of Tripura and Assam, closer to the Hindu image, are absolutely comfortable with their relationship, for they too consist of borderland people who feel that they are on the margins of the large democracy of India. The states of Manipur and Nagaland have suffered for long under the repressive regime of the Indian army that has also been armed with the infamous Armed Forces Special Powers Act (AFSPA) that has led Irom Sharmila, a Hindu Meitei girl of Manipur, to be on fast for more than a decade. Nagaland has also never taken easily what they consider as their forced annexation into India and since India's independence, the relationship between Nagaland and India has been political strained. The media has highlighted the 'separation' and conflict aspects, one way or the other, not adding to the relationship between India and Nagaland. For the majority of people, Nagas remain those, 'with whom we are at war' or those with whom we should sympathise for humanitarian or political reasons (the latter being in a minority anyway). Tünyi (2012: 27) writes that when questioned whether he was for or against the Naga movement for independence, he could not give offhand a straight answer. But in his mind, he identified himself as a Naga who could not bring himself to forgive the Indian army or the Indian government for the wrongs done to his people and the atrocities committed on them. At the same time, as a reflective and educated man, he is also aware that the Naga nationalism that he grew up with was 'based on things like fear, hatred, frustration and other irrational prejudice against the Indian populace' (ibid.: 29), Since this seems to work both ways, one can always see through into the clouds of prejudice and stereotyping of 'the Other' that has vitiated the relationship. But the truth that stands is that such is the situation and to a large extent, the manner in which the people of a place like Delhi tend to treat the people, especially women, from Northeast is a result of mutual distrust and distancing of social relationships.

Again from my own experience, I have seen relationships between girls from Northeast and from the other parts of India soften up and often become cordial when they are put together as a peer group, like in a classroom and in a hostel. Yet, the lack of sensitivity and information about the Northeast often brings up the old hurts and uncaring remarks and small actions may still serve to trigger the feelings of alienation. I had accompanied my colleague from Arunachal Pradesh to the office of the chief engineer of the University of Delhi, who having attended to our issues pertaining to the North Eastern Students'

House for Women on Delhi University campus, turned to my colleague and asked her sweetly, 'Are you from Korea?'. She was nonplussed and only managed to mutter that if she was a Korean then how come she was an assistant professor in Delhi University and also a warden of a hostel. But this small incidence is only one instance of what according to my colleagues and students are a recurrent feature of their lives on the streets of Delhi. Such so-called minor incidences do nothing to improve the image of India in their minds. Another of my colleagues was in tears when a class four employee had asked her to write something in Chinese for her, saying innocently, 'You are Chinese, No?' Although I tried to ease the situation by telling her that the woman in question was ignorant and illiterate, the case of the chief engineer shooting through his mouth could not be condoned so easily. When such remarks become a part of daily harassment and alienation, one cannot expect that the people from Northeast would not type caste the 'Indian' as 'coward, liar, cheater, weakling, beggar, idol-worshipper, rapist, arsonist, and so on' (Tünyi 2012: 29).

It is a fact that whenever a Naga catches a flight from Dimapur to come to Delhi, they say, 'We are going to India'. India will remain forever a foreign country to the people of Nagaland so long as the people of India consider them as aliens.

For the people of the Northeast, the stereotyping and consequent harassments reaffirms their aversion to the local people of the cities like Delhi, and forces them to withdraw further into their shells. Few persons from Northeast include other than Northeast people in their social circles and they always express their mistrust of these persons. Even inside a hostel, I have found that most girls from one region tend to form closer groups with each other. The internal divisions of their own regions also inform the manner in which they form social groups; those most intimate are usually the ones who belong to the closest social point of reference. They also form support groups providing help to each other, often excluding others, even from their peer groups.

Let us take now a brief look at how the women in the Northeast are situated in their own society and how much such 'images' differ from the reality.

5. Gender roles in the Northeast

Although women in the Northeast may not have suffered from the physical restrictions imposed on the women under Brahmanical and Islamic patriarchy, most of the tribes of the Northeast barring some of those from the Khasi and Jaintia hills are patriarchal and patrilineal. The women are relegated to the domestic domain and they play only minor roles in the public affairs of their tribes and communities. The impact of Christianity has worsened the situation of patriarchy and whatever freedom they may have had has been further restricted because of missionary activities in this region. Hümtsoe-Nienü (2012: 69) writes, 'It would be too much of an unmerited observation, if not nearly a lie, to presume that Naga women enjoyed a privileged status equal to the men before Christianity because this is far from the reality'. However, as she describes, they were active members of their village because the men were often away at war. 'They ploughed and sowed and gleaned and reaped. They engaged in agricultural and domestic labors' (ibid.). But they did not enjoy high social or ritual status as they did not go for headhunting, the one key symbol of Naga male social identity. As Hümtsoe-Nienü puts it, the men never gave any thought to the emotions of women who lived in sorrow. 'The glorification of headhunting practice as a passport to manhood is unwarranted, for seen from a woman's perspective, it only doubled her woes as a woman, a wife, and a mother' (ibid.: 71).

The relative freedom was only under the specific conditions of land ownership and community living in which the interpretation that is usually given to patrilineal inheritance, an essential aspect of patriarchy, did not operate. As is well-known, the predominant form of subsistence in these regions is shifting or *jhum* cultivation, where the land is owned not by individuals but by the community; in such a case, there are no rights of possession but only rights of user. Since women play a predominant role in shifting cultivation, this particular form of subsistence is also known by the name of female farming. Shifting cultivation is done by the technology of use of 'hoe' rather than the plough. The hoe is a light instrument that is most often used by the women to turn the top soil after the seeds are broadcast rather than dug in deep, as when a plough is used. Thus, women do the sowing and harvesting and therefore are major stakeholders of cultivation, playing equal if not more important role than men. Other aspects of subsistence include pig-rearing and horticulture (growing of vegetables and fruits), again largely feminine occupations. Thus, women have access to resources like land, trees and animals that they nurture and provide subsistence for the families. The community ownership of land gave equal access to women and did not make them dependent on the men for their subsistence.

As of today, the women still work the fields in most of the Northeast states, and my young colleagues from the northeastern states of Nagaland and Arunachal Pradesh have told me that they work in their fields when they go back home, irrespective of their professional qualifications. When I had dinner at the residence of an engineer from Arunachal Pradesh, I was told that the rice that I was eating was grown in the fields by the family. Another colleague had her mother visiting her after the birth of her baby, but the mother went away in haste, because 'she had so much work back home to do like taking care of fields and animals'.

Earlier the men were occupied in tribal warfare and spent time in the morungs besides engaging in trade and political activities. It is to be noted that while some tribes like Khasis and Garos are matrilineal and women in these tribes hold considerable social power, yet political power has always been held by men. It is only men who were part of the village councils and who negotiated with each other. When I had asked some political leaders from among the Khasis as to why the women do not become part of the tribal councils, they replied, 'It is their choice, they have too much work to do and have no time for politics'. But Khasi women often do not agree on these points although they do agree that they have a handful in terms of ritual and social duties that they need to perform.

Visitors to Manipur are often taken to the Ima market, a market run exclusively by women, and it is quite a sight to see the women, mostly elderly and matronly, zestfully buying and selling various goods. They are cheerful yet sure to negotiate keenly for the best price for their goods. 'The women sell goods ranging from fish, rice, vegetables, jute products, fruits, flowers to things specifically meant as offering to the *Lai* (gods); traditional Manipuri clothes-*phi, phanek, kudei, chaddar* etc., spun and woven with their own hands at their looms' (Brara 1998: 236). Going there one feels, this is a world of women, but when one tries to talk to them, there are tales of sorrow too. The continued conflict in this region, the heavy toll of young lives by the action of the military and also because of drug addiction, has left many families to be headed by women. Many grandmothers are left taking care of their grandchildren whose parents have died of AIDS. The apparent freedom that one sees here has come at a price. The same was true of the Naga women working their fields when the men went 'headhunting' and many a times, a young mother was left to fend for her children when the husband never returned. Hümtsoe-Nienü (2012: 70) has given the sad song of a woman waiting for her husband to return from war, which he never does.

The important difference between the Northeast and the caste-driven peninsular India is that people of the Northeast are not strictly stratified into those who do menial work and those who do not. Here everyone works in their own fields, women weave and make variety of products and men too are adapt and work that involves the use of their hands. 'Sitting in the market was not at all looked down upon. Dignity of labour of such magnitude can be marked as a unique feature of this economy' (Brara 1998: 237).

Again as highlighted by Omvedt and Brara, the Northeast of India has greater geographical and cultural affinity with the Southeast than with South Asia, especially the mainland of the Indian Peninsula that has been dominated by different social values, different forms of patriarchy and subsistence patterns. There are undeniable organisational differences between a sedentary agricultural society with fully formed states and shifting cultivators with mostly what is known as segmental political organisations. The Northeast also did not have the developed caste and social hierarchy that one finds in most other parts of India. Omvedt (1993: 75) writes about Southeast Asian societies:

[They] continue to have one of the most equalitarian village social organizations in the world. There are no caste inequalities and the kinship system of the region is recognized by social scientists to be one of the most equalitarian (least patriarchal) in the world.

However, as noted by scholars who have studied women in this region, the relative independence of women may not be due to simply the nature of subsistence or even as Omvedt believes, the prevalence of Buddhism, but because of the more frequent disappearance of the men from social life. It has been commonly observed that because of the prevalence of drug addiction and HIV/AIDS in recent times as well as continuous political unrest and insurgency, there has been heavy toll on the lives of young men. Many times young women find themselves holding the responsibility of the family, not as a means of freedom or as a statement of liberation but simply as a situation of contingency, due to loss of male members.

6.   Relative value of men and women

But at the same time the contribution of women to the economy did not give them a higher position in society equal to the men. Except for Meghalaya, in all other parts of Northeast, in all the tribal populations, patriarchy is the norm and property is to pass in the male line. When land was held by the community, the women had equal access but when land became private property and also people began to accumulate wealth in the modern economy, the law of only men inheriting has adversely affected the women. According to the revised laws of the Indian nation, women under the amended Hindu Succession Act, inherit equally with their brothers and wives have equal rights. But for the tribes of the Northeast, the customary laws prevail.

The men from the Northeast often point to the use of tradition as a way to maintain their identity and adherence to 'customary laws' is seen as one way to deal with tribal autonomy or assertion of independent identity. In this way, when the 53rd Amendment to the Constitution of India made it mandatory for women to be represented on village councils such as panchayats, the same was not implemented in tribal areas including the Northeast, citing customary laws and the entitlement of tribes to their ways of life. But Naga women have always felt the burden of patriarchy and Naga scholar Hümtsoe-Nienü (2012: 74) writes:

> However as an insider, writing from the 'womb' of the naga context, it is disturbing to assume that retrogression to the past is a readymade solution. This conviction is more intensely felt as a woman member of the naga community where communitarian principles function against the inclusion of women. Be it in the morung tradition, the kinship system, land inheritance practice, or the village administrative set-up; all are basically male-biased.

As already discussed, it is more the absence of men than inherent gender values that gives apparent freedom to women in this and also other frontier regions in South Asia. Thus, gender as a relational construct varies with the presence or absence of the two parties to the relationship, namely men and women. Even strong patriarchal values may be ineffective in real life if the men remain absent. Thus, with respect to the Limbu women, Jones and Jones (1976: 47) write:

> As the Limbu turned to the outside world for new sources of income, especially in military service, the family structure was altered. Because so many Limbu men were now absent from home for long periods, much of the day to day decision making fell to the women.

We can see the recurrence of this theme in several Himalayan ethnographies, where the apparent 'freedom' of women is more a consequence of the 'absence of men' or their inability to be providers than any positive ideology that actually supposes women to be equal agents as men.

Thus, there may be a disjunction between the ideology and the actual situation, one may not correspond one to one with the other. For instance, the traditional Ima market in Manipur was the domain of women past their prime, i.e. elderly grandmothers who, having finished with raising children and housekeeping, turned their attention to buying and selling goods. In recent times, younger women are also entering the market, because they have become sole breadwinners in the absence of the men. The high incidences of HIV/AIDS in Manipur and also the decades-long militancy and police action is taking its toll on the young male population. Thus, what is often regarded as a matrifocal family may be an outcome of circumstances, often negative ones like war, epidemics and displacement.

Channa (2010, 2013a) in her study of the Bhotiyas of Uttarakhand, who are a primarily pastoral community depending on the rearing of sheep and selling of wool and woollen products, has discussed the gender relations in detail. This study was based on her fieldwork in this region from 1997 to 2000 and highlights the ecological and gender relationships of a people whose identity depended not on any stable association with any piece of land, but from their trans-border trade and transhumant lifestyle. The men of this community were primarily traders and sheep herders, and remain absent from the village for long periods of time. In the absence of men, the village is seen as belonging to the women, who carry out most tasks related to subsistence like horticulture, processing of wool knitting and making carpets, rearing domestic animals, making rice beer and generally taking care of all social activities. Although among them, the lineage gods pass in the male line, the actual rituals for them are performed by the women as the men may not be present. The cross-border trade with Tibet that was the mainstay of their economy and also identity was terminated with the political events of the annexation of Tibet and then the Indo-China war in 1962, but the men still engage in such tasks as trading, ferrying tourists or even doing jobs that take them away from the village as the village space is seen as feminine and the men are simply not supposed to be present unless too young or too old.

Channa has shown that the apparent agency of Bhotiya women in central Garhwal is not because the women are seen cosmologically as superior to men, quite the contrary, but simply because of the economy and the nature of ecological relationships. Thus, while men engaged in cross-border trade and pastoral activities, the women stayed back in the village and looked after it. Since men were absent most of the times, the women had to take care of domestic deities like the *kulde-vata* and also perform household rituals. There is also a disjunction between the perceptive cognition of the outsiders, to whom the village life appears to be of greater importance than life in the wilderness, from that of the Bhotiyas, to whom the wilderness where men have supremacy is the more important domain. Similarly, to the people of the Northeast, the symbolic and cosmological value of men's activities, as symbolized in practices such as headhunting, were of greater significance and endowed with much greater cosmological powers than mundane activities like control over the subsistence activities and day to day running of the household and village life. Therefore, the apparent agency of women and their so-called control over the economy may not be interpreted from the point of view of the community and their own world view as translating into a superior position for women. It is the distribution of power between the various domains and their cosmological significance that most often than not determines the manner in which men and women may be perceived.

Practical exigencies such as war and the mode of subsistence, community inheritance patterns and varying norms of modesty and cultural differences may have created an illusion of 'liberation' that may not coincide with ground realties, of both gender construction and the real social position of women. The young women who come to Delhi to study and work are often painfully shy and in awe of the wild urban world they see around them. Coming from small communities with face-to-face relationships, they often find it difficult to anticipate reactions and cannot comprehend the existing stereotypes that people carry. Quite unlike the 'modern' and 'free' women that they are supposed to be, they are often deeply conservative and reticent.[4] Their sense of shock at being accosted and approached by men who expect free and easy access can be assessed by the deep sense of distress that they express.[5]

Thus, the self-image of the women from Northeast is far distant from what they are perceived as, especially in North India that also dominates in the nationalist discourse.

7. Conclusion

While concluding, it is important to make a distinction between the cognitive and the ontological aspects of gender. A part of our understanding of gender and the consequent behaviour informed by and affecting gender relations is the manner in which gender is constructed. These constructions follow cultural, historical and political processes and are a product of collective imagination. They tend to affect the way people behave and also vary according to the constructs one holds in the mind about one's own community and the 'Other'. Women are quite often the boundary markers between communities and the projection of 'Other women' is a means to emphasize how 'they' are different from 'us'. The efforts by men to keep their women in a state of 'purity' (i.e. making them follow 'tradition' while they feel free to change) is typical of almost all societies. Unnithan-Kumar (1997: 20) writes with respect to her study of the tribal Girasia of Rajasthan, 'I see the use of Girasia women as metaphors of identity as reinforcing the notion held by gender anthropologists, that women are markers of boundaries and especially in patrilineal societies are the symbols of tradition'. At another level are the ontological realties of what men and women actually do, how the resources of the society are actually divided, exchanged and negotiated. While conjuring up gender images, people tend to ignore the real for the imagined, especially with regard to the 'Other'. Such negative images are an adjunct of the political relationship and power hierarchy between the segments. A very important factor is the differences in world view and cosmology, like the relative values put on various activities and the parts of the cosmos. For example, the relative value of the habitation and wild may vary from society to society and significant differences in this regard have been presented by anthropological ethnographic works.[6] What may appear to be a significant aspect of high status in one group may not be so in another. Such values and world views are again not static and are liable to change as other conditions change. In other words, gender is also an aspect of history and can change through historical transformations whenever they become possible.

Thus, the disjunction between what 'appears to be' real and 'what is' real is very apparent in the discourse that we have engaged in so far. Even policymakers and planners may get misled by such apparent constructs and the 'freedom' of tribal women often enters into academic discourse. The apparent agency of women from tribal areas such as the Northeast is often a correlate of social, political and economic factors, as already discussed. Such apparent agency certainly does not indicate the lack of patriarchy or gender hierarchy. When taking up a discourse on women or gender in any part of the world, it is to be understood that forms of patriarchy may vary a great deal in response to historical situations and what is normative in one region may not be in another region. Thus, women from the Northeast may have the freedom to wear Western clothes, travel and may eat and drink in a manner not commensurate with the values of Brahmanical patriarchy, yet in their own context, they are as conservative as the Hindu women. In fact, in some aspects, they feel themselves to be more restricted by their customary laws. Women from Nagaland have discussed with me how the modified Hindu law of inheritance that gives equal share of parental property to daughters is more progressive than their own customary laws that denies such rights of inheritance for women. It is therefore imperative to understand that the reality is never any actual situation but only a reflection of deeply embedded social processes and power relations that need to be understood not as unchanging perspectives but always contextually and in the time frame of the present.

Notes

1 The terms 'actual' and 'virtual' have been borrowed from Gilles Deluze (2002: 149), though not quite literally in the same sense.
2 There have been several instances of violence against young men of the Northeast, even resulting in death in a few cases.
3 Tönnies differentiated between Gemeinschaft and Gesellschaft, the former referring to a close knit, homogeneous community and the latter to a loosely knit and complex social organization like an urban city. The former is marked by face-to-face and familiar relationship and the latter by anonymity and alienation.
4 This is an observation based on my interaction with my students from the Northeast who in comparison to girls from other parts of India are particularly shy, do not speak up and try to remain confined to the company of each other. It takes a lot of effort to draw them out of their shell, when they can be like any other.
5 A report published in the *Times of India*, 24 January 2014, based on a survey conducted by the Centre for North East Studies and Policy Research, Jamia Milia Islamia and commissioned by the National Commission for Women, shows that 81 per cent of Northeast women feel harassed in Delhi. This report is based on research that commenced in May 2002.
6 See, for example, Croll and Parkin (1992).

References

Brara, N. V. 1998. *Politics, Society and Cosmology in India's North East*. Delhi: Oxford University Press.
Channa, S. M. 2008. 'Concept of the mainstream', in S. K. Chaudhuri and S. M. Patnaik (eds.), *Indian Tribes and the Mainstream*. Jaipur: Rawat Publications, pp. 69–76.
Channa, S. M. 2010. 'Cosmology, gender and kinship: Role and relationships of Himalayan pastoral women', *Nivedini: Journal of Gender Studies*, 16: 1–25.
Channa, S. M. 2013a. *The Inner and Outer Selves: Cosmology, Gender and Ecology at the Himalayan Borders*. New Delhi: Oxford University Press.
Channa, S. M. 2013b. *Gender in South Asia: Social Imagination and Constructed Realities*. Cambridge: Cambridge University Press.
Croll, E. and D. Parkin (eds.). 1992. *Bush Base: Forest Farm, Culture, Environment and Development*. London: Routledge.

Deluze, G. and C. Parnet. 2002. *Dialogues*, New York: Columbia University Press, Tr. From French by Hugh Tomlin and Barbara Habberjam.

Hümtsoe-Nienü, E. 2012. 'Women's experience of "sorrow": Ending the saga of "Headhunting"', in E. Humtsoe-Nienu, P. Pimomo and V. Tunyi (eds.), *Nagas: Essays for Responsible Change*. Dimapur, Nagaland: Heritage Publishing House, pp. 66–79.

Jones, R. L. and S. K. Jones. 1976. *The Himalayan Women: A Study of Limbu Women in Marriage and Divorce*. Palo Alto: Mayfair Publications. Ltd.

Khan, F. A. 2006. 'Speaking violence: Pakistani women's narratives of partition', in N. C. Behera (ed.), *Gender, Conflict and Migration*. New Delhi: Sage Publications, pp. 97–115.

Klenk, R. M. 2010. *Educating Activists: Development and Gender in the Making of Modern Gandhians*. Boulder, NY: Lexington Books.

Omvedt, Gail. 1993. 'The North-East region and Indian civilization: A view from the East', in B. Pakem (ed.), *Regionalism in India*. New Delhi: Har-Anand Publications, pp. 67–81.

Ramirez, P. 2014. *People of the Margins: Across Ethnic Boundaries in North-East India*. Guwahati, Delhi: Spectrum Publications.

Tünyi, V. 2012. 'Naga nationalism: Where are we heading?', in E. Humtsoe-Nienu, P. Pimomo and V. Tunyi (eds.), *Nagas: Essays for Responsible Change*. Dimapur, Nagaland: Heritage Publishing House, pp. 26–31.

Unnithan-Kumar, M. 1997. *Identity, Gender and Poverty: New Perspectives in Caste and Tribe in Rajasthan*. Oxford: Berghahn Books.

5   Towards a research collaboration with indigenous communities in India

Tara Douglas

1. Introduction

In India, mass media entertainment reaches even the more peripheral areas and young audiences now enjoy the animated programmes that include representations of favourite Hindu myths such as *Little Krishna* (2009), *Sons of Ram* (2012) *Arjun: The Warrior Prince* (2012) and *Mahabharat* (2013) and films such as *Roadside Romeo* (2008), *Toonpur Ka Superrhero* (2010) and *Delhi Safari* (2012) that are inspired by popular imported feature films. Aside from the prime entertainment value of these programmes, they do not represent the rich diversity of indigenous cultures in India. Hence the *Tales of the Tribes* is a research project that sets out to investigate the use of animation as a tool for indigenous representation in India, and it was prompted by my involvement as an animator and assistant producer for *The Tallest Story Competition* (2006), a series of five short animated folktales from Adivasi communities from Central India, produced by the Scottish-based company, West Highland Animation.

This earlier programme was a first attempt to represent indigenous culture in India through the medium of animation. On completion, the series was screened to more than 15,000 children from indigenous and non-indigenous communities in India and in the United Kingdom by the Adivasi Arts Trust (www.adivasiaartstrust.org). The films were enjoyed by young audiences, especially in the regions represented in the programme, where children had never seen animation films of their own folktales before. Within the institutional environment, the programme has also received some criticism regarding the limited extent of indigenous community involvement in the project that was conceived and produced in Scotland (where West Highland Animation has a history of working to preserve the indigenous Gaelic culture through animation). *The Tallest Story Competition* also raised questions about the representation of indigenous cultures in the media, specifically about who would be qualified to determine the representation, and pointing to issues of cultural ownership. This response has motivated a study of historical and contemporary representation of indigenous identities in the *Tales of the Tribes* research project and the production of a new collection of animation films based on indigenous storytelling; this time produced in India and with more engagement from indigenous communities.

The research does not focus on the role of women, either in this project or in larger context of Northeast India where four of the films were developed for the series. There are conflicting views about the position of women in the region (Burman 2012; Das 2012; Roselima 2014) and agreement that Northeastern tribal women enjoy more freedom as equal to their male counterparts but still hold less status than men. I maintain that the feminist research approach is compatible with indigenous research because it can lead to increased sensitivity and shares the aim to create social change, represent human diversity and develop relationships.

2. Representation during the colonial period

A brief discussion on colonial representation establishes the context for the proposal to use animation as a tool for indigenous representation. It also promotes a review of responsive research practices that are suitable for application in the contemporary context. In India, where representation was primarily conducted by authoritative identities positioned outside the local communities, anthropology produced detailed information for the purpose of administering the inhabitants of regions that included the remote hill areas of Northeast India. Critical analysis has since shown how representation, projected by the West as the self-ascribed representer and interpreter of the East, has served the specific purpose of the justification and perpetuation of domination and exploitation (Säid 1978: 247).

The images from the colonial period have influenced the perception of indigenous people on audiences. Descriptions of non-European others have resulted in stereotypical, patronizing views of a timeless orient that does not develop but stays the same, in contrast to progressive European civilisation linked to objectivity, science and facts. The popular representation of the native as the idealised noble savage can be traced back to Dryden's *The Conquest of Granada* (1672). It is a romanticised image that is communicated by particular cinematic representations, two prominent examples being *The Gods Must be Crazy*

(1980) and *Emerald Forest* (1985), and it contributes to an ideology based on the purity of indigenous culture suspended in time where tribal art, perceived by anthropologists to be archaic and a remnant of the past, required preservation in museums (Lenz *et al.* 2003: 115, Coote and Shelton 1992: 20).

3. The neocolonial absence of indigenous representation

The legacy of colonialism did not end with independence. The debates on neocolonialism and globalisation are contentious. In this context, the term 'neocolonialism' refers to the integration of former colonies into the international capitalist economy, and it incorporates hegemony in the political, religious, ideological and cultural spheres. The concept of neocolonialism that was defined by Nkrumah (1965) delineates how control is exercised through economic means commonly associated with the financial interest of multinational companies. It is an analysis that infuses Huggan's (1996: 19) discussion on how colonialism has been transformed into a more insidious form embodied by the global hegemonies exercised by transnational companies and information industries.

It is also a description that echoes Säid's critique on how 'A vast web of interests now links all parts of the former colonial world to the United States' (1978: 285). In India, colonial attitudes are perpetuated in dominant politics and they are accommodated into the contemporary imperial design of globalization, where neocolonial homogenizing processes 'serve the Western market economy to produce a class of educated people whose intellectual formation is directed to satisfy market needs' (ibid.: 325). The relevance of this process of homogenisation can be examined with reference to the dilemmas of indigenous cultures and animation as independent artistic practice.

Capitalist market values have had negative impact on indigenous culture and on the production of animation of the artistic, experimental genre. Indigenous craft has declined with the availability of cheap mass-produced commercial products, which range from clothing and building materials to all kinds of practical items for the home. Commercial production methods have also rendered small-scale animation experimentation out of the competitive market and the representation of indigenous identities in India is conspicuously absent in the animation that is produced.

Storytelling was how cultural values, practices and beliefs were passed on from the elder to the younger generations in traditional societies, and it was through stories that children learnt about the history of their community and the connection to their homeland to establish a sense of belonging, identity and group cohesion. The impact of the new animation industry in India is visible at the periphery where traditional narratives and cultural practices compete with popular television entertainment, so that young indigenous people are now growing up with cartoons that have no cultural relevance to them. The power of the media for normalising ideas and emotions and mobilising action is acknowledged (McLuhan 1994), and in India where animation is targeted at juvenile audiences, the absence of indigenous representation is problematic as the expanding consumption of animation by indigenous children arguably enforces the assimilation of non-indigenous values that are at odds with their cultural paradigms to establish distance from their own community heritage.

The influence of the new exposure is visible both in the fragmentation of previously firm identities and in the evidence of the undeniable local enthusiasm for the animation medium. The encounter with globalisation has exacerbated the challenges to identity and representation that were introduced by colonialism, specifically the marginalization of indigenous peoples in India and the decline of local self-esteem. With particular reference to the Khasi, Kharmawphlang, Nonglait and Rynjah (2006: 13) have pointed out how the influence of globalization has increased the disparity between an urban elite and the underprivileged; Barthakur (2006: 11) has highlighted how the demand for change has created a dilemma between preserving indigenous identities and aligning with the mainstream; Ao (2006: 7) has discussed her concerns for the commodification of Naga cultures and Biswas (2006: 19) has suggested that the representation of Nagas in the media does not match the way they perceive themselves. The silence of the other has undeniably become more pronounced and the absence of indigenous representation poses interpretations about a lack of contemporary relevance of indigenous cultures to mainstream audiences. This further implies the contributive role of the absence of representation to reports of experiences of discrimination that indigenous people commonly face in India.

Turning the lens towards the production of animation in India shows how the commercial animation industry in India is overwhelmingly dominated by production outsourced by European, American and

East Asian countries, with the United States being the most significant market for animation worldwide (Tata Strategic Management Group 2010: 8), in contrast to India, where less than 1 per cent of the animation films that are released are animated (ibid.: 18). Even though just 10 per cent of the animation produced for television in India is targeted for national broadcast, the licensing of multiple cable television channels in India including Disney Channel, Pogo, Nickolodeon India, Cartoon Network and Hungama TV illustrates how animated content also entertains young audiences nationwide.

The aesthetics of animation that have been developed for universal appeal are determined by companies such as Disney according to a strict artistic and corporate protocol (Kunzle 1975: 11). Cuteness, bright colours, fast action and the technical sophistication of Disney cartoons produced with huge budgets have now become standard expectations of animation style in India. Even the representations of Indian culture in animation that are dominated by popular mythological narratives are retold by characters that are based on Westernized aesthetics of cartoon depiction. The popular Hindu mythological renditions such as *Ganesha* (2005) *Chota Bheem* (2008) and *Little Krishna* (2009) therefore cannot be claimed to represent the indigenous communities. The Western universal aesthetic for cartoons contrasts the rich diversity of local traditional art forms that include sculpture, wall painting, miniature painting, jewellery and textiles from classical to tribal and folk sources. However, the high cost of producing animation leads investors to focus on maximum return, resulting in Indian animation companies choosing to adopt tried and tested formulas rather than experiment with Indian content and folk art forms.

This discourse indicates how the dominant approaches to representation inherited from the West continue to have influence in India. In contrast, feminists have challenged the utility of concepts like objectivity and universality. Feminist research promotes a personal, political and engaging stance (Sarantakos 1993) with transformative aims and the goal of raising consciousness and empowering the oppressed (Reinharz 1992: 180–194). I therefore refer to the feminist approach towards readdressing the unequal relationships of dominance and marginalisation for the *Tales of the Tribes* research project.

4.   The politics of self-representation

Self-representation as advised by scholars of post colonial studies including Säid is a path to examine identity. My research is founded on the concept that self-examination is a way to locate a more authentic existence (Bendix 1997: 18), ideology that is relevant and significant to the broader discussion about self-representation by the indigenous people participating in this research, as well as to my representation in the dialogue with indigenous artists and communities. Indigenous identities were traditionally founded on mother tongue languages and connections with the land were recollected and reinforced through stories of origination that even mentioned specific geographical locations: For example, the origin story of the Ao clans are said to have emerged from the rocks at Lungterok. It was a relationship that Chaisie captured when he wrote that 'a Naga derives the essence of his physical existence from his family, clan, khel and village' (1999: 36). The important function of tradition is further corroborated by a study of the work of the anthropologist Malinowski (1948: 39) who also observed how it was of supreme value for the community, and that order and civilisation was maintained through strict adhesion to the lore and knowledge received from previous generations.

The expanding exposure to mass media entertainment and the challenge it presents to traditional indigenous practices and identities need to be examined. Spencer (2006: 26) has linked media consumption and identity in his definition of self-identity as 'a negotiated space between ourselves and others; constantly being reappraised and very much linked to the circulation of cultural meanings in a society', and this indicates how indigenous identities are confronted by media exposure to content that does not reflect indigenous values, stories and creative traditions.

Indigenous communities in Australia and Papua New Guinea have expressed concern about the influence of mass media on local identities (Ginsburg 1993: 97) and it has influenced decisions to provide for media content that reflects local values and cultures. Indigenous media now provides a category of politically engaged film-making practices and images that are controlled by indigenous peoples and that represent their concerns and customs (Martens 2012; Murray 2008a: 18). While there are examples of indigenous productions from indigenous film-makers as diversely located as New Zealand, Australia and Canada, indigenous media programming has yet to be provided for in India.

Young people from isolated regions in India may not have access to literary articulation through the English language to be able to represent themselves in the environment of academia and I stipulate the contribution this has had on the observed silence of the subaltern, identified by Spivak (1988: 78). On the other hand, my research shows that indigenous people have traditionally told their own story and connected to the past through folktales (Scroggie 2009: 77; Smith 1999: 145). The folklore of these communities deliver complex cultural information in a format that is entertaining for children and in India where animation is primarily targeted at juveniles, this presents the idea of its suitability for inclusive dissemination. As a medium that incorporates the dimensions of movement, location, time and sound, it is appropriate for the communication of the multidimensional aspects of folktales to make indigenous culture accessible for both young indigenous and non-indigenous audiences. Coomaraswamy's (1977: 9) theory that the language of metaphysics that informs folklore is imagistic, further reaffirms the idea that the visual medium of animation maybe is more suited to represent indigenous epistemology, oral narratives and visual arts than through literature in the English language.

The *Tales of the Tribes* is a sample collection of five short animation films that are based on themes of indigenous art, culture and narrative traditions. Four of these stories are from the Northeast region, with tales from Nagaland, Sikkim, Manipur and Arunachal Pradesh, in addition to the Adivasi one from the Pardhan Gonds of Central India. The film production has engaged involvement from members of the local community in their conception and development, and this has also led to the investigation of a methodology that is compatible with indigenous outlooks.

Feminist research methods that include interviews and participant observation were brought to this practice-led research as a way to record the development process and to collect material to uncover the issues that have arisen by this engagement with indigenous cultural content and the medium of animation. By using these techniques, this project also examines the relationship of collaboration between the indigenous and non-indigenous participants. The research about this collaboration for the *Tales of the Tribes* project was primarily carried out during the pre-production Animation Workshop that were held in each of the five areas from where the stories originated. The locations for the workshops and the communities that were selected to work with were decided with inputs from regionally based partner organisations, and as the primary researcher for this project, it was my task to identify those partnerships.

The objective of the workshops was to negotiate the representation of the local cultures with groups of workshop participants from the communities and to study cultural nuances with guidance from local cultural elders including artists, musicians, authors and researchers. Most of the invited participants of the workshops were from the age groups of 20–35, on the basis that they would be the most receptive to learning some of the technical processes and developing new interpretive skills. The workshops also included a few Indian student animators or recent graduates, as the resource team to contribute inputs on adaptation from the oral to the audio-visual medium.

There were few female participants in comparison with male in the workshops to develop the animation films. In the case study in Manipur, the twenty-three workshop participants of a proposed tribal animation workshop sourced by the state government through advertisements in the local *Sangai* newspaper were all male and from the Meitei community. I suggest that the format of the advertisement had deterred confidence from female and tribal potential applicants, and that the outcome was a reflection of the current political tensions in the state, which resulted in the appropriation of the indigenous voice by the dominant majority. This example also suggests that while women may be empowered within particular domains, the digital space is male dominated. A parallel situation was reported by animation artist Caroline Leaf who has discussed the male dominance in commercial production studios like Warner Brothers and Disney, and in the new, expensive field of digital animation used for the Internet, games and high-tech expensive special effects (Ajanović 2002).

The Animation Workshops for the *Tales of the Tribes* project were initiated by storytelling sessions, where it was observed that for these young people, the oral traditions are disappearing. The workshop participants had to choose a story for an animation film and the final decision was by vote. The stories that were chosen have generally centred on a male hero and action stories took preference over human interest dramas. This arguably reflects the influence of the popular animation viewed on television that the participants aimed to emulate. It would be fair to accept that the choice of story also reflects the gender equation of the group.

Female-centred folktales from the Northeast region include the tragic genre of unrequited love, suffering and sacrifice exemplified in the tale of Jina and Etiben from the Ao and Khamba and Thoibi from the Meitei. Other folktales that I have documented that have female protagonists have focused on the complex relationship between the stepmother and stepdaughter: An example of this type of tale from the Ao community offers emancipation to a daughter when she transforms into an insect. The Pardhan Gond community of Central India also has several important folktales centred on female characters.

5. The influence of feminist research on the approach to indigenous collaboration

The interest and appreciation of indigenous folk narratives and art forms first drew me to the indigenous groups that are located at the margins in India. The awareness of the historical marginalisation of feminist philosophy in academia (Landau 2012) can precipitate development of an increased responsive approach towards research on disadvantaged communities and cultures. I have been motivated to investigate the similarities between feminist and indigenous research practices.

The debate about objectivity is at the forefront of developing an approach for collaboration with indigenous communities because the research paradigms that have emerged from Western academia have not accommodated the expectations for personal connections (Smith 1999: 149) and the characteristic focus on precision and certainty that was highlighted by Battiste (2000: 2) does not acknowledge the validity of intuition that is upheld by indigenous belief systems. It is logical for social research to demand a level of distance and detachment to promote the inclusivity of the others' experience. Therefore the concept of objectivity as "better research, more investigation, and analysis into the deep causes underlying surface appearances" (Hackett and Zhao 1998: 135) is useful for developing a sensitive approach to indigenous representation and to navigate a more thorough critique of the interpretations. However, critical analysis (Horkheimer 1937) also points to how the commonly accepted objectivity of science is biased against particular thought processes that reduce self assurance about dominant ideologies (Glasser 1992). Therefore to invite receptivity towards indigenous outlooks that exist outside the historical development of Western principles, the researcher must also be prepared to critique his own cultural standpoint.

The self-reflexive practice that is inscribed in feminist research has value to recognise the impact of the researcher on the topic, subject and outcome, and thus challenge attitudes of the so-called value free approach of scientific positivism (Easterby-Smith *et al.* 2008) in favour of socially constructed reality (Berger and Luckmann 1966). Self-reflection also assists us to recognise the typical hierarchy between the researcher and the subject, and to identify the space for mutual learning. In addition, reflective processes are also paramount to the recognition that by adapting the oral tales for the dominant medium of animated film, this is neither a step towards acculturation nor towards the commodification of indigenous heritage.

Researchers have endeavoured to apply indigenous knowledge to existing academic categories of knowledge (Pui-Yin Shiu 2008), an example being "methodological atheism", defined by Berger (1967: 107) as the situation where mystical beliefs are subjected to social scrutiny on the assumption that they are not literally true. However as this approach does not contribute to the respectful research relationships that are important to indigenous culture, a more responsive approach is required. Relating to the *Tales of the Tribes* project, the decision to consult a traditional priest prior to the animation production for the film from Arunachal Pradesh and the subsequent ritual that was performed by him contributes to inspire local confidence and it supports the challenge for the visiting researcher to connect more deeply with indigenous ideologies.

From a Maori perspective, Linda Tuhiwai Smith (1999: 125) highlights the emphasis on the process rather than the outcome for community projects and this reflects the transformative process of creation in traditional art. On this basis the group discussions and the collaborative adaptation processes took priority during the workshops and the animation production was carried out later in a studio environment according to the blueprint that was provided by the script and the storyboard.

Indigenous research also needs to take into account traditional protocols of showing and accepting respect (Smith 1999: 137) and elders from the community were invited to each of the workshops to share their stories and experiences. This process reaffirms intergenerational dialogue and the significance of internal information sources that may become eroded when external information is projected as right through the media. Reciprocity is upheld as a basic moral imperative within the community (Kirkness & Barnhardt 1991: 10) and the reciprocal learning experiences of the indigenous participants and the visiting resource team was the key focus of the workshops over and above the drive to meet production targets. On completion of the production of the series, the commitment for reciprocity makes it essential to first screen the films back in the communities from where the stories originate.

The research relationship is dynamic in the local context and trust must be constantly negotiated (Smith 1999: 136), In practice, this becomes a significant reminder of the vigour that is demanded for collaborations where relationships can become strained because of the difficulty of sustaining long distant communication. In summary, the engagement in indigenous research provides many opportunities to reflect and revise the approach and develop sincere commitment to long term relationships and finally to sharing the research in vernacular languages by education, broadcast, publication and community based programmes.

This discussion has identified some of the complexities of representing indigenous identities in a new medium. Indigenous communities have been marginalized and misrepresented by dominant forces since colonial times and the empirical positivist research practices of academia continue to reinforce this imbalance of power. Therefore a review of feminist approaches is informative towards shaping a methodology to invest practices that are more compatible for research conducted by a cultural outsider to develop self-reflection and sensitivity in the modes of interaction.

Self-reflection also promotes decoding personal incentives and openness to the idea that all interpretations are reflections of the observer's modification. Sustained modes of introspection also lead to increased desire for individual authenticity (Bendix 1997: 47) by connecting with indigenous cultural values and the transformative function of indigenous artistic practice. The consumption of media content through one way transmission is the outcome of expansion of the audience and it enforces impersonality (Williams 1963: 292) in contrast to the transference of indigenous culture by group activities that bind these societies and storytelling practices that encourage intergenerational dialogue. On the other hand, the participatory media practice for the Tales *of the Tribes* project becomes an exploratory process leading to cultural exposure and enrichment to the entire team. The social benefit of this form of practice is visible in the interactions in the workshop environment and can be evaluated by assessing how the knowledge is shared and how this contributes towards re-invigorating indigenous culture for the contemporary context.

I propose that the benefit of approachability is experienced by a female researcher, where dominant practices are frequently associated with the male visibility of the past. Feminist research embodies the commitment to the empowerment of the marginalized in society (Hesse-Biber 2008). Indigenous research also carries the commitment to mobilize the findings for the empowerment of indigenous young people in the space for their voices and identities to be projected. Therefore for this work to be carried forward and bring benefit beyond the duration of this project, a study centre to develop indigenous animation practice would contribute toward the development of indigenous media in India to sustain the stories for the future.

Caroline Leaf (Ajanović 2002) discussed how experimental animation has greater accessibility for women for personal expression in contrast to the applications of digital animation for the Internet, games and high-tech expensive special effects. This further suggests that the experimental genre would be equally suited for expressions by other marginalised groups that do not have access to expensive technology. The short animation film *The Owl Who Married a Goose* (Leaf 1975), produced by the National Film Board of Canada, shows an example of how innovative aesthetic and technical approaches have been used in animation within the context of an Inuit narrative. The technique of 'direct animation' used in this film demanded 'drawing' live under the camera by manipulating sand on translucent glass, lit from below. This method that used the simplest of materials – sand – presents a resourceful solution to the practical dilemma of introducing expensive and complex technology for indigenous artisans.

Leaf alluded to her own initial lack of confidence in her drawing abilities, and the consequent appeal of working under the camera where one image is destroyed to create the next, so that when the sequence has been filmed, there is nothing left except the film, turning the process into 'an one-off performance'. Young indigenous workshop participants in India have regularly communicated their lack of confidence in drawing cartoon characters where assumptions about style are based on their exposure to commercial cartoons. This illustrates how animation workshops that incorporate research on local art forms through visits to museums and private collections provide inspiration that has been viewed positively by workshop participants, as has been communicated by Dogin, who participated in the workshop in Arunachal Pradesh: 'The best thing I found was that it connected me to my culture which is on the verge of extinction' (Dogin, personal communication, 2013).

The Owl Who Married a Goose provides one example of a creative collaboration between an animation practitioner and an indigenous artist – Nanogak is the Inuit artist credited as the designer of the film. Leaf has detailed the aim of involvement by indigenous Inuit artists as far as possible in the making of the film, and she has communicated how the film board later went on to set up a workshop in the Arctic to facilitate film production (Schenkel 1976).

Leaf reported the negotiations that took place in the process of adaptation from the text to the animation medium that included the simplification of artwork for the purpose of the animation; her influence on the interpretation of the animals in the story as more anthropomorphized than was characteristic of the indigenous culture, and the melancholia of the film, when compared to the original folk narrative. The vast resource of original indigenous narratives and folk art styles in India suggests that a method of participatory film-making by indigenous artists and animation practitioners can also lead to the originality of animation produced in India.

Leaf's unconventional approach included the absence of a storyboard and the decision not to use any language other than the Inuit – which led her to eliminate as much of the text as possible and to emphasize the storytelling through visuals. The creation of the soundtrack that engaged a group of female Inuit elders who were able to mimic the sounds of arctic animals meant negotiating issues of cross cultural interaction and language. Contextualisation of this kind illustrates the vitality of experimentation and indicates how parallel collaboration between media professionals and traditional artists can also work to produce local animated representations in India. Leaf disclosed how the films that were developed under the Film Board did not need to address a mass audience, but instead could be made for a small, specialised audience that consisted of people interested in the arts, school children and researchers. A similar approach would work to develop Indian animation that is also targeted at specific rather than mass audiences.

Nina Sabnani's animation films made in India were inspired by the films made by Caroline Leaf, and her film *Tanko Bol Chhe* (The Stitches Speak, 2010) is an example of collaboration with a group of female artisans from Kutch. Sabnani (2013: 80) recorded that the project had generated an unprecedented sense of pride: "they were speaking through their work and sharing their perspectives on life and the world". The exposure to experimental animation had encouraged Leaf and Sabnani to both adopt experimental practices and styles in their own work and in this way establish distance from the commercial animation style and content of the genre of Disney productions. I suggest that parallel exposure to the wide range of films that have been made by artists working independently will develop a comprehensive appreciation of different types of animation in India that can lead indigenous artists to consider the similarities between experimental animation techniques and materials and their own traditional artistic practices.

The National Film Board of Canada films have received worldwide appreciation and Leaf's work is credited with a poetic sensitivity: 'A humanity which one finds all too rarely in animation' and 'A flowing metamorphic quality, narrative and dreamlike' (Schenkel 1976). Developing their own styles of animation design has the potential to bring the symbolic capital that many young people desire, and at the same time this activity can harness the animated medium as a tool for keeping young people interested in traditional culture.

Figure 5.1 The two young Thangka artists, Palzor Sherpa and Tashi Lepcha, from Sikkim creating the artwork for the folktale from Sikkim in the *Tales of the Tribes* animation series.

Source: Author

Figure 5.2 Manipur workshop team.

Source: Author

Figure 5.3 Young animation students of the National Institute of Design experiment with Gond artwork for the animated Gond folktale 'Manjoor Jhali' in the *Tales of the Tribes* collection during a workshop in 2012.

Source: Author

This research investigates how animation can be used by indigenous young people to reconnect to their cultural values and group practices. The activities in the workshops for this project demonstrated that by their involvement in the reinterpretation process, animation is a medium that can reignite interest with young people for traditional narratives and cultures. The process of adaptation for the audio visual medium by local artists is viable with collaboration from students of media. The *Tales of the Tribes* project also engaged young Indian animators and this created opportunities for them to explore original Indian narrative and design. This involvement by student animators and graduates also led to expanded awareness of the value of indigenous culture in their group.

In summary, feminist research practices are relevant for media practitioners to engage with indigenous artists and communities on terms that are sensitive to their practices. Experimental animation techniques can also be used to incorporate traditional skills such as painting, sculpture, bamboo handicraft, textiles and jewellery and the use of such materials in animation may also encourage more women artists from the communities to contribute their skills to the production team.

The critical need for support for art animation and the role that the National Film Board of Canada had towards the supporting artistic animation practice was outlined by Caroline Leaf. For the Indian context, I suggest that collaborative partnerships between a Government institution, a design institute or a university where animation is taught, and regionally based cultural organisations make it possible to organise animation workshops with indigenous artists to explore how original content can be developed to establish the representation of local cultural identities as well as for developing original animation design from India.

References

Ajanović, M. 2002. 'An interview with Caroline Leaf in English', *The Croatian Cinema Chronicle*, 8 (31–32). Zagreb: Croatian Film Clubs' Association, pp. 49–63, Retrieved from: www.ajan.se/index.php?option=com_content& task=view&id=46&Itemid=43 [Accessed 7 December 2013].

Ao, T. 2006. 'Identity and globalization: A Naga perspective', *Indian Folklife*, 22 (July): 6, 7.

Barthakur, R. 2006. 'Winds of change: *Arunachalee* in tradition and transition', *Indian Folklife*, 22 (July): 8, 9.

Battiste, M. 2000. *Indigenous Knowledge: Foundations for First Nations*. Canada: University of Saskatchewan, Retrieved from: www.win-hec.org/

docs/pdfs/Journal/Marie%20Battiste%20copy.pdf [Accessed 24 September 2014].

Bendix, R. 1997. *In Search of Authenticity, the Formation of Folklore Studies.* Madison: University of Wisconsin.

Berger, P. 1967. *The Sacred Canopy: Elements of a Sociological Theory of Religion.* New York: Doubleday.

Berger, P. L. and T. Luckmann (1966) 1991. *The Social Construction of Reality: A Treatise in the Sociology of Knowledge.* USA: Penguin.

Biswas, P. 2006. 'Globalization of folk as a genre in Northeast India', *Indian Folklife*, 22 (July): 16–19.

Burman, J. J. R., 2012. Status of Tribal Women in India. In: *Mainstream*, Vol. 12. [Online]. Available from: http://www.mainstreamweekly.net/article3314.html [Accessed 20 May 2017].

Chaisie, C. 1999. *The Naga Imbroglio (A Personal Perspective).* Guwahati: Standard Printers and Publishers.

Coomaraswamy, A. K. (1939) 1977. 'Primitive mentality', in R. Lipsey (ed.), *Coomaraswamy Collected Papers*, Vol. 1:9. Bollingen Series. Princeton, NJ: Princeton University.

Coote, J. and A. Shelton (eds.). 1992. *Anthropology, Art and Aesthetics.* Oxford: Clarendon.

Das, J. 2012. Women's Human Rights in North-East India. In: *Journal of Humanities and Social Science.* Vol. 3 (4) (Sep–Oct. 2012), pp. 34–37. Available from: http://www.iosrjournals.org/iosr-jhss/papers/Vol3-issue4/D0343437. pdf [Accessed 20 May 2017].

Easterby-Smith, M., R. Thorpe and P. Jackson. 2008. *Management Research.* London: SAGE Publications.

Ginsburg, F., 1993. Indigenous Media: Faustian Contract or Global Village? In: *Indigenous Media, Cultural Anthropology* [online] 92–112. Available from: https://files.nyu.edu/fg4/public/pdfs/Ginsburg%20-%20Indigenous%20 Media%20Faustian%20Contract.pdf [Accessed 25 January 2015].

Glasser, T. 1992. 'Objectivity and news bias', in E. D. Cohen (ed.), *Philosophical Issues in Journalism.* New York: Oxford University, pp. 176–185.

Hackett, R. A. and Y. Zhao. 1998. *Sustaining Democracy? Journalism and the Politics of Objectivity.* Toronto: University of Toronto.

Hesse-Biber, S. 2008. *Handbook of Feminist Research: Theory and Praxis.* US: SAGE Publications.

Horkheimer, M. 1937 and 1982. *Critical Theory.* New York: Seabury Press.

Huggan, G. 1996. *The Neocolonialism of Postcolonialism: A Cautionary Note.* USA: Harvard University.

Kirkness, V. J. and R. Barnhardt. 1991. 'First nations and higher education: The four R's – respect, relevance, reciprocity, responsibility', *Journal of American Indian Education*, 30 (3): 1–15, Retrieved from: www.afn.ca/ uploads/files/education2/the4rs.pdf [Accessed 24 September 2014].

Kunzle, D. 1975. 'Introduction', in A. Dorfman and A. Mattelart (eds.), *How to Read Donald Duck: Imperialist Ideology in the Disney Comic.* New York: International General, pp. 11–23.

Landau, I., 2012. *On the Marginalization of Feminist Philosophy in International Journal of Philosophical Studies* Vol. 18 (4). UK: Routledge, pp. 551–568.

Leaf, C. 1975. *The Owl Who Married a Goose: An Eskimo Legend.* Montreal: National Film Board of Canada, Retrieved from: www.youtube.com/watch?v=fusYZ7eIhps [Accessed 16 May 2013].

Lenz, I., H. Lutz, M. Morokvasić, C. Schöning-Kalender and H. Schwenken (eds.). 2003. *Crossing Borders and Shifting Boundaries*, Vol. 2. Wiesbaden: VS Verlag für Sozialwissenschaften.

Malinowski, B. (1948) 1992. *Magic, Science and Religion and Other Essays.* Long Grove, IL: Waveland Press.

Martens, E. 2012. Maori on the Silver Screen: the Evolution of Indigenous Feature Filmmaking in Aotearoa/New Zealand. In: *International Journal of Critical Indigenous Studies* [online] 5 (1): 1–30. Available from: http://dare.uva.nl/document/2/117154 [Accessed 6 October 2014].

McLuhan, M. 1994 (1964). *Understanding Media: The Extensions of Man.* USA: MIT Press.

Murray, S. 2008. *Images of Dignity: Barry Barclay and Fourth Cinema.* Wellington: Huia Publishers.

Nkrumah, K. 1965. *Neo-Colonialism: The Last Stage of Imperialism.* London: Thomas Nelson & Sons.

Pui-Yin Shiu, D. 2008. *How Are We Doing? Exploring Aboriginal Programs in Surrey Secondary Schools.* Thesis (PhD), University of British Columbia.

Reinharz, S. 1992. *Feminist Methods in Social Research.* Oxford: Oxford University.

Roselima, K. P. 2014. *Customary Law and Women in North East India.* Available from: www.isca.in, www.isca.me [Accessed 21 May 2017].

Sabnani, N. 2013. 'Sewn Narratives', in M. Rohse, J. J. Infanti, N. Sabnani and M. Nivargi (eds.), *The Many Facets of Storytelling.* Oxford: Inter-Disciplinary Press, pp. 79–86.

Säid, E. 1978. *Orientalism.* New York: Pantheon Books.

Sarantakos, S. 1993. *Social Research.* Basingstoke: Macmillan.

Schenkel, T. 1976. *Harvard Film Archive, 2012. Talking with Caroline Leaf*, Retrieved from: http://campus.huntington.edu/dma/leeper/DM101/Readings/@PDF/Women%20in%20Animation%20II-Leaf.pdf [Accessed 8 December 2013].

Scroggie, A. 2009. *Preserving Tradition and Enhancing Learning through Youth Storytelling.* Santa Fe, NM: Santa Fe Community College, Retrieved from: http://himalaya.socanth.cam.ac.uk/collections/journals/jbs/pdf/JBS_20_07.pdf [accessed 23 January 2012].

Smith, L. T. 1999. *Decolonizing Methodologies, Research and Indigenous Peoples.* London: Zed Books.

Spencer, S. 2006. *Race and Ethnicity, Culture, Identity and Representation.* USA: Routledge.

Spivak, G. C. 1988. 'Can the Subaltern Speak?', in C. Nelson and L. Grossberg (eds.), *Marxism and the Interpretation of Culture.* Urbana: University of Illinois Press, pp. 271–316.

Tata Strategic Management Group. 2010. *Market Study on Animation and Gaming Industry in India for Italian Trade Commission*, Retrieved from: http://italiaindia.com/images/uploads/pdf/animation-gaming-industry-in-india.pdf [Accessed 23 September 2014].

Williams, R. 1963. *Culture and Society*. Harmondsworth, UK: Penguin Books.

6 Female MGNREGA workers and poverty reduction in Sikkim

Marchang Reimeingam

1. Introduction

Mahatma Gandhi National Rural Employment Guarantee Act (MGN-REGA) has brought about a rural development scheme which is to enhance the livelihood security of the rural people, especially the poor, by guaranteeing at least 100 days of wage[1] employment in a financial year to every rural household whose adult member volunteer for unskilled manual work. In Sikkim, it was launched and implemented only in the North District on 2 February 2006 after enacting of NREG Act in 2005; it was later covered in the South and East Districts from 1 April 2007. From 1 April 2008, it was implemented in the West District of Sikkim. Since then, the state of Sikkim is fully covered under the scheme. The scheme, which is demand driven in nature, is successfully progressing as a catalyst of rural developmental in general and poverty reduction in particular by strengthening household incomes. The study is based on secondary data, from the Ministry of Rural Development, the National Sample Survey Organisation, the Registrar General of India and the Planning Commission, spreading from the period since the implementation of the scheme till date in Sikkim. It attempts to examine the scheme not only from the linkages between the extent of work participation (emphasizing on women) as casual workers in various developmental activities of the scheme but also as a poverty-reduction programme in rural areas.

2. MGNREGA: employment and asset creation

Employment has a nexus with poverty, especially in the rural areas. In India, people predominantly live in the rural areas. Therefore, rural economy continues to provide the major source of employment and source of livelihood to the people. Sheila Smith and John Sender

(1990: 1334) contended that 'there would be a systematic relationship between poverty and participation in wage labour, so that persons offering themselves as wage workers would be from the poorest household'. Krishnamurthy Sundaram (2007) explicitly showed the changes in the employment and poverty in India. Full employment of human resources is considered as the most important feature and best strategy for poverty reduction or elimination (Sundaram and Krishnamurty 1978). Poverty is closely related to employment and occupational characteristics (Sen 1996). Employment is to be guaranteed in the agricultural sector as well as in the non-agricultural sectors for rural people in order to combat poverty. G. S. Bhalla and Peter Hazell (2003) examined the possible strategies for increasing employment and significantly reducing poverty in rural as well as urban areas in India. J. N. Sinha (1981) asserts that there is a relationship between poverty and employment, unemployment and underemployment. However, the relationship between unemployment and poverty is weak in India. For example, people in the backward regions like the rural areas and underprivileged groups like the scheduled caste (SC) or scheduled tribe (ST) are poor, despite some of them having very little underemployment. Vishnu Mahadeo Dandekar (1986) opined about poverty which is institutional referring to the SCs and STs of India. SCs and STs are not only poor but they also suffer from various social and economic impediments that need to be removed. The Constitution of India safeguards them in the form of reservations in employment. Institutional barrier is to be removed to reach the course of economic development in India. Similarly, protective measures and safeguards should be established for the rural people in general and rural females in particular in order to achieve inclusive growth and development.

It is crucial to liberate women from the bondage of traditional household activities and arrange alternative employment opportunities such as MGNREGA work. Jean Drèze and Amartya Sen (2002) remark that women face lack of freedom to do other things that goes with high frequency of births. Family planning knowledge and practice through education enhances the status of women, well-being and voice. Socio-economic transformation and liberation of women has led to greater involvement of women in the socio-economic activities (Emadi 1992).

Prior to the launching of the scheme, the Maharashtra government formulated the Maharashtra Employment Guarantee Scheme (1972–1973) and Maharashtra Employment Guarantee Act (1977) to provide wage employment to those who demanded employment. Its success story led to the enactment of MGNREGA in 2005. It is implemented by the state governments with central assistance to enhance livelihood security. The model of the scheme is considerably borrowed from the Maharashtra Employment Guarantee Act (Hirway 2004).

It is targeted to those employed as casual manual labour. Its basic objective is to provide work for rural households. It acts as a source of wage income for landless labour and marginal farmers in the lean agricultural season. It also creates assets that raise land productivity. Santosh Mehrotra (2008) opined that the allocations for the scheme could well take an inverted-U trend, i.e. the allocations to the scheme rises initially then falls over time. The region/state's demand for work under the scheme depends on the nature of labour-surplus or labour-deficit in the region/state.

The Ministry of Rural Development (2012–2013) has highlighted that MGNREGA is a supplementary source of income, raises the monthly per capita consumption expenditure of rural households significantly, is a self-targeting programme and creates assets, employment and environmentally sustainable works. Its participation rate among the SCs and STs exceeds their share in the total population. It reduces the traditional gender wage discrimination, vulnerability of production system to climate variability and distress migration. It has a positive impact on the socio-economic status of women.

In Sikkim, MGNREGA was launched and implemented only in the North District in 2006. In the following year, it was covered in the South and East Districts. Later in 2008, it was implemented in all the four districts of the state. Sikkim has received seven national awards for exemplary work done under MGNREGA in a row over the last four years.[2] Through the scheme, the level of poverty has reduced by raising the household income.

The MGNREGA is implemented as a centrally sponsored scheme on a cost-sharing basis between the centre and the states as determined by the act. The financing funding pattern of the NREGS[3] is to be shared by the centre and the states. The central government will bear the entire cost of wages for unskilled manual workers, 75 per cent of the material costs, 75 per cent of wages for skilled and semi-skilled workers, and administrative expenses as may be determined by the centre and the Central Employment Guarantee Council. Meanwhile, the state government will pay unemployment allowance if the state government cannot provide wage employment within 15 days of job application under NREGS, 25 per cent of the material costs, 25 per cent of wages for skilled and semi-skilled workers, and the administrative expenses of the State Employment Guarantee Council.

3.   MGNREGA works

Since the implementation of the programme, MGNREGA works in Sikkim, corroborating with the goals[4] of the scheme, which include water conservation and water harvesting like digging of new tanks/ ponds, percolation tanks, small check dams etc.; drought proofing such as afforestation and tree plantation and other activities; micro irrigation works like minor irrigation canals and other activities; provision of irrigation facility to land owned by SCs and STs, beneficiaries of land reforms and beneficiaries of Indira Awaas Yojana etc.; renovating traditional water bodies such as de-silting of tanks/ponds, de-silting of old canals, de-silting of traditional open well etc.; land development like plantation, land levelling and other activities; flood control and protection including drainage in water logged areas, construction and repair of embankment; rural connectivity; any other activity as approved by the Ministry of Rural Development. In NREGA (2014), some works which were either ongoing or were suspended, for instance the Rajiv Gandhi Seva Kendra, programmes for rural drinking water and rural sanitation were brought under the scheme with a negligible share as shown in Table 6.1.

According to the Ministry of Rural Development, in the beginning (as on March 2007), most of the completed works were flood control measure activities with slightly over 53 per cent followed by micro irrigation, rural connectivity and water conservation and water harvesting. Later in 2010, drought proofing work became the major concern of the scheme. In 2012, the scheme was devoted mostly for land development covering plantation, land levelling and other land development activities with a share of 64 per cent. Presently, land development continues to be the main activity with over 66 per cent of the total 427 number of completed works of the scheme in Sikkim. And most of the ongoing (including suspended) works are on land development and rural connectivity (Ministry of Rural Development 2014). Over the years, there has been a shift in the nature of work, predominantly from flood control, micro irrigation and rural connectivity to drought proofing to land development which indicated a remarkable creation of assets for further development. This has taken place not only with the completion of the prioritised developmental activities and securing livelihood opportunities but also with the proper coordination between the state and the centre as well as implementers and beneficiaries. All the above-mentioned works are pertinent in keeping with the long-term goal of livelihood security and strengthening the sources of income and well-being amongst the people living in and

Table 6.1 Share* (%) of completed work under MGNREGA in Sikkim, India

Work/activities	March 2007	March 2010	March 2012	January 2014 Work			Expenditure		
				Completed	Ongoing/ suspended	Approved not in progress	Completed	Ongoing/ suspended	Approved not in progress
Water conservation and water harvesting	6.80	14.36	7.62	5.15	9.50	5.97	19.73	15.11	–
Drought proofing	0.00	52.48	12.79	6.79	10.00	27.10	14.38	16.93	–
Micro irrigation	21.36	4.23	2.64	6.09	4.79	5.75	6.12	5.98	–
Provision of irrigation facility to land development	0.00	0.00	0.00	0.00	0.21	0.22	0.00	0.25	–
Renovation of traditional water bodies	0.97	0.36	0.30	0.00	0.37	0.77	0.00	0.30	–
Land development	0.97	8.67	64.17	66.51	33.79	25.22	16.16	8.67	–
Flood control	53.40	6.78	5.28	4.22	12.12	7.74	33.08	13.68	–
Rural connectivity	16.50	13.12	7.08	11.24	27.64	24.00	10.53	38.54	–
Any other activity approved by Ministry of Rural Development	0.00	0.00	0.12	0.00	1.33	2.65	0.00	0.52	–
Rajiv Gandhi Seva Kendra	–	–	–	0.00	0.03	0.55	0.00	0.01	–
Coastal areas	–	–	–	0.00	0.00	0.00	0.00	0.00	–
Rural drinking water	–	–	–	0.00	0.08	0.00	0.00	0.00	–
Fisheries	–	–	–	0.00	0.00	0.00	0.00	0.00	–
Rural sanitation	–	–	–	0.00	0.16	0.00	0.00	0.01	–
Aanganbadi	–	–	–	0.00	0.00	0.00	0.00	0.00	–
Play ground	–	–	–	0.00	0.00	0.00	0.00	0.00	–
Total (Number/Rs. Lakh)	103	1,372	1,666	427	3,821	904	153.80†	3,290.92†	–

Sources: Data up to 2012 from http://mgnregasikkim.org and 2014 from http://nrega.nic.in [Accessed 15 January 2014].

*Author's calculation.

around the worksite. For example, the improvement in rural road connectivity with the help of the scheme improves and enhances the efficiency of the means of transportation and accessibility to the markets for the rural marketable surplus products. Such developmental works are made possible with their own labour participation, in return, earning wages. Further it strengthens their economic opportunities and reduces their poverty level.

4.   Women casual workers and MGNREGA

The above-mentioned developmental works are carried out with the help of casual labour who are engaged in the public work. In Sikkim (according to the National Sample Survey Organisation), casual labour households were a negligible 0.2 per cent in 2009/10. It had drastically declined from 6 and 7 per cent in rural and urban areas respectively in 1999/2000 as presented in Table 6.2. The share of casual labour households in Sikkim is significantly lower than the country's size of it. In rural areas, at present, about 13 per cent of the total workers (principal and subsidiary status) are casual labourers in Sikkim, against 39 per cent in India. Casual labourers in the rural areas in Sikkim (following the country's pattern) has considerably increased from just 7 per cent in 2004/5 to 13 per cent in 2009/10, possibly due to the implementation of MGNREGA. The scheme has improved labour participation, especially amongst females. Perhaps with the introduction of the scheme, females employed as casual labour has significantly increased because of the equal wage incentive for males and females, friendly work nature and environment for females, provision of unemployment allowances etc. Prior to the launch of the scheme, the share of females among casual labour (principal and subsidiary status) was significantly lower than the males in rural areas in Sikkim (which is opposite to India). As far as females are concerned, the share of them employed as casual labour in the total employment in principal status (10.2%) is lower in comparison to females employed in principal and subsidiary status (12.9%), indicating that a significant share of females are participating in subsidiary status work like in MGNREGA for their economic empowerment and for supplementing their household income. It not only acts as the catalyst for economic development but also strengthens the economic well-being and (national) income. Females working as causal labour in the scheme reduce the poverty level by raising household income. They are working as casual labour, most likely, due to their inability to get the limited available regular wage or salaried employment or due to the difficulty in getting casual work in other areas.

Table 6.2 Usually employed as a casual labour (%) in the total employment and casual labour households (%) in Sikkim and in India

| State/country | Year | Areas | Usually employed casual labour | | | | | | Casual labour households |
| | | | Principal status | | | Principal and subsidiary status | | | |
			Male	Female	Person	Male	Female	Person	
Sikkim	2009/10	Rural	12.8	10.2	12.0	12.8	12.9	12.9	0.2
		Urban	0.0	0.0	0.0	0.0	0.0	0.0	0.2
	2004/5	Rural	8.4	4.5	7.1	8.3	4.5	7.0	5.1
		Urban	3.0	2.3	2.4	3.0	2.3	2.4	3.5
	1999/2000	Rural	13.6	8.6	12.1	13.5	8.1	11.9	5.9
		Urban	9.0	14.3	10.3	8.1	14.3	10.8	6.8
India	2009/10	Rural	38.3	44.2	39.9	38.0	39.9	38.6	13.4
		Urban	17.1	20.2	17.6	17.0	19.6	17.5	14.2
	2004/5	Rural	33.3	38.9	35.0	32.9	32.6	32.8	11.8
		Urban	14.6	17.4	15.1	14.6	16.7	15.0	11.8
	1999/2000	Rural	36.6	46.1	39.4	36.2	39.6	37.4	14.0
		Urban	16.9	23.1	18.0	16.8	21.4	17.8	14.1

Sources: National Sample Survey Organisation (2001, September 2006 and 2011), Report Nos. 458, 515 and 537.

5. MGNREGA workers

MGNREGA work, one of the public works, was initially implemented only in the North District of Sikkim in 2006/7. Table 6.3 gives in detail, as per the Ministry of Rural Development 2014 data, the employment generated under the scheme in Sikkim. By the end of the financial year of 2006/7, as many as 4,498 households were issued with job cards, of which 96 per cent were STs and the rest were SCs and others. In the beginning of the financial year in 2007, the scheme was introduced to two more districts (South and East) resulting in the significant increase in the number of job card issuance in the households, touching a figure of 30,907. Eventually, there was a drastic change in the share of job card holders amongst the various social groups. In 2007/8, 39 per cent of the households having job cards belonged to the STs and 7 per cent to the SCs. The major share of 54 per cent of the total cards was issued to the other social groups. The cumulative number of households issued with job cards increased to 87,051 in 2013/14. Meanwhile, the Census of India recorded 129,006 households in Sikkim. The share of households issued with a job card was about 67 per cent in 2013/14 (using the 2011 Census household figure). From 2007/8 onwards, the distribution of households issued with a job card among the social groups remains similar. For instance, in Sikkim, in 2013/14, about 37 per cent of the cards were issued to the STs, 5 per cent to the SCs and the rest 58 per cent to the other social groups (against the 2011 Census, population distribution of 33.80% belonging to the STs, 4.63% to the SCs and the remaining 61.57% to the other social groups). It reflects that in Sikkim, job cards are distributed almost in proportion to their share of population among the social groups.

Table 6.4 presents the distribution of MGNREG workers classified by different social groups in Sikkim according to the National Sample Survey Organisation. In 2009/10, about 46 per cent of the rural households were having job cards in Sikkim, against 35 per cent in India. Strikingly, more than half of the entire ST households (both in the state and in India) are job card holders. A very small ratio of about 2 per cent of the entire households sought work but did not get it in Sikkim, as against 19 per cent in India, indicating smooth and fast delivery of employment, resulting in low unemployment rates.

In Sikkim, the share of households who demanded MGNREG employment in the total number of job cards issued has substantially declined from 93 per cent in 2006/7 to close to 68 per cent at present, as presented in Table 6.3 based on MGNREGA data available from the Ministry of Rural Development. This indicates that many of those

Table 6.3 Employment generated under MGNREGA in Sikkim

	Social group	2006/7	2007/8	2008/9	2009/10	2010/11	2011/12	2012/13	2013/14
Cumulative number of HH issued JCs*	SCs	58	2,149	4,995	4,619	4,692	4,043	4,153	4,393
	STs	4,327	11,972	28,728	28,781	30,263	29,025	29,983	31,883
	Others	113	16,786	43,389	36,650	38,620	46,128	47,778	50,775
	Total	4,498	30,907	77,112	70,050	73,575	79,196	81,914	87,051
Share (%) of cumulative number of HH issued JCs in total	SCs	1.29	6.95	6.48	6.59	6.38	5.11	5.07	5.05
	STs	96.20	38.74	37.25	41.09	41.13	36.65	36.60	36.63
	Others	2.51	54.31	56.27	52.32	52.49	58.25	58.33	58.33
Cumulative number of HH DE*		4,179	21,773	52,554	54,156	56,401	55,765	55,596	59,052
DE%JC		92.91	70.45	68.15	77.31	76.66	70.41	67.87	67.84
Labour budget: HH projected up to the month		NA	NA	28,285	55,249	NA	68,127	68,643	59,637
Cumulative number of HH PE*		4,107	19,787	52,006	54,156	56,401	54,464	54,536	50,613
PE%DE		98.28	90.88	98.96	100.00	100.00	97.67	98.09	85.71
PE%JC		91.31	64.02	67.44	77.31	76.66	68.77	66.58	58.14
Number of HH working under NREGA during reporting month		NA	NA	42,626	48,354	51,343	7,806	21,724	22,713
Labour budget: projected person-days up to the month (lakh)		NA	NA	21.58	45.31	NA	61.94	58.92	36.38
Cumulative PDG (lakh)*	SCs	0.02	0.61	1.50	4.18	5.79	1.49	1.48	0.87
	STs	2.38	3.66	11.62	18.41	19.21	11.77	12.43	7.45
	Others	0.03	4.33	13.21	20.68	23.14	19.50	19.24	11.97
	Total	2.43	8.60	26.33	43.27	48.14	32.76	33.15	20.29
	Women	0.61	3.16	9.91	22.17	22.46	14.65	14.80	9.34

(Continued)

Table 6.3 (Continued)

	Social group	2006/7	2007/8	2008/9	2009/10	2010/11	2011/12	2012/13	2013/14
Share (%) of cumulative PDG in total	SCs	0.82	7.09	5.70	9.66	12.03	4.55	4.48	4.29
	STs	97.94	42.56	44.13	42.55	39.90	35.94	37.49	36.72
	Others	1.23	50.35	50.17	47.79	48.07	59.51	58.03	58.99
	Women	25.10	36.74	37.64	51.24	46.66	44.73	44.64	46.03
Cumulative number of HH completed 100 days*		222	2,006	2,863	12,633	25,695	8,731	9,233	1,106
HH completed 100 days (%) to HH provided job†		5.41	10.14	5.51	23.33	45.56	16.03	16.93	2.19
PDG%PE (average number of days worked per HH)		59	43	51	80	85	60	61	40
Number of HH which are beneficiary of land reform/Indira Awaas Yojana		5	91	1,052	235	307	92	89	109
Number of disabled beneficiary individuals		0	1	45	164	5	91	79	80

Sources: Data up to 2007/8 from http://mgnregasikkim.org/ and 2008/9 onwards from NREGA Implementation Status Report of Sikkim http://nrega. nic.in/ [Accessed 22 January 2014].

Notes: SC, scheduled caste; ST, scheduled tribe; HH, households; JC, job card; DE, demanded employment; PE, provided employment; NREGA, National Rural Employment Guarantee Act; NA, not available; PDG, person–days generate. Figure of 2013/14 is up to December 2013. Figures of 2006/7 includes only North District, 2007/8 covers North, South and East Districts; however afterwards all four districts including West District are included in Sikkim.

*Till the reporting month.
†Calculated by the author.

Table 6.4 Share (%) of MGNREG work classified by social groups in Sikkim and in India, 2009/10

State/ country	Social Groups	Households having job card	Households who got work					Sought but did not get work	Did not seek work	All	Average number of days worked*
			<20	20–50	50–100	>100	All				
Sikkim	ST	55.2	6.9	7.9	37.4	0.0	52.2	0.8	47.0	100.0	66
	SC	30.9	5.4	2.1	23.4	0.0	30.9	2.0	67.1	100.0	53
	OBC	48.3	6.1	14.8	26.0	0.0	46.9	2.9	50.2	100.0	54
	Others	2.3	2.3	0.0	0.0	0.0	2.3	0.0	97.7	100.0	15
	All	45.8	6.0	10.3	27.7	0.0	44.1	1.9	54.0	100.0	59
India	ST	54.1	14.3	12.9	12.3	0.3	39.8	19.7	36.3	100.0	42
	SC	45.0	14.8	10.7	7.1	0.3	32.9	22.2	42.9	100.0	35
	OBC	30.6	7.5	6.7	6.6	0.2	20.9	18.3	58.3	100.0	42
	Others	24.0	8.9	4.1	2.0	0.1	15.1	18.1	63.8	100.0	27
	All	34.7	10.2	7.6	6.2	0.2	24.2	19.3	53.8	100.0	37

Source: National Sample Survey Organisation (2012), Report No. 543, 2009/10.

Notes: SC, scheduled caste; ST, scheduled tribe; OBC, other backward class.

*Average number of days worked in MGNREG by households got MGNREG works.

who applied for jobs are neither desperate for employment as they have other means of livelihood (e.g. family support) nor interested to engage in manual work. It means that a significant share of them just got job cards issued for namesake and was not keen to work. However, interestingly, over 98 per cent of households were provided with employment among those who demanded employment in the initial year of launch of the scheme. Later, in 2009/10 and the following year, all households who demanded employment got it. In the subsequent period, some of them did not get employment even if it was demanded. For example, at present, only 86 per cent of those who demand for a job get it. The situation worsens when the share of households provided with employment in the total number of household issued with job cards is observed. At present, only 58 per cent, much lower than earlier periods, of those who hold a job card get employment. The National Sample Survey Organisation also recorded some households who did not get work even if they had a job card among different social groups in Sikkim. The extent of it is more intense at the country level (see Table 6.4). Out of the 45.8 per cent of the rural households who have job cards, only 44.1 per cent of them got jobs in Sikkim. That means, close to 2 percentage points among the rural households with a card do not get a job. The extent of those who do not get work among the job card holders is larger (about 10 percentage points) in India. This situation highlights the following critical issues: that job cards are issued without verifying the eligibility criteria of the beneficiaries, attempts to enlarge the state's budget for the scheme, job card holders do not want to work in manual activities, card holders are engaged in employment with higher earnings (than MGNREG wage) and finally the government is unable to identify and provide adequate avenues for MGNREG work.

Sikkim has not experienced full 100 days of guaranteed employment under the scheme. An average of 85 days (the highest in the history of MGNREGA of Sikkim) of employment was delivered to each household who were employed in it in 2010/11. It gradually declined to 40 days (at present). National Sample Survey Organisation also gives a similar figure of 59 days per worker in a year during 2009/10 (Table 6.4). It is possibly due to the government's inability to generate adequate rural unskilled manual work. It also indicates MGNREGA's work as being considered subsidiary or secondary, e.g. rural agriculturists engage in MGNREGA work during the lean agricultural season. However, studies by C. Dheeraja *et al.* (2010) of MGNREGA in Sikkim found the reasons for not working for 100 days in the scheme as follows: own farming activities, household responsibilities in nursing children and aged, health problems, low wages and hard work involved in the scheme, distance to the worksite etc.

Nevertheless, the scheme is transparent in reaching the beneficiaries such as households which are the beneficiaries of land reform or Indira Awaaz Yojana and even the disabled ones as shown in Table 6.3. It does not depict the situation of excess wage employment generation because all the job card holders who demanded employment did not get job as seen in Table 6.3; in other words, there is a shortage of MGNREGA employment supply.

The associated issue is about the unemployment allowance. According to the MGNREGA, the state government has to pay unemployment allowance if the state cannot provide wage employment within 15 days of job application under NREGS. According to the Ministry of Rural Development, unemployment allowances for the financial rear 2013/14 (as on 31 January 2014) in Sikkim shows that the state is liable to pay the allowances for 57,927 days with a total payable amount of Rs. 38.16 lakhs. This gives only Rs. 65.87 per day which is against the minimum wage rate prevailing in the state.[5] However, ironically, nothing is paid to anybody as unemployment allowance and no reasons are specified for its non-payment. It could partially be because applicants do not fulfill the conditions laid down in the NREG Act 2005. For instance, the period for which employment is sought comes to an end or household completes 100 days of work or workers are not willing to work or workers do not report for work within 15 days of being notified to report for work or continuously absent themselves from work.[6]

In Sikkim, employment generation in terms of person-days has been substantially increased from 2.43 lakhs covering only North District in 2006/7 to 8.6 lakhs in the following year as it covers two more districts. It further increased to 26.33 lakhs by covering the entire four districts of the state in 2008/9. Later in 2010/11, it substantially increased to 48.14 lakhs. However, it declined to 20.29 lakhs in 2013/14 (Table 6.3). The distribution of person-days generated is similar with the distribution of household issued with a job card as discussed earlier. In 2013/14, slightly over 4 per cent of employment generated was made available for the SCs, about 37 per cent of the person-days were performed by the STs and the largest share of 59 per cent of it was given to the other social group. The delivery of employment opportunities is somewhat in accordance with the size of the social groups in the total population. It indicates some sort of social justice and transparency prevailing in the state. The above-detailed data examination gives an impression that the socially disadvantaged group especially the STs are benefitting to a greater extent as the share of person-days generated or the share of households issued with job cards were more than their population composition.

6.   Women's participation in MGNREGA work

Women's participation in the scheme has shown a significant improvement since the launch of the scheme in Sikkim (Table 6.3). As large as 0.61 lakh person-days employment generated under the scheme was delivered to women in 2006/7. It gradually rose to 22.46 lakhs in 2010/11. However, it significantly declined to 14.80 lakhs in 2012/13 and later slipped to 9.34 lakhs following the general trend of the state. The rate of women's participation in the scheme shows a gradual increase from 25 per cent in 2006/7 when the scheme was launched only in one district of the state to 37 per cent when three districts were covered in the following year to 38 per cent in 2008/9 when the entire state was covered under the scheme. In the following year, slightly more than half of the scheme's person-days were provided to women showing the highest women's participation in the history of MGNREGA work in Sikkim. It negates the disguised unemployment and underemployment besides general unemployment problems emancipating from the cocoon of poverty through wage earnings. In the subsequent years, the rate of women's participation declined as the participation of males increased.

In Sikkim, at present about 46 per cent of the employment is occupied by women. The prevailing rate of women's participation engaged in all kinds of work of the scheme is substantial as there is no wage differential between genders. During 2009/10, workers participating in the scheme were mostly women (Institute of Rural Management Anand, 2010). Most importantly, Dheeraja *et al.* (2010: 39) found that in Sikkim 'women are the main workers in MGNREGS and participation of men [are] moderate'. Further, there is no instance of gender or caste/tribe discrimination either in the allotment of work or payment of wages or at worksite which thus portrays a hazel free implementation of the scheme. Moreover, the environment for work participation is conducive for all types of community irrespective of gender or caste/tribe in the state. In Sikkim, the scheme is better implemented due to the good Panchayati Raj Institution system (Panda *et al.* 2009).

7.   Wage rate for MGNREGA workers

Interestingly, the wage rate for the MGNREGA works has been revised upward from time to time for all the states and union territories. This wage rate is linked with the Consumer Price Index for Agricultural Labour. The revised wage rate and index number, a measure of magnitude of economic changes over time, of wage of Sikkim and other states of Northeast is presented in Table 6.5. For Sikkim, wage rate has

Table 6.5 Minimum wage rate for MGNREGA workers (Rs./day) and index number of wage, Northeast India

States	Revised minimum wage rate effect from					Index number (2005/6 = 100)					
	2005/6	01-Jan-09	01-Jan-11	01-Apr-12	01-Apr-13	2005/6	01-Jan-09	01-Jan-11	01-Apr-12	01-Apr-13	
Sikkim	85	100	118	124	135	100.0	117.6	138.8	145.9	158.8	
Assam	62	79.6	130	136	152	100.0	128.4	209.7	219.4	245.2	
Arunachal Pradesh	57	80*	118	124	135	100.0	140.4	207.0	217.5	236.8	
Manipur	66	81.4	126	144	153	100.0	123.3	190.9	218.2	231.8	
Meghalaya	70	100†	117	128	145	100.0	142.9	167.1	182.9	207.1	
Mizoram	91	110	129	136	148	100.0	120.9	141.8	149.5	162.6	
Nagaland	66	100	118	124	135	100.0	151.5	178.8	187.9	204.5	
Tripura	60	85	118	124	135	100.0	141.7	196.7	206.7	225.0	

Sources: The Gazette of India (2013) and http://nrega.nic.in/.

*01-Apr-2009.
†24-Aug-2009.

increased by about 59 per cent in 2013 since the base period (2005/6). A comparison of it with the rest of the northeastern states portrays that the change in the wage rate in Sikkim is minimal because of the larger base (Rs. 85 per day in 2005/6) than all Northeast states except Mizoram. However, the present wage rate is at par with other states. The wage rate for males are always on a higher side than females for regular wage or salaried employees or for any type of casual workers including public work in MGNREGA in India. Remarkably, there is no wage differential between genders for the scheme; although there is for other activities in Sikkim. For example, Rs. 100, as shown in Table 6.6, is paid for MGNREGA workers (15–59 years of age) as wage per day for males and females in 2009/10. The non-discriminatory wage between genders drives females to actively participate in the works.

In Sikkim, wages are not paid on time and are often delayed in disbursement either through the bank or post office accounts or other means. Dheeraja *et al.* (2010) found that in Sikkim, all workers have opened their accounts in banks or post offices; however, about half of them do not timely receive wage payments through their accounts.

8.   MGNREGA, poverty and worker's population ratio

The change in the wage rates of MGNREGA is in accordance with the change in inflationary rate. However, it has a positive implication in the poverty alleviation process. The wage received by the workers raises their purchasing power, affecting the poverty scenario. The level of poverty in Sikkim, following the national pattern, has substantially declined in recent years for both rural and urban areas (Table 6.7). Poverty level in Sikkim is relatively much lower than the level of India. It is about 8 per cent in Sikkim against 22 per cent for the country in 2011/12. As expected, the problem of poverty is more acute in rural than urban areas. However, with the implementation of MGNREGA work, large numbers of rural people are being relieved as number of rural poor persons has declined sharply and systematically. For example, in Sikkim, the number of persons below the poverty line has declined from 1.5 lakh in 2004/5, a period before the launch of the scheme, to 0.45 lakh in 2011/12, a period when the scheme was in full operation. Studies by Dheeraja *et al.* (2010) have established that MGNREGA has reduced the poverty particularly among the poorest of the poor. And the Institute of Rural Management Anand (2010) found that the scheme has attracted not only the rural poor but also those

Table 6.6 Average wage/salary earnings (Rs.) per day received by different employees of 15–59 years in Sikkim and in India

State/country	Year	Gender	Regular wage/ salaried employees (activity status 31, 71 and 72)		Casual workers			
			Rural	Urban	Public work other than MGNREG (41) Rural	Public work MGNREG (42) Rural	Other than public work (51) Rural	Urban
Sikkim	2009/10	Male	365.98	340.33	107.80	100.00	125.33	163.40
		Female	313.19	205.19	99.13	100.00	84.24	–
		Person	351.89	313.53	104.36	100.00	117.37	163.40
	2004/5	Male	203.43	233.39	89.29	–	89.16	121.14
		Female	207.31	224.79	89.29	–	74.22	78.57
		Person	204.23	231.63	89.29	–	86.53	118.88
	1999/2000*	Male	–	–	83.27	–	50.71	57.82
		Female	–	–	–	–	40.60	43.49
		Person	–	–	83.29	–	49.20	54.27

(Continued)

Table 6.6 (Continued)

State/country	Year	Gender	Regular wage/ salaried employees (activity status 31, 71 and 72)		Casual workers	Public work MGNREG (42)	Other than public work (51)	
---	---	---	---	---	Public work other than MGNREG (41)		---	---
			Rural	Urban	Rural	Rural	Rural	Urban
India	2009/10	Male	249.15	377.16	98.33	90.93	101.53	131.92
		Female	155.87	308.79	86.11	87.20	68.94	76.73
		Person	231.59	364.95	93.11	89.03	93.06	121.83
	2004/5	Male	144.93	203.28	65.33	–	55.03	75.10
		Female	85.53	153.19	49.19	–	34.94	43.88
		Person	133.81	193.73	59.33	–	48.89	68.68
	1999/2000*	Male	–	–	48.14	–	44.84	62.26
		Female	–	–	38.06	–	29.01	37.71
		Person	–	–	45.55	–	39.64	56.96

Sources: National Sample Survey Organisation (2001, September 2006 and 2011), Report Nos. 458, 515 and 537.

Notes: Activity status: worked as regular salaried/wage employee – 31; had regular salaried/wage employment but did not work due to: sickness – 71, other reasons – 72; worked as casual wage labour in public works: other than MGNREG works – 41, MGNREG works – 42; worked as casual wage labour in other types of work (other than public work) – 51.

* Age 5 years and above.

Table 6.7 Number and share (%) of population below poverty line in Sikkim and in India

State/country	Year	Rural			Urban			Combined	
		Number of persons (Lakh)	Percentage of persons	Poverty line (Rs.)	Number of persons (Lakh)	Percentage of persons	Poverty line (Rs.)	Number of persons (Lakh)	Percentage of persons
Sikkim	1973/74	1.09	52.67	–	0.10	36.92	–	1.19	50.86
	1983/84	1.24	42.60	98.32	0.10	21.73	97.51	1.35	39.71
	1993/94	1.81	45.01	232.05	0.03	7.73	212.42	1.84	41.43
	1999/00*	2.00	40.04	365.43	0.04	7.47	343.99	2.05	36.55
	2004/5†	1.12	22.30	387.64	0.02	3.30	378.84	1.14	20.10
	2004/5‡	0.85	17.00	387.64	0.02	2.40	378.84	0.87	15.20
	2004/5§	1.50	31.80	531.50	0.20	25.90	741.68	1.70	30.90
	2009/10§	0.70	15.50	728.90	0.10	5.00	1,035.20	0.80	13.10
	2011/12§	0.45	9.85	930.00	0.06	3.66	1,226.00	0.51	8.19
India	1973/74	2,612.90	56.44	49.63	600.46	49.01	56.64	3,213.36	54.88
	1983/84	2,519.57	45.65	89.50	709.40	40.79	115.65	3,228.97	44.48
	1993/94	2,440.31	37.27	205.84	763.37	32.36	281.35	3,203.67	35.97
	1999/00*	1,932.43	27.09	327.56	670.07	23.62	454.11	2,602.50	26.10
	2004/5†	2,209.24	28.30	356.30	807.96	25.70	538.60	3,017.20	27.50
	2004/5‡	1,702.99	21.80	356.30	682.00	21.70	538.60	2,384.99	21.80
	2004/5§	3,258.10	42.00	446.68	814.10	25.50	578.80	4,072.20	37.20
	2009/10§	2,782.10	33.80	672.80	764.70	20.90	859.60	3,546.80	29.80
	2011/12§	2,166.58	25.70	816.00	531.25	13.70	1,000.00	2,697.83	21.92

Source: Planning Commission 2014.

* 30-Day recall period.
† Uniform recall period.
‡ Mixed recall period.
§ Tendulkar method on mixed reference period.

households who are above the poverty level. The scheme enhances economic security in general and food security in particular.

The decline in the level of poverty which is partially attributed by the scheme, if not overstated, has concurrently led to the increase in the extent of economic participation. The extent of participation means longer engagement in terms of the number of days in an economic activity, i.e. workers converging from subsidiary/marginal workers towards principal/main workers. It reduces the level of underemployment. Moreover, despite the non-comparability of the sets of data between the National Sample Survey Organisation and the Census (due to conceptual and definitional differences), the worker population ratio which measures the rate of economic participation is given in Table 6.8. The Census data shows an improvement in the economic participation rate especially in the rural areas of Sikkim, against almost unchanged participation rate at the country level (from 2001 to 2011). The improvement is slightly more prominent for females in the rural areas of Sikkim. It has increased by about 4 percentage points for females against 3 for the males during the same period. It may likely result in a longer period of economic participation per year amongst the workers and also increase the economic participation as marginal workers. However, the National Sample Survey Organisation data does not show any significant change in the rural areas of Sikkim during 2004/5 to 2009/10. It could be argued that this situation arises due to the limited number of 100 days guaranteed for employment under MGNREGA. Hypothetically, 100 days of employment does not sufficiently enlarge the rate of economic participation. It might have largely raised an economically active period, i.e. engaging for longer months in a year, among the principal workers, thereby strengthening and improving annual household incomes which in turn reduces the level of poverty and achieves self-reliance in the rural areas.

9.   Concluding remarks

1 In Sikkim, MGNREGA work has changed in structure and in intensity over the years. Predominant activity such as flood control in the beginning has been replaced by land development and rural connectivity works.

2 MGNREGA activities have enhanced the livelihood and purchasing power of the rural people. It has provided a source of supplementary income to them, thereby reducing the level of poverty, underemployment and unemployment.

Table 6.8 Worker population ratio (%) of Sikkim and India

State/country	Areas	2001*			2004/5†			2009/10†			2011*		
		Male	Female	Person	Male	Female	Person	Male	Female	Person	Male	Female	Person
Sikkim	Rural	57.7	40.6	49.7	55.4	31.8	44.3	55.6	30.9	44.2	61.0	44.6	53.3
	Urban	55.5	21.7	40.2	54.5	16.8	36.9	60.1	15.0	39.8	57.5	24.8	41.9
	Combined	57.4	38.6	48.6	55.3	30.1	43.4	56.2	29.1	43.7	60.2	39.6	50.5
India	Rural	52.1	30.8	41.7	54.6	32.7	43.9	54.7	26.1	40.8	53.0	30.0	41.8
	Urban	50.6	11.9	32.3	54.9	16.6	36.5	54.3	13.8	35.0	53.8	15.4	35.3
	Combined	51.7	25.6	39.1	54.7	28.7	42.0	54.6	22.8	39.2	53.3	25.5	39.8

Sources: Author's calculation based on Registrar General of India (2001 and 2011) and National Sample Survey Organisation (October 2006 and 2012), Report Nos. 516 and 543.

*Worker/population × 100; workers includes both main and marginal workers (for detail definitions please refer to Census of India).
†National Sample Survey Organisation estimates of usual status (principal and subsidiary status).

3 The scheme has changed the traditional rural household workers to wage workers. Assets created through the scheme have resulted in additional income to the rural households apart from wage employment due to increased productivity of land, better irrigation, improvement in transportation, safeguard against landslides, increased farm-based production and increase in access to market.

4 Public workers under MGNREGA in rural areas have considerably increased because of the provision of equal wage for both the genders. Women participation in it is more visible, in comparison to men, and they are prominently participating as subsidiary workers. It is possibly due to their inability to get regular salaried job or causal work other than MGNREGA.

5 As expected, the number of job card holders has significantly increased. The National Sample Survey Organisation (November 2011) recorded that close to half of the rural households have cards. However, at present, it is two-thirds of the households in Sikkim. All of them do not demand for jobs, suggesting that they have other means of livelihood. Some of the households did not get jobs even if it was demanded. Presently, only three-fifths amongst the job card holders got employment under the scheme. It suggests that job cards are issued without verifying the actual eligibility criteria of the beneficiaries to inflate the state's budget for the scheme that requires a correction; card holders do not want to work in manual activities; card holders are engaged in employment with higher earnings than MGNREG wages that may necessitate upward MGNREGA wage revision; and government is unable to identify and provide adequate avenues for MGNREGA work.

6 The state was not able to provide a full 100 days of employment as guaranteed under the scheme to each rural household. It can be attributed to various factors like the government's inability to generate adequate rural unskilled manual work, MGNREGA work considered as subsidiary or secondary economic activity, household responsibilities in nursing the dependent children and aged, health problems, low wages and hard work involved in the scheme and finally distance to the worksite. There is a shortage of MGNREGA work provision that requires immediate attention by the government.

7 Payment of unemployment allowances is absent in Sikkim.

8 MGNREGA employments are delivered in accordance to the size of the social structure of the population.

9   Women's participation rate in the scheme is prominent at a level of close to half of the person days generated, as there is no wage differential between genders. It changes the rural livelihood through increase in household income, leading to alleviation from poverty.

10   There is no gender or caste/tribe discrimination either in the allotment of work or payment of wages or at worksite. The working environment is conducive for all types of community irrespective of gender or caste/tribe.

11   A good Panchayati Raj system prevailing in the state is also held responsible for the better implementation of the scheme, which other states can also adopt and practice.

12   In Sikkim, at present, wage rate for the MGNREGA work has increased by more than half of the wage, since the start of the scheme.

13   Wages are not paid in time and are often delayed in disbursement either through the bank or post office accounts or other means.

14   The increase in wages has a positive implication for poverty reduction. Women in particular received wages and supplemented their household income. It raised their purchasing power and reduced their poverty level.

15   Poverty level in the state has substantially declined in recent years for both rural and urban areas. Poverty level in Sikkim is relatively much lower than at the country level. As expected, the problem of poverty is more acute in the rural areas. However, with the implementation of MGNREGA work, large numbers of rural people are being relieved as the number of rural poor persons declined sharply and systematically. The scheme has enhanced economic security in general and food security in particular.

16   The decline in the level of poverty which is partially attributed by the scheme, if not overstated, has concurrently led to the increase in the extent of economic participation, i.e. workers converging from subsidiary/marginal workers towards principal/main workers, thus reducing underemployment.

17   Hundred days of guaranteed employment does not sufficiently enlarge the rate of economic participation but raises an economically active period among the principal workers, thereby strengthening annual household income which in turn leads to a reduction in poverty levels in the rural areas.

18   Nevertheless, this study does not glorify the work of MGNREGA and poverty reduction in Sikkim. A comparative study across the states also needs to be performed.

10. Recommendations

1 The scheme needs a convergence with other schemes relating to rural livelihood.
2 The scheme should provide sustainable employment linked with economic growth and equity that would solve the problem of poverty.
3 The scheme should create through MGNREGA a decent rural wage employment by developing skills for progression through on-the-job training.
4 The scheme should provide full employment to further reduce poverty and ensure better livelihood.

Notes

1 Wage refers to the minimum wage fixed by the state government under section 3 of the Minimum Wages Act 1948 for agricultural labourers (The Gazette of India 2005: 2).
2 The seven national awards received in a row by Sikkim for exemplary work done under MGNREGA, the National Flagship Programme, are as follows: (1) best performing gram panchayats – Chuba Phong Gram Panchayat for transforming a village reeling under perennial drought for construction of 120 household level water storage tanks of 10,000 L capacity each, (2) best performing district MGNREGA team – North District for excellence in district administration in the effective implementation of MGNREGA, (3) best performing NGO – Voluntary Health Association of Sikkim received the Rozgar Jagrookta Puraskar (Employment Awareness Award) for promoting effective implementation of MGNREGA in Sikkim in 2011 (Zeenews 2011); (4) Deepak Tamang, Panchayat President, Martam Nazitam – Gram Panchayat, Martam Block, East District for his outstanding contribution in 2012 (http://isikkim.com/2012); (5) The Hee Gyathang – Gram Panchayat, Dzongu Block, North District for excellence in the implementation of the programme in 2013 (Voiceofsikkim 2013); (6) The Lamten Tingmo – Gram Panchayat, Wok Block, South District for excellence in the implementation of the programme and (7) Rural Management and Development Department (Sikkim) received the recognition for excellence in convergence initiatives in 2014 (http://isikkim.com/2014).
3 The National Rural Guarantee Act 2005 (NREGA), *Operational Guidelines 2008*, Ministry of Rural Development, Department of Rural Development, Government of India, p. 38.
4 See detail goals of the scheme at MGNREGA 2005, Operational Guidelines 2013, Ministry of Rural Development, Department of Rural Development, Government of India, Delhi, p. 3.
5 As per the MGNREGA 2005, unemployment allowance rate shall be not less than one-fourth of the wage rate for the first 30 days during the financial year and not less than one-half of the wage rates for the remaining period of the financial year (The Gazette of India 2005: 4).
6 See details at The Gazette of India (2005: 3–5).

References

Bhalla, G. S. and P. Hazell. 2003. 'Rural employment and poverty: Strategies to eliminate rural poverty within a generation', *Economic and Political Weekly*, 38 (33): 3473–3484.

Dandekar, V. M. 1986. 'Agriculture, employment and poverty', *Economic and Political Weekly*, 21 (38/39): A90–A100.

Dheeraja, C., P. R. Siva and K. H. Rao. 2010. *Changing Gender Relations through MGNREGS: Sikkim State Report*. Hyderabad: National Institute of Rural Development.

Drèze, J. and A. Sen. 2002. *India Development and Participation*. Delhi: Oxford University Press.

Emadi, H. 1992. 'Women's emancipation and strategy of development in Albania', *Economic and Political Weekly*, 27 (19): 999–1002.

The Gazette of India. 2005. *The National Rural Employment Guarantee Act 2005*. Legislative Department. Ministry of Law and Justice. Delhi: Government of India.

The Gazette of India. 2013. *State Wise Wage Rate for Unskilled Manual Workers*. Delhi: Ministry of Rural Development.

Hirway, I. 2004. 'Providing employment guarantee in India: Some critical issues', *Economic and Political Weekly*, 39 (48): 5117–5124.

Institute of Rural Management Anand. 2010. *An Impact Assessment Study of Usefulness and Sustainability of the Assets Created under MGNREGA in Sikkim*. Anand: Institute of Rural Management Anand.

Isikkim. 2013. *Sikkim Wins National Award in Mahatma Gandhi NREGA Sammelan* [Online]. Retrieved from: http://isikkim.com/ [Accessed 14 January 2014].

Isikkim. 2014. *Sikkim Bags 2 National MGNREGA Awards* [Online]. Retrieved from: http://isikkim.com/ [Accessed 4 February 2014].

Mehrotra, S. 2008. 'NREG two years on: Where do we go from here?', *Economic and Political Weekly*, 43 (31): 27–35.

Ministry of Rural Development. 2012–2013. *Annual Report 2012–13*. Delhi: Ministry of Rural Development.

National Rural Employment Guarantee Act. 2014. *State Wise Notified Wages for MGNREGA* [Online]. Retrieved from: http://nrega.nic.in/nerega_statewise.pdf [Accessed 17 January 2014].

National Sample Survey Organisation. May 2001. *Employment and Unemployment Situation in India 1999–2000*. Report No. 458(55/10/2). Delhi: Ministry of Statistics & Programme Implementation.

National Sample Survey Organisation. September 2006. *Employment and Unemployment Situation in India 2004–05*. Report No. 515(61/10/1). Delhi: Ministry of Statistics & Programme Implementation.

National Sample Survey Organisation. October 2006. *Employment and Unemployment Situation among Social Groups in India 2004–05*. Report No. 516(61/10/2). Delhi: Ministry of Statistics & Programme Implementation.

National Sample Survey Organisation. November 2011. *Employment and Unemployment Situation in India 2009–10*. Report No. 537(66/10/1). Delhi: Ministry of Statistics & Programme Implementation.

National Sample Survey Organisation. September 2012. *Employment and Unemployment Situation among Social Groups in India 2009–10*. Report No. 543 (66/10/3). Delhi: Ministry of Statistics & Programme Implementation.

NREGA. 2014. *MGNREGA* [Online]. Retrieved from: http://nrega.nic.in [Accessed 15 January 2014].

Panda, B., A. K. Dutta and S. Prusty. 2009. *Appraisal of NREGA in the States of Meghalaya and Sikkim*. Shillong: Rajiv Gandhi Indian Institute of Management.

Planning Commission. 2014. *Population below Poverty Line*. Delhi: Government of India.

Registrar General of India. 2001 and 2011. *Census of India*. Delhi: Government of India.

Sen, A. 1996. 'Economic reforms, employment and poverty: Trends and options', *Economic and Political Weekly*, 31 (35/37): 2459–2477.

Sinha, J. N. 1981. 'Full employment and anti-poverty plan: The missing link', *Economic and Political Weekly*, 16 (50): 2043–2052.

Smith, S. and J. B. Sender. 1990. 'Poverty, gender and wage labour in rural Tanzania', *Economic and Political Weekly*, 25 (24/25): 1334–1342.

Sundaram, K. 2007. 'Employment and poverty in India, 2000–2005', *Economic and Political Weekly*, 42 (30): 3121–3131.

Sundaram, K. and J. Krishnamurty. 1978. 'Employment and poverty reduction in the draft plan', *Economic and Political Weekly*, 13 (31/33): 1295–1298.

Voiceofsikkim. 2013. *Excellence in MGNREGA, State Bags 5th National Award* [Online]. Retrieved from: http://voiceofsikkim.com/ [Accessed 14 January 2014].

Zeenews. 2011. *Sikkim Bags 3 National Awards at MG-NREGA Sammelan* [Online]. Retrieved from: http://zeenews.india.com [Accessed 14 January 2014].

7 Women in the land of Jade
Issues and interventions

Reshmi Banerjee

1. Introduction

History has revealed that in Southeast Asia, women were powerful figures who were respected with the region often been defined as an area where women enjoyed 'high status' as compared to the women in traditional India and China. The strength of these women survived colonialism and certain commonalities developed which is shared by the countries comprising this region. These commonalities are: development has encouraged adoption of labour saving techniques which in turn has affected the seasonal employment of landless women; rapid expansion of plantations and deforestation has led to women having less accessibility to forest products for food; they have experienced exploitation in workplaces with low wages, sexual harassment and finally they have often articulated their power through the weapons of 'silence' and 'withdrawal'. Their work is not always visible and the distinction between productive and reproductive labour, between public and private is blurred (Esterik 1995: 248–251).

In ancient times, the name 'Suvarnabhumi' (the golden land) was given to Burma for not only its beautiful golden pagodas but also for its rich natural resources (rice, timber, gems like jade, rubies). At the political level, the monarch exercised absolute power, but he was influenced by custom, traditional etiquette, the Buddhist religion and its teachings with its monastic order, whereas the economy was a subsistence one with the majority of people involved in agriculture. In all judicial matters, customary law mattered and it was instrumental in arriving at acceptable settlements (Myint 2003: 8–10). The Burmese legal literature divided people into four social classes: the rulers or the *min-myo*, the ritualists or the learned or *ponna-myo*, the bankers and the rich merchants or the *thuhtay-myo* and finally the commoners or the poor people or the *sinyetha-myo*. *Myo* was the Burmese word for both the Indian jati and the varna. This above classification of society influenced and decided the rights of inheritance, civil and criminal cases including divorce laws. Polygamy was commonly prevalent and interestingly, in spite of social classification, one could indulge in inter-class marriages (no customary prohibition of inter-class marriage; Myint-U 2001: 31, 32).

Under successive dynasties, the primary task of women was to fulfil the wishes of men. Women were given as gifts to kings and they automatically became the wife of the next one when the king died. However, inscriptions in Bagan would tell us that women were in high positions and they did dedicate land and slaves to monasteries and pagodas. This goes to show that women did possess property and they were in a position to decide for themselves as to what they wanted to do with it. They could own or dispose property as they wished (Nwe 2003). Thus, sexist ideas and customs coexisted with practices which were favourable to women. Chie Ikeya points out that first there were 'regulations on female members of the Theravada Buddhist society (exclusion of women from the sangha since the thirteenth century) & shorter history of Buddhist nuns' and second Buddhist literature did refer to women as temptresses who kept men away from attaining *nibbana* (nirvana) (Ikeya 2005/2006). Mi Mi Khaing in the 1984 book *The World of Burmese Women* pointed out that women were considered to be inferior spiritually in spite of the enjoyment of high status (ibid.).

2.   The colonial period

The defeat of the Burmese king and the coming of the British introduced several politico-economic changes like the introduction of a bureaucratic organisation, legal codes, policy of separation of Burma proper from the border areas along with changes in society like secular education and conversion by Christian missionaries. There was the simultaneous existence of two phenomena which was first reflected in the surprise shown by the British representatives/colonial officers/ Christian missionaries regarding the freedom enjoyed by the Burmese women as there was no sati (seen in the Hindus) and purdah (seen in the Muslims). Some of the statements made by the British officers reiterate it. Sir George Scott (a late-nineteenth-century British officer in Burma) stated: 'The Japanese wife treats her husband as an idol and the Burmese as a comrade'. Another British officer in the late nineteenth century, Harold Fielding Hall stated: 'Burmese woman has been bound by no ties; she has had freedom to come to grief as well as to come to strength'. Second, it was reflected in the attention given by the Burmese and the Indian nationalists to the high status of women in Burma. This was done to prove to the British that social reforms were indeed happening and lack of political reforms was thus a ploy by the British to not give rights to the people (the British had stated that social reforms must come before political reforms). For example, Tilak who visited Burma in 1899 stated after his visit that the British were refusing to grant political freedom in spite of Burmese women enjoying socially advanced status. The British meanwhile felt that the Burmese women lacked refinement, education and child-rearing skills which ultimately resulted in low literacy rates and high infant mortality rates for them (ibid.).

There is no word in the Burmese language for 'Mrs' as her identity does not change when she marries. Wearing of wedding rings is also not necessary or customary, thus removing all signs of patriarchy. There is fluidity and flexibility in spatial relationships which are accepted as the norm and after marriage, a woman can stay with her husband in her own parents' house or can stay with her in-laws or decide to stay separately. They are equal partners with their husbands when it comes to being active in the market as customers and stall-holders. Several acts like the Special Marriage Act of 1872 and 1923, the Buddhist Woman's Special Marriage and Succession Act of 1940 and its amendment in 1954 ensure protection for Buddhist Burmese women (Nwe 2003).

Women could easily inherit family property along with their brothers. She could take on multiple roles like take on responsibility for family finances, could work as traders in the local shops and bazaars, and still help her husband in the fields with weeding, transplanting and harvesting times. One could enter and exit from marriage easily as she could initiate divorce. Women also could hold positions of power – whether it was the queen Shin Saw Pyu of the Pegu dynasty in the fifteenth century or being as heads of villages. Much of the social and economic status that women held was due to customary practice and not due to legal prescription. Thus, Melford Spiro has called these 'extra-structural or informal rights' (Mills 2000: 268).

However, there was ambivalence existing when it came to women. An old proverb listed a thief, the bough of a tree, a ruler and a woman among 'things not to be trusted', women were subordinated in Burmese rituals, male and female clothing were washed and dried separately to avoid pollution and a woman were expected to walk behind her husband. A man's adultery did not carry huge sanction/punishment, but rape was recognised as a crime and could mean loss of all property as a penalty. The birth of a daughter was welcomed (she would stay with her parents in later life), even though a son's birth was celebrated.

According to Spiro, the 'exercise of authority (awza) was a male pre-rogative, so that any social status endowed with authority was by cultural ascription, a male monopoly' (ibid.: 268, 269).

However, things can get complicated in Burmese society, like it did before independence with the Indo-Burmese marriages. There was apprehension in the early 1920s that the Burmese woman would not only lose her Buddhist rights but also destroy her *amyo*, i.e. her race, ancestors and kin, religion, culture etc. (Ikeya 2005/2006). Meanwhile, even now, the concept of *hpon* is relevant (central to the notion of male superiority) to the point that one observes that a monk is called *hpoungyi* (literally great *hpoun* or great glory) with a nun being called *thilashins* (literally keepers of the precepts); the former wielding much more power and importance. Women were excluded from the sangha, which meant that they were also excluded from basic education which the sangha provided. They only enjoyed informal education which was also not universal. However, there are again instances where the wives of powerful people did enjoy significant amount of power like the chief queen of the last king Thibaw, Queen Supayalat, who had huge influence over the king (Mills 2000: 269, 270). Thus, paradoxes and contradictions existed in society.

Women participated along with men in the independence movement and there are several instances/examples which show that women in the country were active agents, trying to bring change. They not only demonstrated in 1927 against a clause which was preventing them from standing for election to the legislative council but also made sure that in 1929, the first woman was elected to the council. There are examples of not only women leaders like Daw Hnin Mya (elected in 1936 to the legislative assembly) and Daw Mya Sein (selected to represent Burmese women at a Burma Round Table Conference in 1931 in London) but also Thakin-ma Ma Aye and Thakin-ma Daw Say who played an equally important role in the 1938 oil field strikes through their membership of the *Dobama Asi ayone* (ibid.: 270, 271). The popularity, credibility and reputation of the female writers and editors also grew in the 1930s; with them being thought as capable of writing critical commentaries on socio-economic and political issues (Harriden 2012: 134).

Organisations like the Burmese Women Union, Burmese Women National Council and Burmese Women Association all played an important role. According to Nang Lao Liang Won, three ethnic Shan women in 1825 and eight ethnic Chin women in 1889 resisted the British. Even after independence in 1948, they not only continued to set up and join resistance groups like the Shan State Army, Karen

National Union but also participated in uprisings like the student's uprising in 1996 and the Saffron Revolution (led by the monks) in 2007 (Nang 2013). History has also shown that the Myanmar Women's Association played an active role in the 1920s to protect women's rights to profession, education and standing for election. Other organisations which played a crucial role are as follows: All Burma Independent Women's Association, Women's Union and Women's Solidarity Association. Women also participated in the university boycotts. Between 1948 and 1962, the Women's Freedom League was closely linked to the Anti-Fascist People's Freedom League. However, it was in 1974 that things changed as all political activities including women's associations were put to an end and around 200 women have been languishing as prisoners since 1998. Meanwhile, women are asking several questions in their various roles in the country. Interestingly, Ma Thistsa Wadee (a Buddhist nun) submitted a complaint letter to the Sangha Association and Myanmar Ministry of Religious Affairs with the question as to why 'Nuns cannot attain the same position as monks in Theravada Buddhism in the country when they can achieve it in Sri Lanka' (FES Gender Team and Gyi 2009). The country continues to see ambivalence being played out in various walks of society.

3. After independence

Statistics often reveal various aspects of a country. The 1953/54 Census data pointed out that women constituted 25 per cent of the total labour force in the urban areas and 31.1 per cent in the rural areas. Around two-thirds of the women in the rural areas were involved in paid employment as agricultural labourers in the mid-1950s. There were also many who were in the informal sector. A government report which was published in 1958 reported that only 9 per cent of the household heads who earned more than 75 per cent of the total family income were women. The country saw elections in 1951, 1956 and 1960, but there was only one elected woman (i.e. Daw Sein Pyu) in the Central Executive Committee, and even the pro-AFPFL newspaper *Bamakhit* did not really encourage the participation of women as it found it to be challenging and corrupt for women. On the other hand, communist leaders not only encouraged women to participate but also provided them with ideological and military training. However, they faced challenges on two counts: women communist members were criticized for their allegedly immoral behaviour and they were asked to focus on their nurturing-procreative side and not on leadership roles; thus, they were seen in fund-raising, social welfare, as nurses and teachers (Harriden 2012: 147–159).

Further, there was complete absence of women in the bureaucracy and the judiciary with only 2.8 per cent women in the governing bodies of Union of Myanmar Federation of Chambers and Commerce. Similar situation also existed in politics with very few women elected as party candidates during the years 1974–1985 (ibid.). Few of the women in public office were Ba Maung Chain who served briefly from 1952 to 1953 in the cabinet as minister of the Karen state, Daw Khin Kyi (widow of the assassinated leader Aung San) became in 1960 Burma's first woman ambassador. Interestingly, one observes an increase in the participation of women during the military rule era, i.e. from 1962 to 1988. This was first on account of women participating in the economy as paid labour force due to the deterioration of the economy and second because of the rising community health and education levels. One finds that between 1973 and 1983, the employment growth was the highest for women in teaching, nursing, clerical and other service jobs as well as in agriculture with the growth being from 33 to 36 per cent (greatest growth in the ages between 20 and 40). Women in the Armed Forces in 1983 were less than 1 per cent of all three services. There were less than 3 per cent women members in the People's National Assembly (*Pyithu Hluttaw*) by 1980s (Mills 2000: 272–275). Women were at the receiving end of a state which witnessed authoritarian military rule, insurgency, violent ethnic armed struggle, extreme poverty and difficult economic conditions. Conflict, masculine regime and militarized exclusive elite society made them even more vulnerable and curtailed their status and independence. The command structure of the military further entrenched the concepts of male superiority and authority, which already existed in the society.

Between 1973 and 1983, there was a significant increase in the percentage of women employed in the agricultural sector (two-thirds in the agricultural sector), but there was a decline in the percentage employed in the manufacturing and wholesale industries. This was against a backdrop of government controlled rice trade, forced procurement, taxation policies, land confiscation, black market, rising inflation (20% in the mid-1970s), food shortages and finally strikes and riots from late 1960s onwards. An average Burmese used to spend half his income on food in 1961, however he had to spend nearly 80 per cent on food in 1976. The economic policies of the government affected women adversely as none of the policies were gender specific. Also women in managerial positions declined in percentage during this period from 13 to 11 per cent. Only 38–41 per cent of senior positions in teaching were occupied by women. One often found that those who did not enjoy influence with the military or did not belong to military families were sent to difficult rural areas which in turn became difficult for lady doctors or teachers. Thus, many were left with no choice but forced into low-paid factory jobs, domestic slavery or prostitution (both within Burma and in the neighbourhood countries). However, women continued to be active which is evident by their participation in the 1974 workers' strike and in the 1988 demonstrations over poor economic conditions. This led to the journalist Denzil Peiris's comment that 'Movements to overthrow governments begin in the kitchen' (Harriden 2012: 186–189). Between 1975 and 1992, expenditure on education declined from 15 to 2.4 per cent and defence expenditure went up from 20 to 40 per cent. Since the government made Burmese as the official language, women in ethnic minority areas remained illiterate in their native language (ibid.: 195).

In current day, 50.3 per cent of the total population in Myanmar consists of women. Many are involved in agriculture, while some work in the factories and mines. Although Burma's laws grant equal rights to women and customary laws grant them equal rights, yet in reality, they do not have equal access to land. The land laws are not only complex and poorly organised, but women themselves do not have proper awareness about their rights as joint owners of family land or about their rights of inheritance. The problem is further aggravated in ethnic minority areas where landlessness is very high. These are also the areas which have been exploited economically by the military for its resources and women, especially rural women, have faced social problems like harassment, sexual abuse (verbal and physical) at the hands of the military.

The rural areas account for nearly 84 per cent of Myanmar's total poverty. In 2012, the government enacted two laws: the Farmland Law and the Vacant, Fallow and Virgin Lands Management Law Both laws are not gender neutral and they do not have any mechanisms for the joint ownership of property between husbands and wives. Both the laws state that the land will be registered in the name of the head of the household which in the country is understood to mean the husband. These laws do not state any use rights for women when it comes to vacant, fallow or virgin land. Women's land rights also vary depending on one's religious affiliation. In customary Buddhist laws, women are not considered as joint owners but they are considered as 'co-owners' of property. The rights for a Buddhist wife varies depending on the type of property: husbands and wives are entitled to one-third of property owned by either spouse at the time of marriage and the property that the spouse inherited (*paryin*), they are both entitled to equal shares of property that they have increased after marriage (*lathtatpwar*), property gifted to the couple after marriage (*khanwin*) and property earned by the work of both (*hnaparson*). Neither spouse is entitled to property brought by the other from the previous marriage into the current one (*ahtatpar*) (USAID Country Profile).

Rural and urban women, Burman and non-Burman women, women living in war-affected areas and those living elsewhere have all had different experiences. Women are taught by their parents to be feminine and respect their 'sons as Masters and husbands as God' – i.e. treat the men as superiors based on religion and tradition. A 1995 report by the Burmese Women's Union found that the society discourages women from higher learning with men's education getting more priority. There is a general ambivalence in society towards women which makes it harder for them to reach positions of authority. There is a paradox in the society which on one side sees women obediently following the traditional Buddhist rules like sleeping on the left-hand side of their partners so as not to pollute the *hpon* (it is located on the right side of men); on the other side, girls as young as fifteen years have joined armed ethnic minority militias (KIO, New Mon State Party, Karen National Union). One finds them working in the fields, stalls and shops, in modern professions as doctors, lawyers, teachers and facing the day-to-day problems with a silent courage and pride. Although they are represented in professions like law, education, medicine, literature, they continue to face discrimination in fields of engineering, mining, agriculture and veterinary science. Since a large number of women work in the small-scale non-organised informal sector, they receive low wages and suffer from insecurity. Many have to bribe their way across the borders to Thailand and China for running their small businesses. Sometimes, they are also arrested. Yet, interestingly, the Buddhist cultural values of Burmese society which sees commerce and trade as related to profit and not spirit, thus sees women as inferior, they being related to economic-entrepreneurial roles whereas men are seen as superior, they being concerned with politico-bureaucratic roles. The common expression often used is 'The man of the family goes to the office to earn, not money, but the neighbour's respect' (Shannassy).

One needs to look at the women of today in the backdrop of a history which did at times show signs of progressiveness. They provided inspiration and strength to many and yet they suffered. The *khit kala* (women of the times), a term used in Burma, however did not take away the fact that women were inserted rather than integrated into the national histories of their country. Barbara Andaya describes it as the 'hegemony of the national epic in Southeast Asian historiography' (Ikeya 2011: 4). Paradoxically, the presence of Burmese women in the urban areas was quite high so much so that the Census commissioner in 1931 Census report remarked that 'apparently Burmese women appreciate the amenities of town life' (ibid.: 22). Also, Burmese women inspired the Indian feminist – nationalist project as stated by Shobna Nijhawan, who recently talked about how the monthly *Stri Darpan* (published from 1909 to 1928) printed many ethnographic accounts of Burmese women just to showcase that gender equality was not based on some Western notion of women but it was more traditional yet progressive (ibid.: 50, 51).

Burmese women face a number of problems/challenges which require interventions in the future.

4. Challenges faced by women

Some of the varied challenges faced by the women of Myanmar are as follows:

Violence against women

This continues to be the biggest problem/challenge facing women in this country. In the Shan state, between 1996 and 2001, 173 incidents of rape and other forms of sexual violence took place which involved 625 girls and women. Rape is being used as a 'weapon of war', and 83 per cent of the rapes were committed by officers in front of their troops, 61 per cent were gang rapes and 25 per cent of the rapes resulted in death. Many of the rapes actually took place when these young women had gone in search of food, outside the relocation sites and it also took place when they were forced to porter or do unpaid work for the military. Rape has also served as a 'reward' for troops fighting in the war and in 24 cases, they were kept up to four months serving as 'comfort women' without fear of any reprisal. Several women who have experienced physical/sexual violence have reported insomnia, loss of appetite, loss of weight, addiction to opium in order to forget, feeling of 'shame', have been at times abandoned by their own family (censure within their own communities) but there is also a strong desire among them to bring these rapists to justice (SHRF and SWAN 2002). Even during the 1988 uprising and in the Saffron Revolution of 2007, women have been physically mishandled. In 1988, women students were sexually assaulted by the special police while in custody. In 2007, at least 19 women disappeared and 131 women protestors including six nuns were arrested by the regime (Women Human Rights Defenders of Burma 2007).

Rape of women porters is quite common. Porters are often made to walk in front of soldiers through minefields and as human shields. Many have got killed, maimed by landmines or have been caught in the crossfire. The psychological trauma that these women face is immense and nothing has been done on a significant level to handle that. The UN special rapporteur on Burma has pointed out that 'the victims, if they are still alive, are ashamed, afraid or choose to obliterate the memory' (Shannassy).

Trafficking of women

Thousands of women are trafficked into China every year to be the wives of men known as *guang gun* or bare branches (these are bachelors in rural areas who cannot find brides) due to the Chinese one child policy and preference for the male child. The women are lured into China on the pretext of jobs and then they find themselves being sold. The Chinese Academy of Social Sciences has predicted that by 2020, some 24 million Chinese men will be unable to find wives (120 boys are now born for every 100 girls). One gets 6,000 to 40,000 yuan for the women from Myanmar, with age and appearance affecting the prices. Most of them are very young (as younger girls are preferred for producing babies) as reported by the Kachin Women's Association of Thailand – with 25 per cent being under 18. The women are living a miserable life of perennial fear with men who subject them to physical and mental torture and whose language they cannot understand. Many are driven to suicide. Their dreams have been converted to a real-life 'marital prison' in a foreign land (Eimer 2011). Also many women are sent to Thailand to work as prostitutes in brothels. They are extremely vulnerable to physical abuse and face danger to their lives as they contract HIV/AIDS. The parents of the young girls, sadly in alliance with police and military personnel, are often involved in forced prostitution in border towns of Chiang Mai, Mae Sai, Kanchanaburi. One finds the traffickers are constantly looking for girls from remote villages as their chances of exposure to the virus are limited. *Asia Watch* in 1993 had pointed out that the rate of infection among Burmese women and girls in the sex trade in Thailand was roughly three times that existing among Thai prostitutes which was said to be over 21 per cent. Those women who escaped often faced charges of unauthorised emigration and participation in illegal prostitution, thus facing imprisonment (Mills 2000: 280).

Migration of rural women

The country in recent times has witnessed the growth of labour-intensive textile and food-processing industries. This has accelerated the movement of young men from the rural to the urban areas to work in factories. The clusters of export-oriented industries readily employ women as they seem to be docile, skilled and open to accepting low wages. The lack of access to land in the rural areas, debt-ridden conditions of the households and the responsibility of younger siblings on their shoulders (who are at school) are some of the reasons for these young women to move out of their villages. Interestingly and increasingly, in the village, decisions regarding farm are taken by men and decisions regarding non-farm are taken by women as strategies of survival. These young women face harassment by even foreign males but even then, many get easy approvals from their families (Chaw 2003).

Recently in 2010, there were factory strikes by textile workers (garment factory in the Hlaing Tharyar Industrial Zone, 11 km from downtown Rangoon), mostly women participated and they were successful in raising their monthly pay by 5,000 kyat. Although the amount was only half of what they had demanded, yet this was a small victory for the women involved (Kaung 2010: 30, 31). Most factory women workers have no family or social life and they are not allowed to venture out. Many resort to abortions in order to keep their jobs (Myate 2008: 25).

Women and livelihoods

In the villages, women's participation in the meetings as well as their accessibility to social networks has been low. The cash economy has added to the rising costs which in turn have added to the burden of women. It was found in a household survey conducted in six villages with a sample of 220 households in 2003 (areas studied were the fragile and resource-poor Dry Zone townships of Chaung U, Kyaukpadaung and Magway) that the following were true for female-headed households: First, there was feminisation of poverty with the female-headed households owning significantly less cultivated land than the male-headed households. Second, 95 per cent of the female-headed households were widows and the rest were divorcees and single women. Third, these households had more number of children school dropouts at the primary education level. Finally, they had poorer livelihood resources like land, cattle and capital and lower per capita income (Kyaw and Routray 2006). Interestingly, a year later, a different viewpoint was also presented in *Integrated Household Living Conditions Survey in Myanmar* (2007) which found a lack of relationship between deprivation and female hardships. The proportion of non-poor households headed by women was found to be slightly higher (19.1%) than poor-women-headed households (18.3%). The causes were attributed to high-remittance income and non-dependency of the urban better-off women (ibid.).

Even in the mining industry, women face challenges as companies enter into business agreements with men rather than women. Also women face numerous other challenges like mines take away farmland without giving proper compensation. Women anyway have poor bargaining powers when it comes to fighting for her compensation rights. It also affects food security and physical violence at home as women are considered responsible for providing food for all in the family and decrease in that leads to increase in domestic violence. Moreover, not only children who accompany their mothers to these mining areas are exposed to chemicals and are prone to accidents as they play but also the working women are affected by handling these chemicals. Exposure to acid mine drainage is much higher for women than men as the former is responsible for collecting water and looking after crops and animals. Moreover, since these mining sites are areas of military supervision with them guarding these areas, women are often subjected to sexual violence. These areas have seen a rise in rapes and institutionalised forms of sexual violence (such as brothels). Interestingly, most campaigns against destructive mining activities either focus on protection of the environment or on the labour rights of workers. Gender concerns however sadly do not get sufficient independent focus (ERI 2004). Seasonal migration to work in mines and other sectors leads to pain and isolation which in turn leads to drugs, prostitution and HIV/AIDS infections. They often thus result in infecting their wives at home when they return.

Since 1997, young women between the age group of 16 and 25 in the eastern Shan state have been forbidden to travel to the Thai border and many have had to bribe the officials to reach the border. Also since 2004, young women need to get a recommendation letter from the local Myanmar Women's Affairs Federation to travel to the border. Often older women who accompany the younger one are harassed and are arrested on false trafficking charges (Women of Burma 2008).

Women and displacement

Myanmar has witnessed massive displacement due to conflict and development projects. According to UNHCR (United Nations High Commissioner for Refugees) 2013 statistics, there is a need to assist

800,000 residents of Rakhine state who are without citizenship; June 2012 communal violence has forced also some 75,000 people to flee their homes. In the southeastern part of the country, UNHCR supports 239,000 people affected by displacement. As of January 2013, there were 2,000 returnees (refuges), 429,200 internally displaced people (IDPs) and 185,640 stateless people (UNHCR). Moreover in the northern Shan state, over 2,000 Palaung villagers from fifteen villages in three townships have been displaced since March 2011. Since the 16th Burma Army Battalions are troubling the men (forcible conscription as soldiers and porters), the men have abandoned their villages and have left the women behind, creating a helpless situation for women. The ratio of women to men (18–35 years) in the IDP camps is 4:1. Tea industry has also failed, leading further to farmers growing opium which in turn has led to drug-addiction on a large scale. Meanwhile, development projects like the transnational gas and oil pipelines from the Arakan coast to China have created large-scale displacement (PWO 2012). Women naturally are at the receiving end of any kind of social and economic upheaval caused by displacement and conflict.

There is no specific institutional mechanism which focuses on gender statistics in Myanmar except the Ministry for Social Welfare, Relief and Resettlement (MSWRR). Senior members of the military are in charge of managing programs for women's advancement and empowerment. THE MSWRR oversees the work of the MNCWA (Myanmar National Committee for Women's Affairs) which was formed in 1996. This committee has identified nine areas of concern for women: need to form the national machinery for their advancement; promotion of education of women and children; focus on health especially on infant and maternal mortality rates; protection of women and children from violence, trafficking; income generation for women; women and media; women and environment; women and culture; and focus on the girl child (MNCWA).

One of the problems facing the country is the lack of gender-disaggregated data on the situation of women. Not only education levels have gone down with more and more girls leaving their schools for supporting their families, but also women face the brunt of the collapse of the health sector with almost a quarter of children expected to die before age 5 and 1 in 12 women expected to lose her life because of pregnancy-related causes in conflict ridden eastern Myanmar (Women of Burma 2008). There are no specific laws (criminal laws) to deal with domestic violence and the 1860 Penal Code sections still handle sexual- and gender-based violence. Also there is absence of women in the Armed Forces, although there was a time when women worked in the nursing corps. The GONGOs (government NGOs) – Myanmar Maternal and Child Welfare Association, Myanmar Women Entrepreneurs Association and the Myanmar Women's Sports Federation – are all composed of privileged women with very close ties with the military regime, thus their influence and role seems questionable. *Hiri* (moral shame) and *ottapa* (moral fear of repercussion) are regarded as cultural obligations of Burmese women – as these are considered as 'twin guardians' of morality in Theravada Buddhism (ibid.). Both these often control the feelings that women tend to go through in the face of adversity.

There were two trends which started emerging over the years: First, there has been a certain connection between privileged businesswomen and the military junta. There are several examples of daughters and wives of government and military leaders enjoying extreme and uncontrolled privileges. Sanda Win (daughter of Ne Win) amassed huge amounts of wealth; Tin U (chief of the National Intelligence Bureau) was also removed in 1983 as his wife was involved in black marketing. Second, many women started seeking employment outside the country. The late 1980s and early 1990s witnessed increasing numbers of women moving to Thailand and other neighbouring countries in search of employment; many choosing to work even illegally in the construction and sex industry, as domestic maids. This was also the result of the lack of growth in the manufacturing, hospitality and tourism industries in Myanmar due to constant unrest and international ostracism. Even educated women emigrated (Mills 2000: 277–279).

Long prison sentences have been given to politically active women like Daw San San Win, an advocate and NLD candidate (given 25 years imprisonment), and Daw Cho Cho Kyaw Nyein, general secretary of the Anti-Fascist Peoples Freedom league (7 years imprisonment). Even professionals have been awarded long prison sentences like Ma Thida, a medical doctor, a short story writer and a friend of Aung San Suu Kyi (20 years imprisonment). Many female writers and intellectuals have been completely banned from publication, e.g. San San Nweh, a journalist, an author and a poet, was detained in 1988/89 and banned from publication (ibid.: 283).

According to the Workmen's Compensation Act of 1924, when compensation is paid for the death of a relative, no lump sums are given to women unless through a commissioner who is appointed by the government. Women are not allowed to apply for Defense Services Academy, Officers Training Course or Officer's Technical Training. Army law seems to override the Penal Code and the army never gives any details as to how it deals with offenders/punishment of the Armed Forces (Sen 2001). A gender assessment by 'Save the Children' in Ayeyarwaddy region pointed out that over one third of the NGO local staff did not know the concept of gender in development or humanitarian interventions/involvement. Women especially as mothers, landless small holders, part of ethnic minorities' are most vulnerable (Wilson and Mwee 2013).

Myanmar is going to face the challenges of climate change and food security. Already one in ten households live below the official food poverty line and the largest number of poor households are concentrated in Ayeyarwaddy, Mandalay, Rakhine and Shan – these four areas account for two-thirds of total food poverty and half of total poverty are found in these four states. Floods in 2008 affected agricultural production and agrarian prices. Already, nearly 50 per cent of poor households are landless. Cyclone Nargis in 2008 further affected rice production since more than 65 per cent of the country's main rice production zone fell in the directly hit area. Cyclone Giri in 2010 struck the Rakhine state. Several parts of the country are also prone to earthquakes with the Shan state experiencing a 6.9 earthquake in March 2011 and Shwebo experiencing a 6.8 earthquake in November 2012. The country is prone to climatic changes and will face increase in temperatures along with rainfall which will be unpredictable. Floods and droughts will be impacting farmers badly and women in the poorer, marginalized households will be at the receiving end (ibid.).

The *silo* (mentality) is present in the country with food security, meaning only the availability of rice. Other aspects of food security like food accessibility, food absorption which includes aspect of nutrition, health which are so crucial especially for women are absent.

5. Interventions attempted

In 1995, the State Law and Order Restoration Council sent a male-led delegation to the UN Fourth World Conference on Women in Beijing. The *Beijing Declaration*, the government pointed out, was going to be implemented in accordance with the political, economic and social objectives. A national machinery for the advancement of women called the Myanmar National Committee for Women's Affairs (MNCWA) was created in July 1996 which identified nine areas of concern: (1) need to form the national machinery for advancement of women, (2) promote education of women and children through formal and non-formal skills-based system, (3) improve heath by reducing infant and maternal mortality rates, (4) protect women and children from violence and trafficking (National Task Force on Trafficking in Women and Children comprising of personnel from the police force, health, social welfare, immigration, border areas departments along with NGOs, attorney general's office was created in August 1998; counselling to be provided in each township and vocational training to be given along with credit and loan schemes to start micro-enterprises), (5) women and economy (impart knowledge of sewing, knitting, weaving and cooking along with stress on non-traditional activities like computer science, fruit carving, driving, costume and jewellery making, English language speaking, secretarial courses), (6) women and culture (to be encouraged to take part in the annual Traditional Performing Arts Competition and summer courses were to be held annually on religion, culture and tradition in schools and in communities), (7) women and environment, (8) women and media (the activities of the community were to be featured in television, radio, periodicals in order to increase awareness and women were to be trained to increase their skills and knowledge along with access to IT) and (9) focus on the girl child (MNCWA).

Working committees were set up at the national, state, district and township levels. In 2000, the government pointed out that the male/female ratio in the national committees was 1:3, but there were various problems:

- Independent observers have pointed out that the males constituted half the membership in all the committees.
- Also the government completely ignored the following areas: the impact of poverty on women, the impact of armed conflict on women, promotion of human rights amongst women and finally women's role and accessibility to decision-making and power sharing.
- The MNCWA received no budget from the government and thus was short of funds.
- The committee members were to work on a voluntary basis and the CEDAW (Convention on the Elimination of All Forms of Discrimination against Women) committee members did point out that the MNCWA leadership lacked expertise in women's issues. Also there was lack of women's presence in the leadership positions. Meanwhile, the government also ratified the CEDAW in 1997. This CEDAW committee pointed out that the government should provide human and financial resources to make the MNCWA work (Harriden 2012: 244–246).

In spite of certain weaknesses/drawbacks, Myanmar has initiated certain positive interventions which could in the future make a difference in the lives of women.

1 In December 2003, the Myanmar Women's Affairs Federation was formed to implement the functions of the MNCWA. Interestingly, the fact that these women are appointed to top positions in Burma does not necessarily translate to increase in the position of women. These women are not able to relate to the issues which affect the ordinary women of the country. They are more loyal to their husbands who are in the top echelons of government. For example, Kyaing Kyaing and Khin Win Shwe were two such women who were held responsible for misusing their leadership positions. Moreover, these women can lose their positions if their husbands do not agree with senior government leaders (ibid.: 258–260). However, women in Myanmar are increasingly coming out in large numbers in the public sphere to assert their rightful position in society. They are much more openly voicing their opinions and expressing their grievances.

2 The Integrated Community Development Project and Community Development in Remote Townships have influenced women positively. It has strengthened 5,473 self-reliance groups where 98 per cent of their members were women as of December 2012. Women have been involved more in decision-making, have increased their awareness of health and social issues and have increased their livelihood options. Again, as of December 2012, the microfinance project has provided financial services in 6,076 villages and urban wards in 25 townships with 583,828 poor people getting benefits from it. Again women constitute 98 per cent of the beneficiaries. The UNDP (United Nations Development Programme) is conducting studies on five themes which are based on the household living conditions survey in Myanmar (June 2011). These themes are regional development, access to finance, role of remittance on poor and non-poor rural and urban households, infrastructure and trade and finally linkage between poverty and environment. The UNDP also supported the Myanmar Positive Women Network, which is composed exclusively of women with HIV (UNDP 2012).

3 UN Women in November 2012 held a peacebuilding and negotiation training course in Yangon for women. This was basically to cultivate their skills and confidence so that they can play a greater role in peacebuilding. Further, courses were held in February and

June 2013 with peer-to-peer monitoring and close to 80 women peace advocates have received such training (UN Women 2013).

4   On the 15 October 2013, Rev Mai Ti, a woman social entrepreneur from Burma, was awarded by the Women's World Summit Foundation for her outstanding work in the Chin state. She was awarded the 'Women's Creativity in Rural Life' award for her work in animal husbandry, community health projects, skills and training courses and disaster and management relief. She has said, 'Wherever I go, I see people having hope and trusting each other. We don't have change yet, but in our hearts we do' (ibid.).

5   88 Generation Student's Group was a group formed after the 1988 student demonstrations and the brutal response of the military towards the students. Their main focus areas are empowerment of the women, human rights, peace in the ethnic areas along with the rights of the workers and the farmers. They created an initiative titled 'Discussion on peace and open society' (Nyein 2012).

6   UNICEF has also trained and deployed over 130 midwives and health assistants, rehabilitated damaged health centres and supported a nutritional surveillance system in 12 high-risk townships (UNICEF). In 61 of Myanmar's most vulnerable townships, it has initiated an integrated package of health, water supply, education, sanitation etc. (UNICEF).

7   The Gender Equality Network was formed after Cyclone Nargis in May 2008 as a response, by focusing on coordination and networking, capacity development and training, data collection and analysis, communication and research. It is a group of sixty national and international NGOs, UN agencies, civil society networks with technical people on it. The steering committee comprises of twelve members who guide the overall strategic direction of the network (LRC).

8   The International Tribunal on Crimes Against Women of Burma has pointed out some recommendations, some of which are as follows: stop attacks on ethnic minority groups (where again women of these ethnic groups are especially vulnerable), give women access to UN agencies and humanitarian groups, abide by rules of customary international law, ratify all international treaties, stress on democratic participation of women, include gender concerns within national development plans and processes, allocate proper resources equitably to women, punish human traffickers of women and children, raise awareness within the country and outside towards the issues of women and violence against women, establish proper, effective judicial mechanisms and finally bring

together all civil society organizations (International Tribunal on Crimes Against Women of Burma 2010).

9   Other interventions: Women's League of Burma formed in December 1999 is promoting the participation of women. The Myanmar Peace Support Initiative (a Norwegian-led international initiative) is trying to build the momentum of peace on the ground. Karen Women's Association in March 2012 initiated the process of involving Karen women's voices in the political dialogue between Karen and Burmese leaders. Kachin Women's Association in Thailand raises its voice against abuses committed against women in Kachin area.

The Strategic Plan/National Plan for the Advancement of Women (2011–2015) is supposedly being implemented with its various aspects – especially women and emergencies, women and economy, women and decision-making, women and human rights, women and media, women and environment. The ASEAN in its ASEAN Committee on Women and Children has Myanmar as its member and there is hope that it will be an active member. The 2008 Constitution of the country in its Article 22 states that all citizens shall be equal before the law irrespective of race, religion, status or sex; will enjoy equal opportunities and will have the right to inherit according to law. Article 32A of the new constitution also points out that the Union shall care for mothers and children.

There is definitely an urgent requirement for education and health facilities along with skill building. Initiatives for education can include focus on human rights, gender equality in school curriculum and scholarships for women; whereas in health, disaggregation of health data along with provision of providing free contraception to poor women is important. Other initiatives which are planned are as follows: research into wage disparities by gender, research into sexual harassment in the workplace, mentoring programs for parliamentarians, strengthen skills for leadership, strengthen the police force, and judicial and health officers to have a better response to violence against women (IPG 2013).

6.   Conclusion

The women of Burma have faced personal fear, psychological trauma, extreme violence and socio-economic discrimination for many years. They have been at the receiving end of an elitist, non-inclusive and abusive military rule. However, changes are slowly beginning to take place in the country and women are readily embracing these much-awaited changes. Improving the condition of women in a social framework of inequality, marginalisation and alienation is not easy. The following measures possibly can improve the current environment for women in Burma:

- Acceptance of past abuses and mistakes is the first step towards long-term reconciliation.
- Legal justice, social rehabilitation, women-centric development initiatives and provision of inclusive institutional mechanisms are some of the immediate steps required in the country.
- Civil society organisations can play a crucial role in addressing the trust deficit which currently exists amongst women and should involve them in preparing a common vision for peace and development. Moreover, media, educational institutions and women leaders need to create more awareness regarding the main grievances and relevant issues, both within and outside the country. Women in Burma have constantly adapted themselves to difficult circumstances in order to survive. They need to share their experiences more and create their own networks.
- Moreover, there are multiple international organisations and humanitarian groups working in the country, but there needs to be a coordinated response to women's issues which is currently being done in a subjective, reactive and ad-hoc manner.

To end,

> The Education and Empowerment of women throughout the world cannot fail to result in a more caring, tolerant, just and peaceful life for all.
>
> (Aung San Suu Kyi)

References

Chaw, C. 2003. *Rural Women Migrating to Urban Garment Factories in Myanmar*, Retrieved from: http://citeseerx.ist.psu.edu/viewdoc/download?doi=10.1.1.202.254&rep=rep1&type=pdf

Eimer, D. 2011. *Burma's Women Forced to be Chinese Brides*, September 4, Retrieved from: www.telegraph.co.uk/news/worldnews/asia

ERI. 2004. *Mining, Gender and the Environment in Burma*, Retrieved from: www.earthrights.org/publication/mining-gender-and-environment-burma

Esterik, P. V. 1995. 'Rewriting gender and development anthropology in southeast Asia', in W. J. Karim (ed.), *'Male' and 'Female' in Developing Southeast Asia*. Oxford: Berg Publishers, pp. 248–251.

FES Gender Team and M. Gyi. 2009. *Country Gender Profile: Myanmar*, Retrieved from: www.fes-asia.org/media/Gender/Country%20Gender%20Profile%20-%20MYANMAR.pdf

Harriden, J. 2012. *The Authority of Influence – Women and Power in Burmese History*. Copenhagen: Nordic Institute of Asian Studies.

IPG. 2013. 'Burma launches national plan to empower women'. *The Irrawaddy*, October 7, Retrieved from: www.irrawaddy.org/burma/burma

LRC. Gender Equality Network. http://lrcmyanmar.org/en/ngo-donor-profiles/inter-agency

MNCWA. August 2001. Status of Myanmar Women. http://mncwa.tripod.com/mncwa/id8.html

Ikeya, C. 2005/2006. 'The "traditional" high status of women in Burma: A historical reconsideration', *The Journal of Burma Studies*, 10: 51–81, Retrieved from: http://www.niu.edu/burma/publications/jbs/vol10/abstract2_ikeyaopt.pdf

Ikeya, C. 2011. *Refiguring Women, Colonialism, and Modernity in Burma*. Honolulu: University of Hawaii Press.

Integrated Household Living Conditions Survey in Myanmar. 2007. June, Retrieved from: www.mm.undp.org/UNDP_Publication_PDF/IH

International Tribunal on Crimes against Women of Burma. 2010. March 2, New York, Retrieved from: www.nobelwomensinitiative.org/wp-content/archive/stories/burma.pdf

Kaung, B. A. 2010. 'Sewing discord', *The Irrawaddy*, 18 (4), April: 30–31, Retrieved from: http://www2.irrawaddy.com/article.php?art_id=18222

Khaing, M. M. 1984. *The World of Burmese Women*. London: Zed Books.

Kyaw, D. and J. K. Routray. 2006. 'Gender and rural poverty in Myanmar: A micro level study in the dry zone', *Journal of Agriculture and Rural Development in the Tropics & Subtropics*, 107 (2): 103–114, Retrieved from: www.jarts.info/index.php/jarts/article/download/104/95

Mills, J. 2000. 'Militarism, civil war and women's status: A Burma case study', in L. Edwards and M. Roces (eds.), *Women in Asia: Tradition, Modernity and Globalization*. Michigan: The University of Michigan Press, pp. 268–283.

Myate, A. C. 2008. 'Problem pregnancies', *The Irrawaddy*, July, p. 25.

Myint, S. 2003. *Burma File: A Question of Democracy*. New Delhi: India Research Press, p. 25.

Myint-U, T. 2001. *The Making of Modern Burma*. Cambridge: Cambridge University Press.

Nang, L. L. W. 2013. *Can Democracy Work for Women in Burma?*, June 27, Retrieved from: www.ned.org/sites/default/files/Tay%20Tay%–

Nwe, T. T. 2003. 'Gendered spaces: Women in Burmese society', *Transformations*, 6, February, Retrieved from: http://www.transformationsjournal.org/wp-content/uploads/2017/01/nwe.pdf

Nyein, N. 2012. 'A woman's (political) work is never done', *The Irrawaddy*, November 10, www.irrawaddy.org/burma/a-womans-political-work-is-never-done.html

PWO. 2012. *The Burden of War: Women Bear Burden of Displacement*, Retrieved from: http://eng/palaungwomen.com/Report/The%20Burden%20 of%20War.pdf

Sen, B. K. 2001. 'Women and law in Burma', *Legal Issues on Burma Journal*, 9, August, Retrieved from: www.ibiblio.org/obl/docs/LIOB09-women_and_ law_in_burma.htm

Shannassy, T. O. *Burma's Excluded Majority: Women, Dictatorship and the Democracy Movement*, CIIR, Retrieved from www.progressio.org.uk/sites/ progressio.org.uk

SHRF and SWAN. 2002. *License to Rape*. Report by the Shan Human Rights Foundation (SHRF) and the Shan Women's Action Network (SWAN), May, Retrieved from: www.burmacampaign.org.uk/reports/License_to_rape.pdf

UNDP. 2012. *UNDP Report: Myanmar*, Retrieved from: www.mm.undp. org/UNDP_Publication_PDF/UNDP%20Myanmar%20Annual%20 report%202012.pdf

USAID Country Profile, Retrieved from: http://usaidlandtenure.net/sites/ default/files/country

Wilson, S. and N. E. Mwee. 2013. *Food and Nutrition Security in Myanmar*, Retrieved from: http://fsg.afre.msu.edu/Myanmar/burma_background_ paper_4_food_security_rev.pdf

Women Human Rights Defenders of Burma. 2007. *Courage to Resist*. Report by the Women Human Rights Defenders of Burma, Women's League of Burma, November, Retrieved from: www.womenofburma.org/Report/courage- to-resist.pdf

Women of Burma. 2008. *In the Shadow of the Junta: CEDAW Shadow Report*, Retrieved from: http://womenofburma.org/in-the-shadow-of-the- junta-cedaw-shadow-report/

UNHCR. www.unhcr.org/pages/49e4877d6.html

UNICEF. www.unicef.org/har09/files/har09_Myanmar_countrychap. . .

UNICEF. www.unicef.org/myanmar/about.html

UN Women. 2013. www.unwomen.org/ca/news/stories/2013/

Index

Acharya, M. 56
Adivasi Arts Trust 102
Adivasi women 3
Agarwal, Bina 2, 52–4, 71, 72
ahal 46
Ahmed, Sarah 52, 54
Andaya, Barbara 154
animation 8, 102–5, 108, 111, 113, 114, 117
annual floods 70
Anti-Fascist People's Freedom League 151
Ao, T. 105
apex Tribal Hohos 6
Armed Forces Special Powers Act (AFSPA) 91
ASEAN 165
Aye, Thakin-ma Ma 150

Bahuns 44
Bamakhit 151
Banda Aceh 4
Banerjee, Paula 5
Barthakur, R. 105
Battiste 110
Beijing Declaration 161
Benares Recension 27
Benedict, Paul 21
Benedict, P. K. 22, 26
Beyond the Nature/Society Divide: Learning to Think About a Mountain (Freudenburg, Frickel, and Gramling) 59
bhagi system 78
Bhalla, G. S. 122
Bhotiyas 97

biodiversity 82
Blumenbach, Johann Friedrich 13
Blust, R. 26
Borah, Bharati 2
Bory de Saint-Vincent, Jean Baptiste 14
Brahmins 86, 88
Brara, N. V. 86
Buddhist Burmese women 149
Burma Round Table Conference 150

capabilities 6, 68, 77, 81, 82
capitalist market values 104
Central Employment Guarantee Council 123
Chain, Ba Maung 152
Channa, S. M. 97
Chant, Sylvia 5
Chettris 44
Christian Tangkhul Nagas 86
climate change 1, 4, 53, 58, 68, 81, 161
communities 3–6, 8, 17, 23, 31, 32, 44, 46, 48, 50, 55, 70, 72, 93, 102–17
conflict 90
The Conquest of Granada (Dryden) 103–4
Conrady, A. 26
cosmological powers 98
cultural barriers 56
customary land rights 2
customary laws 96, 99, 100, 147, 153

Dandekar, Vishnu Mahadeo 122
devithan 46
Dheeraja, C. 132, 134, 136
disaster 1, 4, 5, 8, 71, 75–9, 82

discrimination 46, 55, 56, 105, 123, 134, 154, 165
displacement 4, 9, 97, 158–61
diversification 3, 76
Drèze, Jean 122
Dublin Principles 42
Dzuvichu, Rosemary 6

East Asian homeland 28–33
East Asian linguistic theory 21–7
Eastern Himalaya: defining 12
Eastern Himalayan homeland 28–33
East Garo Hills 2
eco-feminism 53
employment 45, 72, 80, 121–3, 128, 132–4, 140, 151, 152, 160
empowerment 1, 2, 5, 6, 54, 112, 126, 159
enlightened citizen 90
Erxleben, Johann Christian 13
ethnic language 70
ethnolinguistic phylogeography 17
exclusion 7, 51–4, 68

farming system 70
farm-scapes 79–81
Father Tongue correlation 17
father tongues 17–19
female farmers 69
feminist environmentalism 53
feminists 43, 52–3, 103, 106, 108, 110–17
feminization 157
flood of 2012 75–9
food security 3, 71–3, 77, 79, 80, 140, 158, 161
Fortescue, Michael 28
Freudenburg, William 59
Frickel, Scott 59

Gandhi, Indira 88
Garos 94
gender: constructed images of 85–100; discrimination 56; education reforms 6; paradox 6; reform 6
gender rights 42–64; methodology 43–4; mountain women, narratives 54–6; narratives in India 52–4; preliminary framework 43–4

gender roles 85–100; in Northeast 92–5
genes 16–17

Hall, Harold Fielding 148
hazard resilient communities 5
Hazell, Peter 122
hierarchies 3, 85, 88, 95, 99, 110
Hindu Succession Act 96
historical linguistics 16
Hmong-Mien populations 31, 32
Homo sapiens asiaticus 14
households 5, 42, 44, 57, 69, 70, 73, 76, 80, 123, 126, 128, 132, 133, 157
Huggan, G. 104
human population genetics 16
Hümtsoe-Nienü, E. 93, 94, 96

Ikeya, Chie 148
inclusion 6, 81, 96
indigenous communities 102–17; collaboration 110–17; colonial period, representation 103–4; feminist research, influence 110–17
indigenous peoples 16
Indo-Aryan communities 44
inequalities 1, 4, 56, 68, 95, 166
inheritance rights 2
Institute of Rural Management Anand 136
Integrated Tribal Development Authority 3

Jayalalitha, J. 88
jhum cultivation 93
Jones, R. L. 96
Jones, S. K. 96
Jones, William 16

Karafet, T. M. 17
Karan, Pradyumna P. 55
Karbi Anglong 2
Khaing, Mi Mi 148
Khan, F. A. 90
Khan, Genghis 14
Khasis 86, 94
khetala system 45

khit kala 154
Klaproth, Julius von 16
Klenk, R. M. 87
Kukis 86
Kumar, P. 54
Kyi, Daw Khin 152

Lahiri-Dutt, Kuntala 53
land rights 2
language 16–21, 28, 31, 32, 107,
    108, 112, 114, 149
Leaf, Caroline 112, 114, 117
Leduc, Bridgette 55
Lepchas 3
Leyden, John Caspar 20
liberation 98
Limbu men 96
Limbu women 96
linguistics 16
Linnæus, Carl 13
liquidity 69
livelihoods 79–81; diversification 3
Lynch, O. J. and Maggio,
    G. F. 55

Magars 44
Maharashtra Employment
    Guarantee Act 122, 123
Mahatma Gandhi National
    Rural Employment Guarantee
    Act (MGNREGA) 44, 77,
    121–44; employment and asset
    creation 121–3; poverty and
    worker's population ratio
    136–40; wage rate, workers
    134–6; women and 126–7,
    134; workers 128–33; works
    124–6
Malagasy 32
male-female employment
    opportunities 45
marginalization 5, 7, 88, 105, 106,
    110, 166
massive floods 67
Matisoff, Jim 21
Mayangs 86
Mehrotra, Santosh 123
Meiners, Christoph 14
migration 4, 9, 17, 23, 56, 76–7, 79,
    80, 82, 123, 157

Ministry of Rural Development
    123, 124
Mishra, Deepak K. 3
Mizos 86
modern reductionist science 52
Mongoloid myth 13–16
mountain village, Sikkim 42
mountain women 54–6
mul 46
Müller, Friedrich Max 16
mulphutnu 45
Myanmar National Committee for
    Women's Affairs (MNCWA) 161

Nagas 3, 6, 86, 91, 105
Naga women 89, 93
National Film Board of Canada 117
National Sample Survey
    Organisation 132, 140, 142
Niger-Congo languages 18
Nijhawan, Shobna 155
Nkrumah, K. 104
Northeastern Himalayas 85–100; in
    'Indian' imagination 89–90
Northeastern woman 86
Nyein, Daw Cho Cho Kyaw 160

Omvedt, Gail 95
opportunities 1, 2, 4–6, 45, 68, 69,
    77, 82; inequalities of 4–5
Ostapirat, Weera 23

Palaeomongoloids 15
Panchayat Raj Institutions 5
Pangals 86
participation 1, 5, 6, 8, 9, 53, 54,
    57, 80, 121–3, 126, 134, 140,
    151–3, 156, 157
patriarchy 8, 52, 54, 56, 85, 86, 92,
    93, 95, 96, 99, 149
Peiris, Denzil 153
Peiros, I. 26
periodic flooding 67
Poloni, E. S. 17
Pontic-Caspian steppe 18
popular mythological narratives 106
poverty 136–40; alleviation process
    136; reduction, in Sikkim 121–44
practical exigencies 98
Pyu, Shin Saw 149

Rais 44
Raju, Saraswati 6
reciprocity 111
rehabilitation 4, 166
Reid, Lawrence 26
Relandus, Hadrianus 21
representation 5, 8, 52, 102–8, 110, 114, 117
resilience 3, 77, 82
resource management 54, 55
Roy, Kartik C. 2

Sabnani, Nina 113, 114
Saffron Revolution 151
Säid, E. 104
salais 86
Say, Thakin-ma Daw 150
Scheduled Caste Development Corporation 3
Schlegel, Gustave 22
Schmidt, Wilhelm 26
scientific positivism 110
Scott, George 148
self-help groups (SHGs) 81, 82
self-reflection 112
self-representation, politics 106–9
Sen, Amartya 6, 80, 122
Sender, John 121
Sen, Gita 1
Sharmila, Irom 91
Shiva, Vandana 52, 53
Sikkim Himalayas 44
Singhal, R. M. 54
Sinha, J. N. 122
Sino-Tibetan myth 19–21
Smith, Linda Tuhiwai 111
Smith, Sheila 121
social development index 6
social reform 5
socio-economic systems 67
Special Marriage Act 149
Special Marriage and Succession Act 149
Spiro, Melford 149, 150
Starosta, Stanley 27
state monopoly 52
storytelling 105
strategies 5, 79, 81, 82, 122, 157
Sundaram, Krishnamurthy 122
Systema Naturæ (Linnæus) 13

Tales of the Tribes 103, 106, 111, 117
The Tallest Story Competition 102
Tanko Bol Chhe 114
tea tribe 69–70
The Owl Who Married a Goose 113
Tibeto-Burman 20, 21
Tinsukia district 67–83
Tiwari, Archana 43
topography 7, 42, 43, 45, 49, 50, 53, 56
Trans-Himalayan family 19–21
tribal communities 55
Tungids 15
Tünyi, V. 91

Unnithan-Kumar 99
unpredictable floods 67
Unterhalter, Elaine 6
upper caste Hindu Meiteis 86
upper caste Hindu women 88

Vaishnavism 44
Varietas Caucasia (Blumenbach) 13
violence 4, 5, 9, 90, 155–6, 158, 159, 162
Virey, Julien-Joseph 14
vulnerability 1, 5, 7, 8, 123

Wadee, Ma Thistsa 151
water, access to 42–64; narratives in India 52–4; state-made provisions, policy decisions 51–2; use and management 50–1
water collection 49–50
water management system 45–9
water managers 56
water resource management 54
water sources: in Ahley Gaon Ward 47–8; in Dumi Gaon Ward 48–9
wet terrace fields 3
Win, Daw San San 160
Witsen, N. 21
women: after independence 151–5; alternative livelihood sources and migration 76–7; challenges 67–83, 155–61; climate and nature 4; colonial period 148–51; coping with change 77–9; disenfranchisement of 53; and displacement 158–61; farmers

and food managers 71–5; floods, context 67–83; food and food distribution, access 73–4; food utilization and consumption 74–5; gender-disaggregated farming system 67–9; horticultural crop cultivation 72; imaginary reconstruction of 87; interventions, attempted 161–5; in land of Jade 147–66; and livelihoods 157–8; migration of rural 157; Mongoloid 88; relationship with nature 53; risk and disaster managers 75–9; role as producers 71–3; study area and predominant features, farming system 69–71; trafficking 156; violence against 155–6
women's empowerment 2
Women's Freedom League 151
women's insecurity 4
Workmen's Compensation Act 160
World Disasters Report 4
World Health Organization 2
The World of Burmese Women 148
Wulff, K. 26
Wymann von Dach, Susanne 54

Yayoi people 31
Y chromosomal introgression 16

www.ingramcontent.com/pod-product-compliance
Ingram Content Group UK Ltd.
Pitfield, Milton Keynes, MK11 3LW, UK
UKHW020414010325
455677UK00029B/883